# Friends of the Court

## Lawyers as Supplemental Judicial Resources

Alexander B. Aikman
Mary E. Elsner
Frederick G. Miller

National Center for State Courts

A Project Sponsored by the National Institute of Justice

© 1987 National Center for State Courts
Printed in the United States of America
NCSC R-100

**Library of Congress Cataloging-in-Publication Data**
Aikman, Alexander B.
    Friends of the court.
      1. Courts—United States—States—Officials and employees.
2. Court administration—United States—States. 3.
Lawyers—United States—States. I. Elsner, Mary E., 1948-
II. Miller, Frederick G. III. National Center for State Courts.
IV. Title.
KF8795.Z95A38    1987    347.73′1    86-33312
ISBN 0-89656-082-1    347.3071

This report was prepared under Grant 83-IJ-CX-0021 from the National Institute of Justice, Office of Justice Assistance, Research and Statistics, United States Department of Justice. The opinions, recommendations and conclusions contained in this report are those of the authors and do not necessarily represent the official policy or position of the National Center for State Courts, the National Institute of Justice, the Office of Justice Assistance, Research and Statistics, or the United States Department of Justice.

# Contents

Foreword, xi

Précis, xiii

Acknowledgments, xvi

Introduction, xix

  *The Evaluation Effort, xx*

**PART ONE**
**General Summary and Conclusions**

**Chapter One: Quantitative Analysis of Adjuncts' Use, 3**

  *Number of Dispositions Increased, 5 • Improved Case Processing Times, 7 • Secondary Impact of the Program, 8 • New Procedures in Oregon, 9 • The Effect of Judicial Adjuncts on Case Outcomes, 10*

**Chapter Two: Qualitative Assessment, 11**

  *Appearance of Justice, 12 • Nature and Quality of Decisions, 13 • Improved Relations with Adjuncts, 14 • Litigant and Litigating Attorney Support, 15 • Types of Cases Adjuncts Should Hear, 15*

## Chapter Three: Costs and Administrative Consequences, 18

*Costs for Courts, 18 • Costs to Adjuncts, 21 • Administrative Consequences, 23*

## Chapter Four: The Adjuncts' Perspective, 31

*Lawyers Provide Useful, Complementary Expertise, 32 • Permanent Versus Temporary Programs, 32 • Number of Hours Adjuncts Are Willing to Volunteer, 33 • Functions Adjuncts Are Willing to Serve, 34 • Conclusion, 34*

## Chapter Five: Key Considerations in Designing a Judicial Adjunct Program, 36

*Planning, 36 • Initiation of the Program, 39 • Operating the Program, 41 • Guidelines for the Use of Lawyers to Supplement Judicial Resources, 42*

## Chapter Six: Conclusion, 45

## PART TWO
## Evaluation Reports for Six Sites

## Chapter Seven: The Tucson *Pro Tem* Judge Program, 51

*Description of the Program, 51 • Program Goals, 53 • Quantitative Evaluation, 53 • Qualitative Evaluation, 60 • Costs and Administrative Issues, 63 • Overall Assessment, 65*

## Chapter Eight: The Portland *Pro Tem* Judge Program, 68

*Problems That Led to Creation of the Adjunct Program, 69 • The Program, 70 • Goals, 73 • Quantitative Evaluation, 73 • Qualitative Evaluation, 76 • Costs and Administrative Issues, 78 • Overall Assessment, 80*

## Chapter Nine: The Arizona Court of Appeals Judge *Pro Tem* Program, 84

*Background, 84 • Developing the Program, 86 • The Program, 87 • Goals, 89 • Quantitative Evaluation, 90 • Qualitative Evaluation, 99 • Costs and Administrative Issues, 103 • Overall Assessment, 106*

## Chapter Ten: The Connecticut Trial Referee Program, 112

*Goals, 113 • Operation of the Program, 114 • Quantitative Evaluation, 116 • Qualitative Assessment, 124 • Costs and Administrative Issues, 127 • Overall Assessment, 128*

## Chapter Eleven: The Minneapolis Mandatory, Court-Annexed Arbitration Program, 131

*Developing the Program, 131 • Description of the Program, 133 • Program Goals, 135 • Quantitative Evaluation, 135 • Qualitative Evaluation, 146 • Costs and Administrative Issues, 152 • Overall Assessment, 154*

## Chapter Twelve: The Seattle Early Disposition Program, 157

*Description of the Program, 157 • Goals, 159 • Quantitative Evaluation, 160 • Qualitative Evaluation, 168 • Costs and Administrative Issues, 173 • Overall Assessment, 175*

**Appendix A: The Use of Judges *Pro Tempore* as Mental Health Judges in the Pima County (Tucson, Arizona) Superior Court, 179**

**Appendix B: Administrative Orders of Division One of the Arizona Court of Appeals, 187**

**Appendix C: Rules and Guidelines for Connecticut Trial Referee Program, 194**

**Appendix D: Fourth Judicial District Court (Minneapolis, Minnesota) Rules Regarding Mandatory, Nonbinding Arbitration, 202**

**Appendix E: Analysis of King County Superior Court Early Disposition Programs 1983 and 1984, 208**

## LIST OF TABLES

Table 1: Types of civil court-trial and jury cases disposed by *pro tem* judges and regular judges, January 1984 to March 1985, 54

Table 2: Point when court-trial cases assigned to *pro tem* and regular judges were disposed, January 1984 to March 1985, 55

Table 3: How cases assigned to *pro tem* and regular judges were disposed, January 1984 to March 1985, 56

Table 4: Trials concluded in the Pima County Superior Court, 1984 and 1985, 57

Table 5: Estimated costs of *pro tem* judge program, January 1984 through June 1985, 64

Table 6: Multnomah County Circuit Court filings and terminations, 69

Table 7: Number of cases listed for summary judgment motion hearing, 74

Table 8: Results of summary judgment motion hearings, 75

Table 9: Filings and terminations, Division One, 1983 through 1985, 85

Table 10: Time interval statistics for memoranda cases disposed July 1983 to June 1984, 91

Table 11: Number of civil appeals disposed by court July 1983 through September 1985, 92

Table 12: Disposition of civil appeals with oral argument, by percent, 93

Table 13: Disposition of civil appeals without oral argument, by percent, 94

Table 14: Change in time-to-disposition for civil appeals (median days), 96

Table 15: Change in time-to-disposition for civil appeals with oral argument disposed by memo (median days), 98

Table 16: Department E program personnel requirements in start-up year, 104

Table 17: Distribution of types of cases disposed by refereed trial with state totals, fiscal year 1985, 115

Table 18: Changes in the court-trial list, 1983 to 1986, 115

Table 19: Manner of disposition of cases assigned to trial referees, January 1984 through June 1985, 116

Table 20: Motions to correct, exceptions, and objections filed at the three study sites, January 1984 to June 1985, 123

Table 21: Distribution of time referees spend disposing of one case, 124

Table 22: Trend in pending civil cases, September 1980 through September 1983, 132

Table 23: Civil filings, 1980 through 1982, 132

Table 24: Types of cases referred to arbitration, September 1985 through June 1986, 137

Table 25: Results of arbitration, September 1985 through June 1986, 137

Table 26: Arbitration program results compared with original dollar demand, September 1985 through 1986, 138

Table 27: Average original dollar demand for various outcomes, 138

Table 28: Percent of cases with final disposition in arbitration process. Case outcomes for casetype/trial-type pairs, 139

Table 29: Settlement figure as a percent of original demand for 10 percent of cases, 139

Table 30: Arbitrator's award as a percent of the original demand, 140

Table 31: Actions of parties in response to arbitrator's award, 141

Table 32: Average percent awarded of original demand, 141

Table 33: Disposition compared with estimated trial length, 142

Table 34: Likelihood of arbitration or trial request, 142

Table 35: Outcomes of requests for trial between September 1985 and July 1986, 143

Table 36: Outcomes of cases requesting trial according to original dollar demand, by percent, 145

Table 37: Distribution of cases in EDP evaluation, 1983 and 1984, 161

Table 38: Trials in EDP and control cases, 162

Table 39: Age at EDP hearing date for EDP and control cases, 1983 and 1984, 163

Table 40: Comparison of days to reach disposition, by percentiles, 166

Table 41: Percentage of all cases disposed within 90 days of EDP hearing dates, by case type, 1983 and 1984, compared with dispositions in control group, 167

Table 42: Percentage of all cases disposed within 90 days of EDP hearing dates, by age of case, 1983 and 1984, compared with dispositions in control group, 168

## Appendix A

Table A-1: Mental health hearings, January-June 1984, 180

Table A-2: Mental health hearing dispositions, 184

## Appendix E

Table E-1: Distribution of cases included in study, 209

Table E-2: Distribution of dispositions by end of study period, 210

Table E-3: Cases disposed by time of disposition and volunteer/assignment status, 213

Table E-4: Percent of cases disposed within 90 days of EDP hearings, by type of case, 214

Table E-5: Civil cases disposed by time of disposition and type of case, 215

Table E-6: Percent of cases disposed within 90 days of EDP hearings, by age of case, 218

Table E-7: Civil cases disposed within 90 days of EDP hearing, by age of case, 219

Table E-8: Cases in which trials were held, by EDP involvement, 220

Table E-9: Cases in which trials were held, by type of case, 222

Table E-10: Distribution of cases among case types, 223

Table E-11: Distribution of cases among case types and between volunteer/assignment status, 224

Table E-12: Cases included in study, by age of case, 225

## LIST OF FIGURES

Figure 1: Civil caseload history, 1978 through 1985, Pima County Superior Court, 58

Figure 2: Median time-to-disposition for civil court-trial cases disposed by regular and *pro tem* judges, January 1984 through March 1985 (days), Pima County Superior Court, 59

Figure 3: Median time-to-disposition for civil appeals, Court of Appeals, Division One, Arizona (days) July 1983 through September 1985, 95

Figure 4: Pending trial list history, 1979-1986, Bridgeport Superior Court, 118

Figure 5: Cases added to and disposed from trial lists, 1979 through 1986 Bridgeport Superior Court, 119

Figure 6: Court-trial list, median age of pending cases (months), Connecticut Superior Court, 120

Figure 7: Court-trial list cases disposed FY 1983 through FY 1986, Bridgeport median time-to-disposition (days), 121

Figure 8: Jury trial list, FY 1983 through FY 1986, Bridgeport median time-to-disposition (days), 122

Figure 9: Opinions of program participants toward referee program, 126

Figure 10: Arbitration caseload history, September 1985 through June 1986, Hennepin County District Court, 136

Figure 11: EDP and control cases disposed 1983, 30-day periods, all cases, 164

Figure 12: EDP and control cases disposed 1984, 30-day periods, all cases, 165

Figure 13: Opinion chart, King County settlement program, 170

## Appendix E

Figure E-1: EDP and control cases disposed 1983, 30-day periods, all cases, 211

Figure E-2: EDP and control cases disposed 1984, 30-day periods, all cases, 212

# Foreword

The widening gap between expanding workloads and available judicial resources is creating serious problems in many courts. Justice is discounted when the pressure to reduce backlogs and delay results in an increase in plea bargains. Traditionally, the most common response to concern about case delay and increasing volume has been to increase the number of judges. In a period of fiscal restraint, however, the nation's courts are faced with tight budgets. There has been little room in public budgets to support increases in judicial resources proportionate to the growth in caseloads. There is an urgent need to find ways of reducing what ought to be temporary backlogs without the permanent and costly response of increasing the number of judges.

This report offers a solution: the use of volunteer lawyers to augment judicial resources. Based on evaluation of six programs that use volunteer lawyers in a judicial capacity, the report is optimistic about the benefits of such programs in reducing case backlog and delay in our nation's courts. These programs complement an overall delay reduction plan of a court and offer the opportunity to improve bench-bar relations.

The success of the concept can be seen both in reductions in the time to disposition of cases and also in the positive reactions of the judges and attorneys involved. There is little or no financial cost, and attorneys report no discernible difference in the quality of adjudication.

The spirit of volunteerism tapped by these programs can serve both individuals and the community. It has the capacity to resuscitate our justice system and the American bar.

Now that effective models have been demonstrated, how can we integrate volunteerism into the justice system? State bar associations provide continuing education for their members, and some require it. Courses could include the role of the judge, addressing judicial conduct and procedures. Lists of attorneys who completed the course would then be provided to requesting courts. These courts could in turn verify other criteria for selection as a judicial adjunct, such as a time requirement for law practice.

Such a program has the potential of providing useful information when vacancies on the bench occur. Because training occurs beforehand, it can also improve the quality of judicial appointments.

By participating in judicial adjunct programs, an individual attorney invests in both his or her own future and that of the court being served. The court recognizes this individual initiative and applies the resources both to meet its current needs and also to plan for the future with a pool of potential judges.

The National Institute of Justice is pleased to have supported this useful evaluation by the staff of the National Center for State Courts, guided by an active and highly qualified Advisory Board. The entire effort would not have been possible without the innovative spirit and commitment of the cooperating courts.

The results shared by these courts offer a stimulus for change and reason for optimism. This new program promises significant benefits for our judicial system and better options for state and local governments as they meet fluctuating demands for judges.

JAMES K. STEWART
*Director*
*National Institute of Justice*

# Précis

Judicial adjunct programs,[1] when well managed and especially as part of a broad effort to attack civil case delay and growing case backlogs, can

- increase the number of dispositions over previous years;
- reduce the time to disposition of cases handled by adjuncts;
- improve bench-bar relations; and
- provide attorneys new understanding and appreciation of judges' duties and problems.

While using lawyers as judicial adjuncts is not a panacea for either delays or backlogs, there are significant direct and indirect benefits achievable by a court with an effective adjunct program.

The National Center for State Courts has evaluated six uses of lawyers as supplemental judicial resources over a 30-month period. This report contains general findings and conclusions regarding the use of lawyers as supplemental judicial resources, in addition to detailed descriptions and evaluations of the six programs. Three courts used lawyers as judges *pro tempore.* In the Pima County (Tucson, Arizona) Superior Court, judges *pro tem* were used to dispose of a block of civil nonjury trials. In the Multnomah County (Portland, Oregon) Circuit

---

1. The term "judicial adjunct" encompasses courts' myriad uses of lawyers to supplement judicial resources, whether or not the lawyers are paid for their services and whether they are used temporarily, for a defined period of time, or indefinitely.

Court, lawyers sit as judges *pro tem* to hear and resolve motions for summary judgment. In the Arizona Court of Appeals division located in Phoenix, judges *pro tem* sit on special panels with a regular appellate judge to help reduce its backlog. In addition to these three judge *pro tem* programs, the National Center evaluated the use of lawyers as trial referees in the superior court of Connecticut, the use of lawyers as arbitrators in a court-annexed arbitration program for civil cases in the district court in Minneapolis, and the use of lawyers to evaluate and make recommendations regarding settlement of civil cases awaiting jury trials in the King County (Seattle) Superior Court. Following is an outline of the key conclusions, beyond those above, of the National Center's 30-month study.

1. Judicial adjuncts are useful in a wide range of programs.
2. The improvement in statistics observed in some of the evaluation sites cannot be attributed solely to the use of judicial adjuncts; there also was evidence of a "Hawthorne effect"—the phenomenon that positive results are achieved because attention is being paid to a problem, almost regardless of the solution adopted. But the existence of the Hawthorne effect does not detract from the value of the adjunct programs. The adjunct programs were the catalyst for the coming together of positive factors and the focus that produced improvement. The incidental positive aspects of the bench-bar interaction remain a unique byproduct of these programs.
3. The trial bar generally likes and supports the use of judicial adjuncts in programs that resolve cases more quickly, result in earlier trial dates, or help to reduce a court's backlog.
4. Litigants' attitudes toward the use of judicial adjuncts generally reflect the attitudes of their attorneys; because most litigating attorneys support the use of judicial adjuncts, most litigants do not object to their use.
5. With a few exceptions, neither litigating attorneys nor clients discern any difference in the quality of adjudication in proceedings conducted by judicial adjuncts. In some instances, mainly in domestic relations cases, litigating attorneys expressed the opinion that the quality of adjudication is improved by using lawyers who specialize in the subject area over which they are presiding.

6. Potential problems in judicial adjuncts programs involving conflicts of interest and violations of judicial ethics are not manifested in practice in programs studied or, when they appear, are identified quickly and resolved so as to avoid affecting either the quality of justice provided or the appearance of justice. Nor were instances found of adjuncts using their position as an adjunct for economic advantage.
7. The fresh perspectives on and respect for judges' tasks and problems gained by judicial adjuncts result in increased support of the bench. Adjuncts also gain insight that makes them more effective advocates.
8. Lawyers will volunteer time, sometimes substantial amounts of time, without compensation to help courts address identified and recognized problems. Nonetheless, courts must be sensitive to the matter of not asking for too many uncompensated hours from individual attorneys.
9. Few judges or lawyers expressed concern that the use of adjuncts might make it harder in the future to obtain needed full-time judgeships. There is no evidence to date in the six sites that their adjunct programs have reduced the chances of adding needed full-time positions.
10. The orientation and training of judicial adjuncts should receive more attention from courts, regardless of the skill level and number of years at the bar of the lawyers used.
11. The support and interest of the presiding judge is very important in assuring acceptance and successful implementation of a judicial adjunct program.
12. Judicial adjunct programs involve additional and new administrative responsibilities, normally assumed by court staff and the chief or presiding judge. There are two types of costs associated with judicial adjunct programs: direct and indirect. The direct, out-of-pocket costs are relatively small, covering such items as copying and postage; in two programs they also included adjuncts' fees for service. The indirect costs are the salaries, fringe benefits, and associated overhead of staff and judges. These indirect costs can be substantial but normally represent a reallocation of resources and priorities, not new outlays. In all six sites additional administrative duties and costs were accepted and acceptable.

# Acknowledgments

In a project spanning two and a half years and involving six jurisdictions, the list of people deserving special recognition and thanks far exceeds the limited capacity of these acknowledgments. Yet recognition of their assistance is required, even if each is not named individually.

The project's genesis is attributable to the shared vision of James K. Stewart, director of the National Institute of Justice, and Advisory Board member Edward A. Dent, III, who were concerned with the seemingly intractable problems of pretrial delay and the growing backlog of cases in some courts. They believed that the use of attorneys as supplemental judicial resources could have a positive effect on these problems. As director of the National Institute of Justice, Mr. Stewart recognized the value of testing the hypothesis that lawyers can help courts, before deciding it was valid. Thus, this project was initiated. We have been spurred and encouraged throughout this project by Mr. Stewart's enthusiasm and his interest in our research efforts and Mr. Dent's gentle prodding and advice.

Project staff were helped immeasurably throughout the evaluation effort by the chief or presiding judges in each evaluation site, their court administrators, and, in some locations, key people on the administrators' staff. In each site, these people supplied caseload data in support of the evaluation, provided generously of their time, and offered invaluable assistance in arranging the interview schedules of project staff.

Hundreds of judges, judicial adjuncts, other lawyers, and court staff generously gave of their time and, more important, their views regarding the use of judicial adjuncts. In all cases the time spent with project staff was above and beyond their normal busy schedules. Their generous contributions imparted clarity of understanding to project staff, and are responsible for any useful insights this report offers.

Special acknowledgment is required of the Advisory Board on the Use of Volunteer Lawyers as Supplemental Judicial Resources.[1] Beyond the hours and days devoted to development of the *Guidelines on the Use of Lawyers to Supplement Judicial Resources*, originally published in 1984, the insight and general guidance of the Board directed and fashioned the evaluation effort. Project staff particularly appreciate the commitment of the Advisory Board reflected in their willingness to review a draft of this manuscript after they had formally disbanded. Their careful reading and advice measurably improved the quality of this report.

In addition to the special assistance of the Advisory Board, we wish to acknowledge the assistance of three former National Center staff members, John M. Greacen, Douglas C. Dodge, and Charlotte A. Carter. Each participated in development of the *Guidelines* and volunteered time to review and comment upon a draft of this report. In addition, Douglas Dodge participated in this evaluation effort for a year before leaving the National Center for State Courts to become a court administrator. We deeply appreciate their commitment to the project long after their formal affiliation with the National Center ended. Larry L. Sipes, former Regional Director of the National Center's Western Regional Office, also deserves special thanks for his careful review of a draft of the manuscript and his thoughtful comments.

Throughout this project we have benefited from the patient support and guidance of Bernard Auchter, project monitor for the sponsoring National Institute of Justice. Mr. Auchter was an effective liaison with the National Institute of Justice and a valued counselor regarding both procedural and substantive aspects of the project.

Two appendices contain the special contributions of others. Roberta L. Tepper, at the time a third-year law student at the University of Arizona, undertook a special study of the use of judges *pro tem* in mental health matters by the Pima County Superior Court in Tucson, Arizona. Her report is Appendix A. Three members of the staff in the Office of the Administrator for the Courts of Washington, Sharon L. Estee, manager, Research and Statistics, and Robert Anson and Jenni A. Christopher, of the Research and Statistics section, spent countless hours designing the statistical evaluation of the Seattle program and then collecting, reviewing, and analyzing the data and preparing the final statistical evaluation reports. Their report is Appendix E. The authors of *Friends of the Court* greatly appreciate these authors' time and effort, the insights they added to our work, and their willingness to allow us to use their papers in this report.

---

1. See footnote 1, page xxiii, for a list of Advisory Board members.

A report of this length and complexity requires the patience and skill of dedicated administrative staff. We are especially thankful to Maxine Rhodes, project secretary, for her assistance in project administration and in assuring the professional appearance of all our work products. Helen Ogata, Rochelle Rodgers, Brenda Jones, Patricia Maddox, Stacey Healy, Catherine Meek, and Louise M. Harris persevered with good humor through numerous drafts and the vagaries of both modern technology and project staff. We sincerely appreciate their skill and constant support.

Final editing and printing of this report were completed under the careful eye and guidance of Carolyn McMurran of the National Center's Publications Department. Her skill and attention to detail improved both the readability and the appearance of the report. Tina Beaven, art director for the Center, designed the book and made valuable suggestions for the effective presentation of tabular material and illustrative figures.

Although many have contributed to this report in positive ways, we alone are responsible for any deficiencies or inaccuracies it contains. The reader also is reminded that the views expressed are those of the authors and do not necessarily represent the views or opinions of the United States Department of Justice, the National Institute of Justice, or the National Center for State Courts.

ALEXANDER B. AIKMAN
MARY E. ELSNER
FREDERICK G. MILLER

# Introduction

Almost all courts can use temporary judicial assistance from time to time. The need may arise from inevitable scheduling problems, while waiting for new judicial positions to be created or filled, or because of a new, legislatively imposed program. In some of these situations it is not possible for the court to get full-time judicial positions created, while in others it would be inappropriate; the need is real but not sufficient to justify full-time judicial resources. Many courts in these circumstances struggle as best they can, devoting their limited resources to the highest priority items and postponing lesser priority matters to another day. Since August 1983 the National Center for State Courts, with funding from the National Institute of Justice and with the assistance of an Advisory Board on the Use of Volunteer Lawyers as Supplemental Judicial Resources,[1] has studied whether the use of practicing lawyers offers courts a practical means of dealing with these extra demands for resources.

The Advisory Board adopted the term "judicial adjunct" to encompass courts' various uses of lawyers to supplement judicial resources, whether or not the lawyers are paid for their services and whether the services are used temporarily, for a defined period of time, or indefinitely. The term and its definition are used throughout this report.

The study has had three components: (1) an initial survey of some existing judicial adjunct programs; (2) the development of guidelines for the use of judicial adjuncts; and (3) the evaluation of several different uses of judicial adjuncts. The first two parts of the study were accomplished with publication of the Advisory Board's *Guidelines for the Use of Lawyers to Supplement Judicial Resources* in the summer of 1984.[2] The Advisory Board concluded:

- Court systems should consider using lawyers in a variety of capacities as supplemental judicial resources when full-time judicial resources are inadequate to meet demands. Such use should not be a permanent alternative to the creation of needed full-time judicial positions.
- Except for serious criminal trials and child custody proceedings, most types of cases are appropriate for assignment to judicial adjuncts.
- All judicial adjunct programs should have carefully defined objectives, be subject to court control, involve lawyers in planning as well as implementation, and include evaluation and monitoring.
- The court should maintain control over the selection of judicial adjuncts; the quality and background of lawyers selected should be appropriate for the task assigned.
- Assignment of cases to judicial adjunct programs should not be subject to the consent of the parties or their counsel, but appropriate mechanisms should be established to provide the parties an option concerning the particular judicial adjunct before whom they will appear.
- The court and the adjuncts should be sensitive to identifying and resolving actual and possible conflicts of interest affecting the provision of justice or the appearance that justice is being done.

It was discovered in the first phase of this study that very few courts have attempted to evaluate the impact of judicial adjunct programs. Accordingly, project staff worked with six jurisdictions over 30 months in an effort to evaluate a variety of judicial adjunct programs to see what impact, if any, the programs had on the court and what problems, if any, are associated with the use of adjuncts. This volume reports the results of those evaluations.

# The Evaluation Effort

Six jurisdictions, each using adjuncts in a different way, participated in the evaluation effort:[3]

### *Judge* Pro Tempore *Programs*
- Pima County (Tucson, Arizona) Superior Court: use of judges *pro tem* to dispose of a block of civil nonjury trials (hereafter referred to as "court" trials).
- Multnomah County (Portland, Oregon) Circuit Court: use of judges *pro tem* to hear and resolve motions for summary judgment.

- Court of Appeals, Division One, Phoenix, Arizona: use of judges *pro tem* sitting on special three-member panels, each with a regular judge presiding, and deciding cases through unpublished memorandum opinions.

## Other Programs
- Trial referee program in the Superior Court of the State of Connecticut, in which trial referees conduct civil court trials, write memorandums of decision, and recommend to regular judges that judgment be rendered accordingly.
- Mandatory, nonbinding, court-annexed arbitration for civil cases in the Fourth Judicial District Court (Minneapolis), Minnesota, using a single arbitrator.
- Settlement program for civil jury cases awaiting assignment of a trial date in King County (Seattle, Washington) Superior Court, in which pairs of lawyers sat on panels, each with a sitting judge, to evaluate the cases and make recommendations regarding settlement.

The arbitrators in Minneapolis are paid $150 for each hearing day in which they participate. Trial referees in Connecticut receive, upon request, up to $100 per day of hearing, but few have asked to be paid. The judicial adjuncts in the four other programs participate without compensation.

The Tucson, Connecticut, Portland, and Seattle programs were conceived and operating prior to implementation of the National Center's evaluation effort. The National Center worked with the two other jurisdictions to design an evaluation plan before their programs started. The general approach to the evaluation was similar in each of the six sites, however. In each case, project staff members visited the court to explain the National Center's interest in the use of judicial adjuncts and to explore the court's willingness to participate in the project. The respective roles of the court and the National Center were discussed and defined. Each court was asked to articulate goals for its program and, in conjunction with National Center staff, to establish the procedures for the evaluation, including the data to be collected, how data would be collected, who would be responsible for the data, and who would serve as the principal contact or contacts between the National Center's project staff and the court. Finally, project staff and the court agreed upon a general time frame for the evaluation.

In each site it was agreed that the evaluation would have three components: a quantitative analysis focusing on caseload data, a qualitative analysis designed to understand participants' opinions and attitudes, and a fiscal analysis to estimate the direct and indirect costs of the program to the court. In each site the qualitative analysis was undertaken through interviews of judges, judicial adjuncts, litigating attorneys, and court staff. In two of the sites, Seattle and Connecticut, the interviews were supplemented by written questionnaires sent to judges, judicial adjuncts, litigating attorneys, and clients. In Seattle, Phoenix, Tucson, and Minneapolis, National Center staff also observed proceedings in which judicial adjuncts presided or participated.

The time frame for each evaluation differed; the specific length of each evaluation is indicated in the site reports. In no site are the statistical indicia of success unambiguous; real-world evaluations in environments that shift and change seldom can produce clear answers to all the questions asked initially or subsequently raised by the data. There is sufficient consistency among the sites on key issues, however, to cause us to share our conclusions with a measure of confidence. When more data might affect a conclusion, that fact is noted in an individual court's evaluation report.

Each site in the program had its own specific evaluation questions, but we sought to answer some common questions in all sites. Many of these were part of the qualitative evaluation rather than the quantitative, although there were some common quantitative issues, as well. These questions were common to all sites:

1. To what extent did the program achieve the individual court's goals?
2. Did the program produce unexpected positive or negative results?
3. What do the litigating bar and citizens think about lawyers assisting the court in this program?
4. Did the use of judicial adjuncts produce "appearance of justice" problems that affected the quality of justice the court was seen to be providing?
5. Does the use of judicial adjuncts free judicial time and thus have incidental impact on the processing of cases not handled by adjuncts?
6. Will lawyers offer their services on a *pro bono* basis; if so, does their willingness to volunteer their services depend on the type of program or the number of hours requested of them?
7. What new administrative burdens does the use of adjuncts impose on a court?
8. What extra costs are associated with the program that the court would not otherwise bear?

Each of these questions, together with our conclusions based on the answers to these questions, is discussed in the following pages of this report, presented in two parts: (1) a general summary of the quantitative, qualitative, and administrative lessons learned from all evaluation sites and a review of key considerations for courts designing a judicial adjunct program; and (2) a detailed description of the program in each site and the evaluation results from that site. The reader interested in detailed information about any of the individual adjunct programs should consult the descriptions in the second part of the report rather than the first part.

## Notes to Introduction

1. The Advisory Board was chaired by former Chief Justice of Connecticut John A. Speziale. Its members were the Honorable William D. Blue, Judge, Lancaster County District Court, Nebraska; Edward A. Dent, III, Washington, D.C.; Sue K. Dosal, State Court Administrator, Supreme Court of Minnesota; the Honorable Pat Irwin, Magistrate, U.S. District Court and former Chief Justice, Oklahoma Supreme Court; James R. Larsen, former Court Administrator, Supreme Court of Washington, representing himself and then-Chief Justice William H. Williams; the Honorable H. Carl Moultrie, Chief Judge, Superior Court of the District of Columbia (deceased); Robert D. Myers, Esq., Arizona; Kenneth Palmer, State Court Administrator, Supreme Court of Florida, representing then-State Court Administrator Donald P. Conn; Peter J. Rubin, Esq., Maine; Alan Slater, Executive Officer, Orange County (California) Superior Court.

2. Williamsburg, Va., 1984; hereinafter cited as *Guidelines*. The Guidelines, without supporting commentary, are reproduced at the end of Chapter 5.

3. Initially, the district court in Ft. Lauderdale, Florida, expressed interest in joining the project as an evaluation site testing one-person settlement conferences; this would have allowed comparison of the three-member panel in Seattle with the one-person conference in Florida. The bar in that district indicated to the court that it would rather put its limited resources into other programs to reduce delay, so the court decided not to implement the settlement conference procedures. Courts in Maine, Nebraska, and the District of Columbia also expressed preliminary interest in starting judicial adjunct programs, but circumstances in each jurisdiction led each to direct its resources to other programs.

PART ONE
# General Summary and Conclusions

CHAPTER ONE

# Quantitative Analysis of Adjuncts' Use

All six programs studied by the National Center for State Courts had one similar aim, to introduce judicial adjuncts into the civil adjudication process. A number of factors specific to each study site helped determine the scope of the program and the design of its evaluation. These factors were the following: the procedure(s) to be assigned to the adjuncts; the expected capacity of the program; the state of the caseload of the court; the goals set for the program; the quality and quantity of historical statistical caseload data available; and the ease with which new data directly related to the evaluation could be collected.

Three major evaluation designs were discussed in *Guidelines for the Use of Lawyers to Supplement Judicial Resources:* the controlled experiment, the before-and-after design, and the case study.

A controlled experiment yields the best information about the effects of a new procedure, but it requires the most stringent conditions for implementation. There must be a sufficient pool of cases from which to draw experimental and control groups. It must be possible to continue to handle some cases in the traditional manner even as the new treatment is being introduced. There must be sufficient recordkeeping capacity to permit the identification and follow-up of specified individual cases for an extended period of time. Finally, there must be no ethical objections to treating similar cases in two or more different ways and to deciding upon the treatment of each specific case by using a random allocation method. All these conditions were met at one study site—the Superior Court of King County (Seattle), Washington, where a classic controlled experimental design was used to evaluate its settlement program.

When all the conditions necessary to support a controlled experiment are not met, consideration should next be given to using a before-and-after design. In this evaluation design, it must be possible to identify and compare the experiences of two similar groups of cases that were processed during consecutive periods of time. Data on the "before" group may be collected in one of three ways, listed in descending order of preference: the data may be constructed specifically for the evaluation from individual case data already collected for another purpose; they may be gleaned from historical statistics already compiled; or they may be reconstructed manually from stored primary data sources. If none of these three methods is possible and the court still wants to proceed with a before-and-after design, implementation of the new program should be postponed until sufficient "before" data are collected on current procedures. Postponing the implementation of a new program that may improve the outcome of cases may raise practical, political, or ethical concerns that must be weighed against being able to discern whether the new program has the desired effect.

Data collection for the "after" group is considerably easier to manage since it may proceed as the new program is implemented. Each case must be followed individually, just as for the controlled experiment. Additional data may be collected from the "after" cases in order to construct a more detailed description of how the program functions. Four of the study sites used modified before-and-after designs: the Court of Appeals in Phoenix, Arizona; the Connecticut Superior Court; the Superior Court of Pima County (Tucson), Arizona; and the Fourth Judicial District Court in Hennepin County (Minneapolis), Minnesota.

If it is not possible to identify separate "before" and "after" groups or if the capacity to reconstruct or collect data on the "before" group does not exist, then the program may be described in a case study. This design requires only that detailed information on all facets of a program be collected and compiled. The conditions which brought about the implementation of the program and its stated goals should be included, but they only need to be quantified in the most general terms and not with the detail necessary for a before-and-after design. The major drawback of using a case study is that it cannot provide sufficient information to actually evaluate a program. At the end of a case study, the participants may have formed an opinion about whether or not the new program was an improvement over the traditional method, but even if their opinions are correct, it will not be possible to state statistically the degree to which current practice is better or worse. A decision on the outcome of a program—whether to continue, modify, or terminate it—can be made with a case study only, but this decision must be based on something other than statistical results.

The use made of judicial adjuncts to hear summary judgment motions by the Circuit Court of Multnomah County was evaluated using a case study format. It probably is safe to assume that simply by using adjuncts rather than regular judges to hear these matters the judges are able to spend more time doing other things. Saving time for judges was one of the primary goals of this program. A more complex evaluation design might have been able to determine how much judge time was saved (not necessarily the same as the amount of time the adjuncts spent), but such additional information was not very important to the court.

Even if it is not possible to carry out a comprehensive evaluation for every new program introduced, data collected in the course of a case study can serve as the basis for a more extensive evaluation or periodic program monitoring conducted in the future to determine whether the program is continuing to meet the goals set for it. Details on the design and results of individual evaluations are given in the chapter for each study site. The remainder of this chapter reviews conclusions or results common to two or more sites.

Although each program was unique, some achieved common results. The focus in the discussion that follows is on *statistical* gains and changes. A full understanding of these results in some instances requires a "qualitative" explanation. Although noted below, these qualitative factors are discussed more fully in the next chapter.

## Number of Dispositions Increased

The primary strategy of judicial adjunct programs is to add judicial resources to the court. In most instances this ensures an increase in the number of cases disposed by the court, although precise quantification of the adjuncts' contribution to the increase is not always possible.

1. More civil cases were disposed during the first year, 1984, of expanded use of *pro tem* judges in the Pima County Superior Court. The increase over 1983 was 6.5 percent, or 419 more cases disposed. *Pro tem* judges contributed about 200 dispositions to this total. (Between January 1984 and March 1985, *pro tem* judges conducted 240 civil court trials.) Civil filings increased almost 10 percent during the same period, however, so the civil pending caseload rose 11 percent from the number pending at the end of the previous year despite the increase in dispositions.
2. The number of cases disposed from the court-trial list for the year after implementation of the trial referee program in Connecticut (1984) was larger than the number disposed during the previous year for each of the three sites studied. This increased level of dispositions continued

through 1985. Combined with lower numbers of cases added to the court-trial list for this same period, the increased dispositions reduced the size of the pending caseload in each of the three sites. The contribution of the trial referees to this trend is apparent and seems to be significant (see Chapter 10), but is hard to quantify because increasing dispositions and a decrease in the number of pending court-trial cases started before the trial referee program went into effect.
3. Division One of the Arizona Court of Appeals started its *pro tem* judge program in September 1984. This was the second year in a row that the division's civil and total dispositions exceeded filings, despite a 9.4 percent increase in civil filings and a 6.7 percent increase in total filings. In 1985, with the *pro tem* judges' assistance for a full year, there were 10 more civil dispositions in 1985 than in 1984, but total civil dispositions fell 10 short of total civil filings. The court issued 30 more memorandum opinions in 1985 than in 1984, but its 274 memo opinions were seven shy of the 1983 total. Although the *pro tem* judges' contribution to this improvement in total dispositions and the number of memo opinions written is discernible, it is less than might be expected from changes that occurred in the time from at-issue to oral argument and oral argument to decision (see Chapter 9).
4. The Hennepin County District Court switched from a master calendar system to an individual calendar system at the same time the arbitration program began in July 1985. Increased dispositions since that date cannot be attributed to the new calendar system or the arbitration program individually. Nevertheless, in the first year of operation, the arbitration program has been credited with the disposition of 685 cases. Dispositions through arbitration occur when a case has settled after assignment to arbitration and before the expiration of the time the parties have to appeal the arbitration award or through acceptance of the arbitration award. The figure of 685 dispositions is equivalent to the number of dispositions that would be reached by 2.78 of the 14 judges presently hearing civil cases in the Hennepin County District Court.
5. The contribution of the judicial adjuncts to a court's (or state's) total disposition figures is most likely to be apparent in these four sites rather than in Portland and Seattle. Positive changes were noted in all four sites; the changes exceeded the adjuncts' dispositions in Tucson and Connecticut. Some of the balance of the change may be attributable to regular judges' having time to devote to other cases. Some also is attributable to what social scientists refer to as the "Hawthorne effect": the improvement that occurs which is associated with paying attention to a problem, regardless of the specific solution applied. The apparent presence of a Hawthorne effect does not detract from the value of the adjunct programs. They seem to have served as a catalyst for the

improved times to disposition in Phoenix. The adjunct programs contributed to the courts' improved positions; the fact that the improvement observed seems to have resulted from more than their contribution alone is to be noted but does not require dismissing the programs or their value.

## Improved Case Processing Times

Reducing case processing times for specific groups of cases was one of the primary goals at most of the study sites. This goal proved to be more demonstrably achieved than other goals by most of the courts studied.

1. The court of appeals division in Phoenix reduced the median time from at-issue to oral argument by 19 percent for cases handled by the newly created Department E panels (the *pro tem* judge panels) when compared to the baseline time frame for similar cases decided before the program was implemented. Time from oral argument to decision also was reduced by 28 percent for all the cases in the court, although the Department E cases alone took longer between argument and decision than the court had taken in the baseline period. This latter result seems to reflect the extra time taken by some *pro tem* judges to write opinions. These data reinforce the conclusion that a significant portion of the improvement in Phoenix is attributable to a Hawthorne effect.
2. In Connecticut there were dramatic improvements in time-to-disposition for court-trial cases. Here, rather than a Hawthorne effect, the improvement probably reflects the positive effect of an adjunct program that is but one part of a multi-faceted, well-managed program to reduce pretrial delay. The time from being placed on the court-trial list to disposition was reduced between 14 percent and 41 percent for the three court locations studied in the evaluation of the Connecticut Superior Court trial referee program. The median age and the size of the court-trial pending caseload also were reduced at each of the three courts studied. Some of this improvement is probably due to the concurrent positive effects of the fact-finding program that was introduced at two of the three Connecticut study sites shortly before the trial referee program began; it is not possible to separate the effects of these two programs using the evaluation design that was selected (see Chapter 10). Improvement may be attributable to a concerted emphasis by state officials to reduce pretrial delay, with the use of trial referees being an important element of the overall program.
3. Median time from settlement conference to disposition in the Seattle superior court was reduced 55 days for cases assigned to the program in 1983 and 150 days for those that volunteered for the program. The savings at the 75th percentile were 105 days and 210 days for these two

groups of cases, respectively. Similar reductions were found for cases in the 1984 program.

## Secondary Impact of the Program

Two courts began to experience a measurable positive effect on portions of the caseload not directly touched by the program. This "spillover effect" was identified in the court of appeals in Phoenix and the superior court in Connecticut.

1. As noted above, time from filing to disposition decreased for all cases processed by the court of appeals during the evaluation period, not just those cases heard by Department E panels. It was reduced even more for cases not directly involved in the program than it was for Department E cases. Some of the general reductions can be explained by the fact that when the Department E panels were created, they removed some of the cases waiting for oral argument before other departments of the court. Just as happens when an additional service line is opened at a store, all the waiting lines get shorter. But most of the lines were still being served by the same amount of judge-time. To the extent that their sitting on Department E panels took the regular judges of the court away from the other departments, some of the lines may have been served by a smaller amount of judge-time, and, as a result, could have been slowed down but were not.

    All judges of the court were sitting on Department E panels; thus they became especially aware of the goals of that program. They seem to have carried over the spirit of court improvement from the *pro tem* program to the rest of their caseload. The bar association also may have participated in creating conditions conducive to a spillover of benefits from one part of the court to the rest of its caseload. Whatever the basis for or the size of the spillover effect, it was a consequence of the program in Phoenix.

    Although not directly related to the Department E program, the court also changed a rule during the study period that had the effect of reducing the number of motions for reconsideration and for review. This was probably responsible for much of the across-the-board reduction in time from decision to mandate observed in all categories of cases.

2. Changes in the condition of the jury-trial caseload in Connecticut are more directly related to implementation of the adjunct program than is the generalized improvement observed in Phoenix. When the trial referees began hearing civil court trials in the Connecticut courts, the courts were able to transfer at least some of the judges who had been hearing civil *court* trials to civil *jury* trials; the evaluation site that experienced the largest drop in the size of its civil-court-trial pending

caseload had, at the same time, transferred all its civil judges to the jury trial list.

While the number of court-trial requests in Connecticut has been declining steadily since 1980, the number of jury-trial requests generally has increased since mid-1980. The increase in the number of judges transferred from the court-trial list, and thus available to hear jury trials, was sufficient to turn around the growth of the jury-trial list in two of the court locations studied, and has stemmed the growth in the third site. None of the other courts that demonstrated progress in meeting primary goals has as yet demonstrated the existence of any spillover effects.

3. Even though the uses made of judicial adjuncts in the Pima County Superior Court, Arizona, and in the Connecticut Superior Court are quite similar—*pro tem* judges conducting civil-court trials versus trial referees conducting civil-court trials—the effects of these two programs on case processing were quite different. These different results are a direct consequence of the differences in the two programs. Cases have been assigned steadily to trial referees in Connecticut since early 1984. The steady influx of additional judicial resources has helped each court studied there to bring its court-trial list under control. The court in Tucson assigned a large number of cases to *pro tem* judges in six-case blocks when the *pro tem* judge program began. Since then few court-trial cases have been assigned to *pro tem* judges; regular judges of the court have continued to hear these cases as well. And the court in Tucson did not adjust its calendaring of jury trials to reflect removal of the court trials, so some trial judges' time was not used optimally. The crisis that was developing in early 1984 for the civil-trial list in Tucson was averted, but the court has yet to reap any other benefits from this program.

## New Procedures in Oregon

A few years ago, new rules of civil procedure were adopted in Oregon allowing summary judgment motions for the first time. When these first began to be filed in the circuit court in Multnomah County, they were assigned individually to the judges hearing civil cases. Normally these motions were scheduled early in the morning before the start of trials. As the number of summary judgment motions filed increased, the court began to use judicial adjuncts to hear and dispose of them. During 1983, judges heard 41 percent of the motions filed; early in 1984 all motion hearings were transferred to the judicial adjuncts. There were 1,040 cases with motions for summary judgment assigned to *pro tem* judges during 1984; during 1985, 727 were assigned to them. It is not possible to estimate how the court would have handled these motions had *pro tem* judges not been available, or the impact this would have had on the court's total civil dispositions. Even so, it is likely that the adjuncts' use had a positive even if unmeasurable effect on civil case processing.

## The Effect of Judicial Adjuncts on Case Outcomes

1. It was feasible to examine the outcomes of cases in only one evaluation site, Portland, where there was a measurable difference in outcome attributable to the use of judicial adjuncts. Trial attorneys interviewed in the other sites that used *pro tem* judges or trial referees indicated that outcomes were the same or, especially for domestic relations cases with an adjunct who practices family law, qualitatively better because the adjunct specialized in that area of the law, whereas most judges did not.
2. The outcomes of summary judgment motions filed by plaintiffs and defendants in Portland are different, whether the motion is decided by a regular judge or a *pro tem* judge. But when one adds in the factor of who decided the motion and who filed it, there are still some small differences attributable to whether a regular judge or a judicial adjunct heard the motion. *Pro tem* judges granted a larger percentage of motions; regular judges denied a larger percentage. One explanation for this difference suggested during interviews is that the *pro tem* judges may feel freer to grant motions for summary judgment because they are not so concerned about being reversed on appeal as a regular judge of the court may be. These data compare *pro tem* judges' current rulings with rulings made by regular judges in 1984 and earlier; this time difference may be a factor in the different outcomes, too. Other explanations offered can be reviewed in more detail in Chapter 8.

CHAPTER TWO

# Qualitative Assessment

At each project site a qualitative assessment of the program was made. The project staff interviewed judges, adjuncts, litigating attorneys, and in some instances parties who participated in the adjunct program. In Connecticut and Seattle questionnaires were developed and sent to these persons to elicit their opinions about the adjunct program. In general, all the adjunct programs were highly regarded. Admittedly, people involved with the program want to see it succeed. Furthermore, at each project site the program itself or certain aspects of the program were new, and the qualitative assessments were made without an extended period of observation. Nonetheless, the degree to which judges, adjuncts, and litigating attorneys in all sites approved of the programs reduces the risks associated with assessment of subjective responses.

There were a few respondents in some sites who were not in favor of the program and did not believe it was providing a significant service to the court. Those who voiced negative qualitative assessments of the program during interviews seemed generally to favor judges' performing the duties assigned to the judicial adjuncts. Therefore, in their eyes no judicial function performed by extra-judicial persons, however productive, beneficial, or popular, would receive a positive qualitative assessment.

The philosophical perspective that underlies this negative view of all adjunct programs must be acknowledged. Many judges and lawyers have worked for decades to remove part-time and temporary judges from the courts in favor of full-time judges. The use of judicial adjuncts is seen as a step back. The philosophical perspectives supporting only a full-time judiciary cannot be addressed fully here. It should be emphasized, however, that in the six evaluation sites and the other jurisdictions studied during the first phase of this study, the temporary and part-time assistance provided by judicial adjuncts was never seen as an acceptable permanent substitute for needed full-time help. And the project's advisory board was equally clear when it stated in its first guideline that the use of judicial adjuncts "should not be a permanent alternative to the creation of needed full-time judicial positions."[1] Nonetheless, when a need arises that cannot be met—either immediately or in the near term—by full-time judgeships, as in most of the evaluation sites, the use of judicial adjuncts is in large measure supported by both bench and bar.

There is another distinction between the *pro tem* judge and trial referee programs evaluated and the use of *pro tem* judges that traditionally has been opposed by some attorneys and judges. Traditionally, "part-time judge" has meant a lawyer (or non-lawyer) who spends a significant portion of available work time (from a few days a month to half-time or more) as a judge, usually on a regular schedule. Almost always these part-time judges are paid salaries or stipends. The use of judicial adjuncts evaluated and reported on here involves lawyers serving, normally, once or twice a year for one to four days at a time. In four of the six sites all lawyers served without compensation and in a fifth many lawyers did not request a fee even though one was available.[2] In the "traditional" model, part-time judging is a job assumed by someone who has another, primary job, often the private practice of law. In this study, part-time judging was not seen as a job by any adjunct interviewed and for a substantial majority it was seen solely or largely as a public service. A few *pro tem* judges in each evaluation site served an above-average amount of time, averaging two days or more a month, but these were exceptions and even these lawyers did not view their service as a "job." The distinction noted here does not moot the policy issues associated with part-time judges, but it suggests a different context in which the issues need to be discussed and resolved.

There were some variations in the qualitative assessment of the adjunct programs from site to site. In those sites where quantitative improvement in case processing had been documented the qualitative assessment seemed to be higher. Those who assessed the quality of these programs could point to a statistical basis for their views. Similarly, in project sites where a presiding judge or the judge who administered the program was strongly in favor of the project, the qualitative assessments tended to favor the program more strongly.[3]

## Appearance of Justice

There was concern in several sites that criticism would surface that the use of adjuncts adversely affects the appearance of justice. Very little is done on an institutional basis to reassure litigants that judicial adjuncts are providing the same justice that would be received were parties to go before judges of the court. Litigating attorneys may explain to their clients that they will be appearing before a judicial adjunct and express an opinion that the adjunct is competent, but very little conscious "selling" of the program occurs. In some instances, litigating attorneys indicate to clients that their chances of receiving an informed, intelligent, and unbiased judicial officer are the same whether they appear before a judge or a judicial adjunct. Often, though, litigating attorneys simply explain the mechanics of the program to which their clients are being exposed. Interestingly, in the appellate project in Phoenix, most litigating attorneys do not inform their clients that they are appearing before a panel composed of one court of appeals judge and two judicial adjuncts. It is unknown whether this says something about the acceptance of the use of adjuncts in Phoenix or about the attorneys' view of the appellate process and clients' involvement in that process. Our understanding from other exposure to the adjunct programs in the trial courts in Phoenix suggests the latter explanation, as most attorneys who appear before adjuncts in the general jurisdiction trial court advise their clients that the judge is an attorney sitting as a judge *pro tem.*

## Nature and Quality of Decisions

Some litigators—in a few instances more than one might hope—commented on the relative lack of formality in proceedings presided over by judicial adjuncts. Although they claimed that this did not negatively affect their own perceptions of the process, they feared citizens might judge the proceedings less favorably because of the relative lack of formality. No attorney in any site reported that a client expressed displeasure at the courtroom or hearing atmosphere (as opposed to the outcome), but several feared the intangible perceptions these clients would take from the proceedings.

With rare exceptions litigating attorneys were positive about the quality of decisions by judicial adjuncts. In most cases they said there was no discernible difference between regular judges' and judicial adjuncts' decisions or courtroom handling of the issues. When differences were cited, they almost always fell into three categories:

1. Because adjuncts are "fresh" and sitting on the bench is a new or sporadic experience, they are very attentive to lawyers' arguments and concerns. Because of the special nature of their service and also because they are "closer" to practicing law than judges with years on the bench, adjuncts might give each case more time in court or might devote more time to a written decision.[4]
2. Particularly in domestic relations and medical malpractice cases, adjuncts who are matched to these cases as a result of their specialization bring expertise and interest in the subject area to the dispute reso-

lution process that judges normally do not have. Some litigators felt better-informed or more imaginative results were achieved by adjuncts.
3. Some adjuncts were not as well qualified as litigators desired; but virtually always this criticism was directed to individual adjuncts and not to the program.

In Portland, the nature of the summary judgment motion process has changed significantly as a result of the program. Prior to the adjunct program, summary judgment motions were being heard by judges the same day as the case was scheduled for trial. Using adjuncts allows the court to schedule these motions at an earlier date, thus alleviating the need to prepare fully for trial when the motions are granted in full or in part.

Since the summary judgment procedure has only been allowed under the Oregon rules for a little more than ten years, there are some judges on the circuit court bench who had no experience with the procedure when in practice. Adjuncts who have active civil practices have had years of experience with summary judgment motions and may have a keener sense of when the motion should be granted than judges who have been on the bench for ten years or more. Litigators generally and the courts have gained experience with the process over these ten years, so the issues raised and the quality of arguments made may be higher today than when regular judges alone decided these motions.

The judicial adjuncts in Portland granted either in full or in part a higher percentage of summary judgment motions than the judges. The dispositions in a number of cases have been appealed to the Oregon Court of Appeals; through early 1986 all judicial adjuncts' decisions had been upheld by the court of appeals.

Litigators who argued before the Phoenix court of appeals' Department E uniformly were pleased with the quality of preparation and with the *pro tem* judges' focusing quickly during oral arguments on the key issues. Opinions by *pro tem* judges were thought by litigators to be appropriate in length, tone, and analysis. Through early 1986, the decisions in Department E cases that have been appealed to the Arizona Supreme Court have been affirmed; in one case the Supreme Court adopted the opinion written by a *pro tem* judge.

# Improved Relations with Adjuncts

One of the significant benefits of judicial adjunct programs is that they improve relations between the court and the attorneys serving as judicial adjuncts. The adjuncts have a much better understanding of the operations of the court, its difficulties, and the limitations it faces. In almost every instance there is increased empathy among the adjuncts for the work that is performed by judges.

In cases where the program is designed so that judicial adjuncts and judges perform their duties together, such as the Early Disposition Program (EDP) in Seattle and Department E of the Arizona Court of Appeals, a new basis for understanding is developed between judges and litigating attorneys. They are exposed to the practices and concerns of each other as they conduct the program. The program also provides a time of equal footing between the adjuncts and the judges. The adjuncts and judges are able to consider themselves as colleagues rather than as being cast in specific roles of judge and attorney. The end result of these improved relations is that the court has more spokespeople for its operation, and the local legal community has more voices able to express the concerns, frustrations, goals, and aspirations of the court.

## Litigant and Litigating Attorney Support

The litigants and litigating attorneys who appear before the judicial adjunct programs support the programs very strongly. The support of the litigating bar is remarkable because it is not uncommon for the litigating bar to oppose procedural changes that require change in its habits of practice. This opposition was not found in any of the project courts. On the contrary, the litigating bar appreciates the fact that through a new program the court is attempting to alleviate its backlog, speed disposition of cases, or explore alternatives such as arbitration.

The litigating attorneys' support for the program is not blind, however. They voiced concern that in particular instances the court had not screened cases effectively to assure that only appropriate cases are sent to the program. They also sometimes indicated they desired the court to screen adjuncts more effectively so that the program would be assured of only the highest-quality attorneys serving as adjuncts. Litigating attorneys were concerned further that those programs designed to alleviate backlogs should not become permanent programs; were programs to be expanded in their scope and become permanent, it is feared by some attorneys that adjuncts could become overburdened with their work for the court or that the court might be denied needed permanent judgeships. Some attorney criticism of any court program is to be expected; the concerns expressed about adjunct programs were within the range expected, both in number and in kind.

## Types of Cases Adjuncts Should Hear

The advisory board's third guideline on the use of judicial adjuncts states that adjuncts can hear all types of cases except serious criminal and child custody cases. All of the evaluation programs involved general civil cases, but in Tucson judges *pro tem* preside over felony jury trials and for a six-month period in 1984 presided over mental commitment hearings. (As to the latter, see Appendix A.) In Portland, judges *pro tem* resolve motions affecting child custody.

To test the advisory board's conclusion about appropriate case types for adjuncts and to see if litigating attorneys felt any particular case types should be excluded from the programs in the evaluation sites, in each site we asked whether there are any case types that should not be part of the particular judicial adjunct program being evaluated or, more generally, should not be heard by judicial adjuncts. The responses were surprising.

Most responses fell into two categories: (1) felony (or criminal) cases and child custody cases, as the advisory board concluded, should be excluded or (2) adjuncts should be able to hear and determine all case types. When those giving the latter answer were asked in a follow-up question specifically about criminal cases and child custody cases, most agreed there are sound policy reasons for excluding these case types, but that conclusion was apparent only after an initial reaction that there is no reason to exclude any case type. Judges more often wanted to exclude criminal and child custody—or all family—matters than attorneys.

Adjuncts in response to these questions seemed to focus as often on the number of consecutive days they might have to serve as on the types of cases they might be asked to hear. Two judges *pro tem* in Tucson indicated adjuncts should be spared "high visibility/high publicity" cases because they might hurt attorneys' practices, but this concern applied whether the cases were felonies, condemnations, or injunction actions. A related concern was expressed by a Connecticut judge, who feels referees should not decide tax or zoning cases because of the potential these cases carry for pressure on adjuncts.

Almost all agreed, either with or without reminder, that felony and child custody cases should not be assigned to judicial adjuncts but this was a consensus, not a unanimous opinion, and it applied more strongly to felony cases than to child custody cases. No general civil case category was identified by judges, adjuncts, or litigators as inappropriate for adjuncts to hear.

## Notes to Chapter Two

1. *Guidelines*, p. 3.
2. In Minneapolis, all lawyers are offered payment. Virtually all thought *some* payment was an appropriate recognition of the time and effort expended, but several also believed they and others—enough for a substantial panel—would volunteer their time if payment were not offered.
3. In each site most of the people interviewed by National Center staff were suggested by the court. The National Center requested that a cross-section of the bar be included among interviewees, but there was no independent means of

assuring that diversity. In a few instances we went to court files and called attorneys at random. There was no noticeable difference in opinions of these latter interviewees from those identified by the court.

4. This observation was made in Tucson, but some Tucson *pro tem* judges also claimed they are "tougher" on lawyers who seemed to wander in their presentations or present duplicate evidence than are regular judges because the *pro tem* judges do not want to "waste" their donated time.

CHAPTER THREE

# Costs and Administrative Consequences

There are costs inherent in implementing and running a judicial adjunct program, but they usually are less than the cost of creating new judgeships or quasi-judicial positions. In some instances, no new costs are incurred, but rather, some costs are incurred earlier than they would have been as the program begins to increase the pace of litigation in the court.

## Costs for Courts

The following cost elements may be incurred by a program:

- Judge time for participation and administration
- Staff time
- Design and production of new forms
- Postage
- Copying files
- Accoutrements
- Facilities
- Compensation for adjuncts

Not every program incurs costs in each of these categories. Further, and most important to understand, many of these "costs" do not involve new or increased budget items; they are "indirect" or "accounting" costs indicating staff and judicial time devoted to a program but not cash outlays. Thus, although each evaluation site incurred indirect costs because of staff and judge time spent on its program, only one site,

Minneapolis, incurred staff costs solely attributable to its program that had a budgetary impact. And in Minneapolis, the program's establishment occurred following legislative authorization for and encouragement of the program.

**Judge Time for Program Participation and Administration**
One or more judges participated from the start in developing the judicial adjunct programs at all six sites studied. They conducted the initial meetings between representatives of the court and the local bar association at which the general focus and type of program to be implemented were determined. They were instrumental in identifying attorneys to serve as adjuncts, either by recruiting them directly or by screening those who volunteered. They helped determine what types of cases would be eligible for the program. They also served as the program's public relations representatives, speaking before various groups and issuing press releases in support of the program.

At some of the study sites, one or more judges participated in ongoing program administration, matching cases for assignment to judicial adjuncts. They have maintained control over case assignment at all sites by reserving for themselves the responsibility for deciding whether specific cases can be excused.

In two of the study sites, Seattle and Phoenix, judges sat on panels with judicial adjuncts to hear cases. In Seattle, the time taken up by judges' participation on the settlement panels was hoped to be offset by an eventual reduction in the trial rate. In Phoenix, however, the judges' participation on Department E panels was recognized as an additional assignment for the judges that they were willing to undertake if it would result in the reduction of case processing times.

Finally, the judges in most of the sites studied have reviewed the results of the program evaluation and decided whether to continue, modify, or end the program.

**Staff Time**
Support staff in each of the courts have been responsible for implementing the program. At most sites one or more of the staff (e.g., the clerk of the court, the court administrator, or the state court administrator) have been involved in program design and development along with the judges.

Day-to-day administrative responsibility is assigned to a program administrator. This administrator usually directs a small staff, located in the clerk's office or the administrative office of the court, responsible for performing all tasks necessary to run and evaluate the program. In most of the programs studied, the administrator and staff schedule the procedures to be held in the courthouse, send out notices and duplicate files, collect materials needed for hearings and collect data on the outcome of each hearing, monitor receipt of reports from the judicial adjuncts, and administer their compensation. Another task that is required by court staff is monitoring and evaluating the adjunct program. If the court's management information system is not efficient, the time consumed in collecting and analyzing data to monitor the program can be significant.

**Design and Production of New Forms**
There usually are a few new forms needed to support administration of a judicial adjunct program. The court may need to design a form for lawyers to use in applying as judicial adjuncts and another for cases when inclusion or exclusion is sought. If the program involves new or modified procedures, new notices may need to be developed. Communication between the court and the judicial adjuncts will probably be more complicated than it is between the court and its regular judges, if only because the judicial adjuncts' offices are outside the courthouse. This may require that more forms be developed and used to ensure that adjuncts are kept fully informed.

**Postage**
Notices and reminders must be mailed to plaintiffs, defendants, and judicial adjuncts for each procedure scheduled as part of the adjunct program. If the program includes steps that are not a part of traditional case processing, there will be new costs for the court. In addition, the cost of sending notices to the judicial adjuncts will be extra.

**Copying Files**
Some courts do not allow case files to be removed from the courthouse. In these courts, it may be necessary to duplicate the applicable portions of the file, either because the hearing will be held somewhere other than the courthouse or to give the judicial adjunct the opportunity to review the file before the hearing.

**Accoutrements**
In order to provide the appropriate atmosphere, courts may supply judicial adjuncts with some of the outward symbols of judicial authority—robes, gavels, state and national flags for their courtrooms, etc. Some of these may need to be purchased.

**Facilities**
Space within the courthouse may need to be modified to accommodate the program. One courtroom of the Court of Common Pleas of Allegheny County (Pittsburgh), Pennsylvania,[1] for example, has been divided into a central waiting room surrounded by a series of small hearing rooms to accommodate its arbitration program. The administrative judge at one of the study sites in Connecticut mentioned that he would like to have a portable bench that could be moved into a hearing room when a refereed

trial was scheduled. None of the study sites spent any money on new facilities, but expenses for facilities may be incurred by some judicial adjunct programs.

## Compensation for Adjuncts

Two of the study sites elected to pay the judicial adjuncts for their service. Adjuncts in Connecticut are paid up to $100 per trial day upon request; all those serving in Minneapolis are paid $150 per day.

The courts studied considered several factors in deciding whether to offer compensation to judicial adjuncts: how much time each adjunct would be expected to contribute; whether payment was offered to attorneys performing other services for the court; what proportion of the local bar would be needed; whether the court could expect to recruit enough attorneys of the necessary caliber if compensation were not offered; and available budget funds. Four of the six sites decided not to offer compensation; this decision has not affected their ability to recruit adjuncts.

If compensation is offered, it may be one of the major, if not the largest, costs of the program. And, unlike judge and staff costs, the compensation of judicial adjuncts requires cash outlays. Obviously, the court will not be able to pay judicial adjuncts the rates they charge to clients. Some courts have based compensation either on the fee paid to active or retired judges for a day or a token figure that is treated more as an honorarium than comparable compensation. Arbitration programs generally pay between $100 and $200 per day or per case.

# Costs to Adjuncts

Costs incurred by judicial adjuncts do not appear in the public budgets of courts, but they are real and in some cases can be substantial. When costs are uncompensated or only partially covered by a court, the contribution by the adjuncts not only can be significant to each individual but in sum may equal or exceed both the direct and the indirect costs of the court. The elements of costs incurred by adjuncts in the evaluation sites are reviewed here. The National Center was unable to estimate the dollar value of these costs at any site, but was able to obtain estimates of adjuncts' time commitments in all programs. Those estimates are included in the individual evaluation reports.

## Time

As noted above, judicial adjuncts receive some compensation in two of the six study sites. But instead of being regarded as payment for their time, they see it as helping them or their firms cover overhead costs incurred during their service. The time the adjuncts spend can be separated into three categories: case related, administrative, and travel time.

*Case-related.* Case-related time includes the time the judicial adjunct spends preparing for the proceedings, conducting all hearings necessary, and preparing reports or opinions to complete the service. Although most programs ask a judicial adjunct to serve for one day, if a case is continued or taken under advisement, or if additional hearings on a case are required, service can extend over several days. Programs may also require that an adjunct serve at intervals during the year. Each court should be aware of how much time it expects adjuncts will be asked for and will be willing to contribute. In the three *pro tem* judge programs and the trial referee program in this study, attorneys' case-related time generally involved a day or so of preparation and a day or two of court proceedings.

*Administrative time.* Judicial adjuncts are responsible for handling administrative details in some of the programs, scheduling hearings and trials with the litigating attorneys and completing forms designed to facilitate caseflow or support evaluation of the program. At some sites administrative staff of the court were available to assist the adjuncts; at other sites these responsibilities were handed over to the support staff of the adjunct's law firm. No compensation was offered at any of the study sites to cover adjuncts' administrative time. No attorney indicated during interviews that compensation should be provided for staff administrative time.

*Travel.* Some lawyers found they were asked to serve as adjuncts in courts some distance from their offices. Lawyers from as far away as Tucson served in Department E of the Phoenix Court of Appeals, traveling 110 miles, one way. Some Connecticut lawyers also found that they were asked to serve as trial referees at more than one court location. No compensation was made by any of the programs for travel time or expenses. Only a few lawyers, generally those who had traveled far to serve, mentioned that payment of travel expenses might be appreciated.

**Staff**

Numerous judicial adjuncts reported that they asked the administrative staff of their law firm to assist them by handling the administrative details of the program and typing the letters, memoranda, and decisions or reports necessary. Some used law clerks to help them prepare for their service and do legal research related to report and opinion writing.

In the two locations that offered compensation to the judicial adjuncts, that compensation was regarded in part as reimbursement for the overhead expenses of the adjuncts. In effect, a lawyer contributing services to the court was also contributing some of the support services of his or her law practice to the court.

## Supplies and Other
In addition to contributing law firm staff time, some programs encouraged lawyers to donate the facilities of their law firms. When there was not sufficient room available in the courthouse, some programs asked judicial adjuncts to schedule hearings in their law firms' conference rooms. Lawyers' staffs used the equipment and supplies of their law firms to prepare the reports and briefs required.

As a result of their different designs, the programs studied required different amounts of time and commitment of resources from the adjuncts, but all required that each adjunct contribute something to the program. This did not appear to be a barrier or problem for any adjunct.

# Administrative Consequences

## Selection of Adjuncts
The procedures used to select adjuncts varied considerably. There were, nevertheless, similar elements in the selection processes. The differences in procedure represented each site's individual attempt to accomplish the same goal: the selection of the best possible attorneys to serve as judicial adjuncts.

In Portland, *pro tem* judges have been used for a number of years, so it was not necessary for the court to develop new procedures for the selection of attorneys for the summary judgment program. The local bar association recommends names to the court for consideration as *pro tem* judges. The presiding judge selects names from the bar-recommended list and submits these names to the Oregon Supreme Court for approval.

As in Portland, *pro tem* judges have been used for a number of years in Tucson. To undertake the block assignment of court-trial cases in Tucson, the presiding and assistant presiding judges selected attorneys for the program and then forwarded these names to the chief justice for formal appointment. Starting in 1984, attorneys selected for adjunct service have been reviewed by a committee of the local bar association, also, before names are submitted to the chief justice.

In Phoenix, each Division One judge named 20 attorneys for possible adjunct service. The chief judge maintains a master list of all names submitted by the judges. When a new list is needed of people to serve on the adjunct/judge panels, names of *pro tems* are selected at random from the master list. As with trial court *pro tem* judges, formal appointment is made by the chief justice. In both Tucson and Phoenix, *pro tem* judge appointments are for six months.

The Connecticut referee program is a statewide program; the adjunct recommendation was made by the administrative judge of each judicial district with the appointment of nominated attorneys by the chief justice. Approved adjuncts are sworn in for service as referees for a one-year term.

The Seattle Early Disposition Program was developed with the support and participation of the local bar. The attorneys who were selected to serve on the EDP panels were named by a group of senior bar members and accepted by the court.

A pool of available attorneys was formed for the Minneapolis arbitration program through a general solicitation. Local attorneys who meet minimum qualifications are asked to apply for service as arbitrators. The response was more than adequate to create a sufficient pool. Each week the arbitration coordinator randomly selects the names of attorneys to serve.[2] The arbitration coordinator also has a list of attorneys who are on an on-call status to fill in for cancellations, oversettings, and other emergencies.

It was almost unanimously thought in all six sites that the success of adjunct programs depends largely upon the quality of those selected to serve. Because this is widely recognized, it is often recommended that judges maintain control of the selection process to assure adjuncts meet or exceed required qualifications.[3] Another recommended quality-control measure is the participation of the local bar in the process, since it is very important that adjuncts be respected by their peers. As noted above, Portland, Tucson, and Seattle used bar nomination or review in their selection process.

Bar involvement in adjunct selection helps avoid criticism that the court is biased in the selection process. Although there was only extremely isolated criticism of selection of adjuncts, bar involvement can protect the court from accusations of cronyism, elitism, or other prejudices. (See Chapter 9 for problems that can develop.) In the minds of some, the bar association members themselves have these same prejudices, so bar involvement may not totally allay such criticism.

Those sites that employed a two-tier selection process—with the judges approving bar selections or the supreme court approving or accepting lower court judges' selections—did not suffer undue complexity or delay from the two-level process.

Whatever selection process is used, it should be understood that it is impossible to please everyone. In fact, a court can burden itself unduly by attempting to strike a perfect balance of attorney types for its program. In many programs there was an attempt made to have a mix of plaintiff and defense attorneys serve on the adjunct panel. Maintaining such a mixture over an extended period of time can be difficult. It is simply the nature of civil practice that there are more small-firm and sole-practitioner offices with plaintiff practices and more large firms with defense practices. If adjunct programs demand considerable time from the adjunct, the burden is greater on the plaintiff attorney since the large firm can more easily absorb the loss of income than the sole practitioner.

The importance of having a pool of highly qualified adjuncts is recognized at each site. Nevertheless, it is thought that some attorneys are not of the highest quality even in sites where the pool is small and the adjuncts virtually hand-picked. But those who criticize a few individual adjuncts are quick to point out that the pool as a whole is of high quality. In each project site there are only a certain number of attorneys whose practices and reputation would place them in a "blue ribbon" status. Programs using fewer adjuncts had a higher percentage of "blue ribbon" attorneys serving. Logically, programs that use fewer adjuncts have less difficulty drawing from the highest ranks of the legal community.

The pool of adjuncts that was closest to a "blue ribbon" panel was in Portland. Three factors combined to make this possible: the bar association recommended names, the presiding judge selected highly qualified attorneys, and the pool was limited to approximately 40 attorneys. Those who thought there were some attorneys not of "blue ribbon" caliber in Portland were critical of attorneys who represented opposite sides of the bar, i.e., certain defense attorneys thought that certain plaintiffs' attorneys were not "blue ribbon." Also, some of the adjuncts hearing domestic relations cases in Portland were thought to have been chosen more for their breadth of experience in domestic relations than their stature within the entire legal community.

Those who participated in the Seattle Early Disposition Program were almost unanimous in their opinion that attorneys chosen to sit on the panels were of high quality. Somewhat less concern was demonstrated for the quality of the adjuncts in Seattle, however, as the EDP panels' opinions were only recommended settlements. Litigating participants were pleased that the personal injury panels were composed of one plaintiff-oriented and one defense-oriented adjunct.

In the remaining four sites, the adjunct pool was considered to be composed of high-quality attorneys, but they were characterized more often as a good cross-section of the bar rather than as a "blue ribbon" panel.

Arizona courts have used judicial adjuncts extensively for a number of years. The metropolitan bars of Phoenix and Tucson are accustomed to this practice. By early 1985 Tucson had approximately 70 attorneys in its adjunct pool. Every indication is that the attorneys are well chosen and represent the best attorneys in Tucson, but their peers did not necessarily consider them "blue ribbon" attorneys, in part because the practice of using *pro tem* judges is relatively common and quite a few Tucson attorneys have served as *pro tem* judges. Perhaps, also, the Tucson bar does not have the stratification of members that is found in larger urban areas and its members are reluctant to classify any group of attorneys as elite or "blue ribbon."

The attorneys selected to serve on Department E of the Phoenix court of appeals were selected by the individual judges and then randomly drawn from this pool. The court made an attempt to create a pool of attorneys representing a broad cross-section of the bar. Unfortunately, there were some who viewed the results as giving in to "special interest" groups of the bar; these same critics regarded the quality of the adjunct pool as tarnished. (See Chapter 9.)

In each Connecticut judicial district, the administrative judge nominates adjuncts, who then are considered and appointed as trial referees by the chief justice. In most districts, the attorneys thought that the adjuncts were some of the most highly regarded attorneys in the community, but in isolated instances there were comments that some adjuncts were not qualified.

Since the Minneapolis arbitration program is a large-scale program, the court has not made a significant attempt to control the quality of its arbitrators. At present, all attorneys applying who meet minimum requirements are placed in the pool of available attorneys. Parties who do not want to accept the arbitration award can go to trial without any penalty, so there is less concern that arbitrators meet exacting standards.

When a court considers the quality and background it desires in an adjunct, it should not overlook the psychological phenomenon of attorneys "rising to the occasion." Service as an adjunct is unique and often regarded as an honor by attorneys. They take their responsibility seriously and work to justify their selection by the court. They also do not want to appear inept or be discredited in front of their peers. Thus, adjuncts not regarded as the "best" lawyers may be highly conscientious and perform more than adequately.

As we have seen, one of the major factors in selecting adjuncts is the number of attorneys required in the pool of available attorneys. The presiding judge in Portland indicated that he was trying to keep the pool to a relatively limited size so that he could draw from only the best attorneys in the Portland area. The balance that he had to create was a limited, high-quality pool, but he had to include enough attorneys so as not to overuse them; if the adjuncts thought the court was asking too much of them, they might terminate their service. As attorneys in Portland withdraw as adjuncts, the presiding judge adds additional attorneys to the list.

In continuous adjunct programs the courts maintain a pool by adding adjuncts from time to time. For those projects that are more temporary or cyclical, such as the Phoenix court of appeals project and the Seattle Early Disposition Program, the judges or bar association select a new group of attorneys for each new cycle.[4]

**Training and Orientation**

The Minneapolis arbitration program was the only one that provided formal orientation and training for its adjuncts. Other project sites conducted orientation sessions when adjuncts were sworn into service or supplied them with written material on certain aspects of the program.

In Minneapolis, arbitrators were invited to attend an orientation session conducted by judges of the Hennepin County court and attorneys familiar with the arbitration process. This orientation session was videotaped for subsequent use. The court also developed a comprehensive procedural manual that was given to each arbitrator before his or her service.

In the other five evaluation sites, the adjuncts acknowledged that there was a lack of training or orientation. But there also was very little enthusiasm for expanded training. Most adjuncts reasoned that there was little need for substantive training. When attorneys hear matters involving law with which they are not familiar they view it as an opportunity to learn new areas of the law or update their knowledge in a particular area rather than as an inappropriate or difficult assignment. Such an assignment was especially attractive for some who saw their adjunct service as a break from their day-to-day practice.

Even though adjuncts do not believe substantive training is necessary, in most sites they thought the courts could have provided more thorough orientation in the "nuts and bolts" of the adjunct program, such as help on maintaining a proper judicial demeanor and attitude.

Judges do not see any greater need for training and orientation than the adjuncts do. It is recognized, however, that in isolated instances the adjuncts are not using the procedures the judges had envisioned. If the court had provided the adjuncts with an orientation manual outlining what was required of them, this oversight might have been eliminated. Unfortunately, providing adjuncts with written instructions and orientation will not always eliminate inadequate performance. In Phoenix the court provided the adjuncts with a letter indicating what the court expected of them; yet in some instances the adjuncts did not pay attention to the letter.

When a program is in its initial stages it is difficult for the court to foresee all procedural elements. Therefore, the appropriate approach for training and orientation is to develop an orientation manual before initiation of the program and plan to update it after the initial months to include procedures that were unforeseen or became problem areas for the adjuncts.

The court should also recognize that there are written materials already available that can be supplied to the adjunct. For instance, in Tucson a number of attorneys, especially those adjuncts who heard jury trials, found that the judge's benchbook was a very helpful tool. Some highly experienced litigators admitted they do not pay attention to what judges do at the start of jury trials because they are focusing exclusively on their openings. For them, the benchbook was invaluable. In Phoenix, the court of appeals supplied its adjuncts with the court's style sheet to help standardize opinion writing. Other existing court documentation may be available that would assist adjuncts that could be either given or loaned to them.

**Facilities and Accoutrements**

*Facilities.* In each site, adjuncts served in courtrooms. In all the sites except Phoenix, other rooms within the court such as jury deliberation rooms, conference rooms, and libraries were also utilized for the adjunct program.

In Seattle, each Early Disposition Program panel sat at the counsel table in the middle of the courtroom or arrayed themselves at the judge's bench. The former instances were most common, with the tables arranged in conference room style so that litigating attorneys, parties, adjuncts, and the judge could sit around them. In certain instances, when the EDP panel thought the settlement discussion would benefit from an even more intimate setting, jury rooms were used to make the session more private. In Portland, attorneys prefer to hear summary judgment motions in courtrooms, but it is necessary from time to time to use other courthouse rooms. The situation was very much the same in the referee program in Connecticut.

The Minneapolis arbitration program uses courtrooms in the old court building. The program has grown more rapidly in its first six months than expected, and rehabilitation of existing courtroom facilities in the old courthouse has sometimes resulted in the use of conference rooms, jury rooms, or judges' chambers.

The adjunct program in Tucson is the only one of the six programs where adjuncts scheduled cases outside the courthouse. When court facilities were not available, they held the court trials in their law offices. In these situations court support staff traveled to the adjunct's office.

It was unanimous among judges that adjunct program proceedings should take place in the courthouse. Most lawyers serving as adjuncts felt strongly that the court should supply adequate facilities; a courtroom was seen by them as the best facility. Some adjuncts thought it hindered their ability to proceed when they were forced to use a less-than-adequate room within the courthouse. On the other hand, a few adjuncts, including some serving as judges *pro tem*, preferred the greater informality of a law office.

With court facilities at a premium, it might be necessary to have adjuncts report to one specific office, such as the office of the program administrator or the clerk of the court, for assignment to available facilities at the time of the hearing. This is the procedure followed in Minneapolis, where the arbitrators, litigating attorneys, and parties report to the arbitration director's office for assignment to individual courtrooms. This assignment process can make maximum use of available space as well as facilitate last-minute changes in assigned cases, since adjunct program calendars, like other court calendars, are subject to last-minute settlements and other developments that prevent proceeding as scheduled.

*Accoutrements.* The judicial decorum with which the judicial adjunct program is conducted varies depending upon the program and the overall philosophy adopted for it. In Seattle, as noted, the tactic that was used by most panels was to have the judge and adjuncts sit at a table with the litigating attorneys and parties to discuss the case at hand. In most cases the judge and in all cases the adjuncts did not wear robes and they conducted themselves relatively informally. The other end of the spectrum is represented by the philosophy of the arbitration program in Minneapolis, where the arbitrators are asked to wear robes, sit at the bench, and conduct the arbitration hearing in a formal manner, even though the rules of procedure and evidence are relaxed. The arbitrators in Minneapolis understand the philosophy that to a certain extent the arbitration hearing is providing the parties with "their day in court," and so the court wishes the hearing to have regular judicial decorum. Some arbitrators initially opposed or felt uneasy about the use of robes, but after serving almost all came to see that their wearing robes was important to the litigants and added appropriate formality to the proceeding. In the more relaxed atmosphere of the Tucson and Portland programs, some adjuncts think it is appropriate to wear robes and do so, while others do not. The Department E panel of Division One of the Arizona Court of Appeals conducted itself exactly as a regular division of the court.

The staff support that adjuncts receive depends both on the ability of the court to supply clerical support staff and on demands of the particular adjunct program. In the Seattle EDP program the judge's clerk and bailiff attended the settlement conferences and assisted in handling the logistics of the sessions. In Portland, the summary judgment adjuncts receive no clerical support and conduct the motion hearings on their own. In Connecticut and Minneapolis, the situation is much the same; the adjuncts do not have clerical support staff provided by the court, although the arbitration administrator's staff may do some of the clerical work for arbitrators after the hearing is concluded. In Tucson, the court has provided court clerk and court reporter support for the adjuncts and has the support staff travel to the individual adjunct's law offices when the court trial is conducted at those offices rather than the courthouse.

In most instances the adjuncts' use of their own staff to support their service is quite limited. In most programs, some cases will require the preparation of memoranda. The adjunct almost always calls upon his or her office staff to serve in completing these tasks. Naturally, correspondence between the court and the adjunct regarding the program is completed with the assistance of the lawyer's staff, but beyond this standard correspondence and report preparation, very little is done by adjuncts' own support staff in any of the sites. The main exception is the isolated use of legal staff to do research for the adjuncts. Instances of junior attorneys or law clerks doing research for the adjuncts were reported in Portland, Phoenix, and Tucson. The vast majority of the adjuncts, however, thought it was necessary to do their own legal research.

## Notes to Chapter Three

1. This court was studied in Phase I of the project. See *Guidelines*, p. 35.
2. The random process is adjusted to assure that the arbitrator and litigating attorneys are in different firms and, in some cases, to provide an arbitrator familiar with the type of cases assigned.
3. *Guidelines*, pp. 7 and 15.
4. In Phoenix unused names from previous six-month appointments were used on subsequent panels.

CHAPTER FOUR

# The Adjuncts' Perspective

Lawyers serve in adjunct programs primarily because they believe they have a duty to do so. Some attorneys view this service as part of the tradition to contribute a certain amount of time to the legal system with minimal or no compensation. Others, particularly those whose practices have been quite successful, believe they owe a debt to the judicial system for having enabled them to develop and maintain lucrative practices.

In each project site there was significant concern with delay in getting cases through the system and the backlog of civil cases that perpetuates this delay. Although most adjuncts view their participation as a service to the court, a significant minority also see that any reduction in backlog or case processing time would benefit their own practices. In Portland, for instance, where it was taking as much time to get a summary judgment motion scheduled as a trial, attorneys saw that they could have their own summary judgment motions heard at a much earlier date through the adjunct program. Similarly, in Phoenix, where there was a two-year wait from at-issue to argument in the court of appeals, attorneys saw that their own cases on appeal could be heard much more quickly if the backlog were reduced and case processing time decreased.

In isolated instances attorneys stated their belief that serving as an adjunct would be beneficial to their own aspirations to be selected as a judge in their jurisdiction. The vast majority of attorneys, though, indicated that they had no ambitions to judicial office.

Almost all the attorneys who served as adjuncts indicated that they had gained new perspective on what it was like to be a judge. To some, this new perspective provided useful insight on how they might improve their own presentations as advocates in court. Others reported that they simply had gained considerably more respect for the task of judging.

Adjuncts also were able to gain a better perspective on the general quality of preparation within the local bar. Many adjuncts were dismayed with the poor quality of preparation by their peers.

## Lawyers Provide Useful, Complementary Expertise

A number of adjuncts believe that by bringing their perspective as a current practicing attorney to the bench, they bring a useful perspective to the judicial position. To the extent that judges become removed from the realities of an attorney's everyday practice, the judicial adjuncts add this perspective.[1] The adjuncts also bring an enormous wealth of experience in a variety of areas of the law. The Seattle EDP program, to a limited degree the Minneapolis arbitration program, and, for motions in domestic relations cases, the Portland program tried to match attorneys to cases involving their particular specialties. The other sites did not make such attempts. Nevertheless, by sheer numbers, adding adjuncts to the bench brings a vast variety of expertise in the law.

## Permanent Versus Temporary Programs

As each adjunct program becomes established within the community, a sense develops that if the program is not explicitly limited in its duration, it will become permanent. For the most part, attorneys do not see this as a negative but think that if the adjunct program is able to relieve the court of backlog and reduce case processing time it nonetheless could be reduced in scope but maintained for future use on a more limited basis.

In Tucson, for instance, where the adjuncts were given a block of civil cases to dispose of, the adjuncts believe the need for *pro tem* judges will continue well beyond disposition of this initial block of cases. Although most originally thought the program would be temporary, they are not concerned that it now appears to be needed indefinitely.

In Portland, attorneys think that the summary-judgment-motions program has become institutionalized to the point that it will continue at least for the foreseeable future. In Seattle, the judicial adjuncts saw the EDP program as a stopgap type of program but one which could—and should—be repeated at least annually, if not twice a year.

In Phoenix, there was an understanding that the program was developed to deal with a severe backlog of cases and that it probably would be discontinued once this backlog had been worked through, but even here the adjuncts saw the possibility that the program could be continued on a permanent basis. Several hoped it would be maintained, believing appellate filings would continue to increase faster than judgeships and thus that the court would continue to need help for a number of years. There was a similar feeling among adjuncts in Connecticut, as in Phoenix, that they were serving during a particularly critical period when there were not adequate judicial resources and that the legislature might remedy this by authorizing new judgeships.[2] Yet the program *could* continue indeterminately. In Minneapolis, it is clear that the adjuncts think that if the arbitration program is successful, it will become institutionalized within the court. Many attorneys in Minneapolis favor a permanent program because they favor arbitration as an alternative dispute resolution process, whether or not the court has enough judges.

## Number of Hours Adjuncts Are Willing to Volunteer

The attorneys in Seattle, Phoenix, Tucson, and Portland volunteered their services. The service was limited in Seattle to a day or two once a year and in Phoenix to a maximum of twice a year. Although adjuncts in Phoenix sat and heard arguments on only one day, preparation for the arguments, writing opinions, and reviewing the opinions of others often involved a number of extra days. The typical judge *pro tem* in Phoenix donated between three and four days of time each instance of service; a few donated seven and more days.

In Portland and Tucson, attorneys may be called on to serve considerably more often than in the other sites. In Portland the question of the maximum number of hours an attorney is willing to volunteer is of very real concern. The median time attorneys spend in preparation for a day's summary judgment hearings is seven to eight hours. The day that is scheduled for hearing summary judgment motions involves another seven to eight hours. If attorneys take a number of cases under advisement, there are additional hours in writing memoranda that are necessary to conclude the one day's service. In a typical instance, this time volunteered to the court could consume up to three days of an attorney's time. In spite of this, most adjuncts in Portland think that it is appropriate to schedule them for service once every three months.

In Tucson the adjuncts' chief concern seemed to be presiding over trials that required more than two or three days of their time. One sole practitioner presided over a court trial (before the block-assignment program went into effect) estimated to be four to five days long that actually required ten trial days and almost as much time after the trial to reach a decision and write an opinion. That amount of time severely affected that adjunct's practice. He said he could not take a case like that again. Although no other judge *pro tem* in Tucson had a similar experience, several are careful to check on the estimated length of individual trials and/or to limit the number of times a year they serve. A few said if the court sought more days a year from them they would withdraw from the list.

In Connecticut, some litigating attorneys as well as adjuncts expressed the hope that the court would limit its calls on individual trial referees to avoid driving away some of the well-regarded referees.

On the other hand, in Tucson, Portland, and Connecticut a few adjuncts donate a truly significant number of days each month (up to four or five days a month regularly) and are happy to do so.

In all six sites, adjuncts seem to have little trouble donating three or four days during a year. Service significantly beyond six days a year might seriously restrict the pool of attorneys from which a court could draw.

## Functions Adjuncts Are Willing to Serve

Judicial adjuncts are willing to assume almost any function if they perceive a need, although the function served may affect who volunteers and how many hours the adjuncts are willing to volunteer. For instance, in Seattle where the adjuncts serve on a three-person panel to provide litigants with a possible settlement determination, it is understood that the disposition reached by the panel is only a recommendation; therefore, the adjuncts are willing to volunteer only a limited number of hours to this program. When the Seattle EDP adjuncts were asked if the program should be repeated more frequently in future years, many indicated they would not be willing to expand their service.

In the Phoenix court of appeals program, some adjuncts expressed dismay that the memorandum opinions they wrote would not be published. They implied they would be willing to devote more hours to their service if their opinions were published.

In some of the project sites, adjuncts perceived that the cases they heard were cases the judges of the court did not want to hear. When asked whether the judges were "dumping" cases on them, the most common response of the adjuncts was that this might be, but that it was an appropriate allocation of resources. If the court as a whole were able to improve its civil case processing, then the type of case allocated to the judicial adjuncts would be of little or no concern. On the other hand, some adjuncts clearly looked for *some* challenging matters as "compensation" for their assistance.

## Conclusion

Adjuncts seem to feel the benefits they receive far outweigh the loss of several days of practice a year. These benefits include (1) psychic satisfaction in helping the "system"; (2) reducing the size of the backlog or the time to disposition so their own clients' cases move faster; (3) a better understanding of what is and what is not important to a judge in a trial or hearing; (4) for some, an opportunity to meet with and get to know judges as colleagues; and, finally, (5) for a few, the opportunity to test or advance their interest in becoming a judge.

## Notes to Chapter Four

1. To the extent that judges are appointed after years of practice as a government attorney, often as a prosecutor or public defender, the judges may have little or no exposure to private practice.

2. Since the program started in Connecticut six additional judgeships have been created and six more were recommended in the Governor's budget for 1987.

CHAPTER FIVE

# Key Considerations in Designing a Judicial Adjunct Program

A judicial adjunct program should be approached in three phases, each equally important: planning, initiating, and operating and adjusting the program. The key components in each of these phases are reviewed in this chapter.

## Planning

Each new program a court undertakes should be planned carefully; a program using judicial adjuncts is no different, but there are a few steps in the design and planning process that are unique to judicial adjunct programs. Following is a checklist of items that should be considered. A particular adjunct program or a particular court environment might require expanding this list, but a court considering an adjunct program should at least address each of the following items. It also should be recognized that some of the items listed below overlap; the order in which they are discussed may not be the order in which a court would address them.

**Define Real Problem**
Judicial adjuncts can be effective in dealing with some problems, but not all. The responsible judicial authorities and court staff should seek to identify the exact nature of the problem(s) facing the court, either through an evaluation of statistics or a series of in-depth, confidential interviews, or both. When the cause and nature of the problem are identified, it should be easier to determine if judicial adjuncts can provide all or part of the solution. For example, if the court is considering

establishing a judge *pro tem* program, but the true problem is that lawyers are not prepared when they reach their first trial date, having more judges to try cases may not be as effective a solution as a plan to assure that lawyers are prepared when the trial date is reached. If the problem is the need to attack a backlog of cases ready for trial, however, the use of judges *pro tem* would be an appropriate response. In light of the experience in our evaluation sites, a court might also consider the use of adjuncts as one part of a multi-faceted attack on the problem(s).

**Check Statutes and Rules**
Before lawyers are considered for use as supplemental judicial resources, it is important to check existing statutes and rules to be sure that there are no legal impediments. If lawyers' use in the manner being considered is prohibited, or if it is not explicitly permitted and the court wants some positive sanction for the program, it may be necessary to seek new statutory or rule provisions.[1]

**Define Goals**
Specific and, if possible, quantifiable goals should be established for the program. Several benefits derive from setting goals. Developing and agreeing on goals within the court and broader justice community focuses attention on the true problem or problems, helps to identify and refine solutions, and builds a constituency for the new program. Goals will help all to understand the program's purposes, may help define the appropriate duration of the program, will help establish the evaluation approach and process, will enable an evaluation to provide useful answers to the court about the impact of the program, and help a court to measure expected benefits against projected costs. Goals also provide a benchmark against which the court can measure its progress during the life of the program. Comparison of results to a predetermined goal often provides positive reinforcement to participants and serves as an ongoing inducement to maintain the efforts required by the program.

**Obtain Judges' Support**
Whether or not all of the judges on the court will be involved with or affected by the use of judicial adjuncts, the program is much more likely to be successful if all or a significant majority of the judges support and approve of the new program.

**Consult with the Bar**
A program involving judicial adjuncts must have bar support. Very early in the planning process key members of the bar—the principal bar association, several bar associations, or a bar association and key individual lawyers—should be consulted. If the need is clearly defined and

understood by the bar, the court can expect full, and in most cases enthusiastic, support.

### Involve Staff
Often more staff than judicial time is involved in running the judicial adjunct program. Even if this is not the case, staff have important expertise that might affect program design decisions. The court administrator, clerk of court, and other key staff people should be involved early in the planning process to avoid including features that will cause judges, lawyers, or staff unnecessary difficulties during implementation.

### Define Program Elements
The elements of the program should be defined carefully. They might include types and number of cases to be included; age of cases to be included, if relevant; number of judges and adjuncts needed; facilities to be used; staff to be assigned; and the point at which cases are assigned to adjuncts. This definition process provides further understanding of what is involved so the potential administrative burden can be determined in advance.

### Estimate Costs
In determining estimates of costs for the program, a distinction should be made between new, out-of-pocket costs that would not otherwise be incurred and indirect costs associated with using staff diverted from other tasks. Based on the goals and program elements, the court should estimate any additional out-of-pocket costs and indirect costs associated with the program. Just as caseload and case processing data should be monitored during a program, so too should costs. A court might find indirect costs to be acceptable but impose limits on new, out-of-pocket costs.

### Establish Evaluation and Monitoring Procedures
Undertaking evaluation and monitoring of a program enables the court to assess its success or failure with more certainty than through anecdotes or "feelings." Monitoring procedures also enable the court to see the impact of the program as it proceeds, thus providing early warning of impending problems or early notice of growing success.

### Establish Expected Duration
An initial projection should be made of how long the program will be needed. Some programs may be needed for only a few months, some for a year or two, and some indefinitely. Establishing the expected duration of the program enables both the court and the bar to understand more fully the obligations they are undertaking.

## Consider a Pilot Project
Depending on the nature of the problem being attacked and the program being established, it may be advisable to test the use of judicial adjuncts on a portion of the problem or only some of the eligible cases. The results of using judicial adjuncts can be compared with the results in cases processed in the normal fashion in order to determine whether the adjuncts' use has been beneficial. A pilot project also serves to limit initial costs and may mute some initial opposition.

## Establish Adjunct Selection Criteria and Procedures
The nature and duration of the program will help to define how many adjuncts will be needed and, in general terms, the time commitment to be asked of adjuncts. Once these items are known, the criteria for those serving as adjuncts and the procedures for selecting them can be established. Most successful adjunct programs have included members of the bar in the selection process, although the court should reserve the final authority for appointing or designating adjuncts.[2]

## Determine Location of Proceedings and Use of Accoutrements
Depending on the nature of the program, it may or may not be appropriate to allow adjuncts to use their own offices or conference rooms. If adjunct proceedings are held in the courthouse, it may or may not be appropriate for the adjuncts to use courtrooms, have robes, and have courtroom staff. To the extent possible, the court should decide its preference on these issues and advise adjuncts before the program is implemented.

# Initiation of the Program
After all elements have been planned, several steps must be concluded before the program actually starts. As with the discussion of planning, steps below are listed for ease of reference and not necessarily in the order in which the steps would be undertaken.

## Allow Sufficient Lead Time
A court faced with an immediate problem, and in some cases a critical situation, may wish to implement a judicial adjunct program at the earliest possible time. If, however, sufficient time to plan and start the program is not provided, the court risks either not gaining the benefits it desires or having to invest substantial administrative time after the program is started in correcting problems caused by an insufficient planning effort. A little extra time spent planning and initiating a program can save substantial time and problems after it gets started.

### Announce Program and Goals

The program and its goals should be announced to both the bar and the general public. The bar needs to know that the court is undertaking a new program and the parameters of that program. Members of the public should be advised so that they are aware of the court's efforts to address a problem and of the court's expectations for the new program. If the judicial adjunct program also involves the bar donating its time to the court, the public should be made aware of this public service by the bar. There might be more than one announcement: one when the program is agreed to by the court, one shortly before it starts, and one on the first day of the program.

### Select Adjuncts

Judicial adjuncts must be identified, screened for qualifications, invited to participate, and appointed.

### Establish Committee to Monitor the Program

A committee composed of judges, staff, and bar members should be established to monitor the program and, if necessary, adjust its parameters or procedures. A committee offers two benefits: (1) it provides a variety of perspectives on the operation of the program and (2) the bar will have a continuing involvement with and commitment to successful operation of the program.

### Orient Litigating Bar

Although the program may be announced in writing in a number of media that reach members of the bar who will be litigating before judicial adjuncts, it is useful for some programs to have in-person orientation programs. The experience in Connecticut can be contrasted with the experience in Minneapolis with respect to the effectiveness of written announcements versus orientation programs. Not every judicial adjunct program requires meetings or workshops, but many would benefit from bringing members of the litigating bar together to discuss the program with judges and court staff.

### Train and Orient Adjuncts

Despite the protest of some judicial adjuncts in the programs the National Center evaluated and the skepticism of many judges in the evaluation sites, training and orientation for adjuncts appears to be necessary. The components of that training and orientation will be determined by the nature and scope of the program being undertaken, but we are confident, based on interviews of adjuncts in all six evaluation sites, that adjuncts will accept training and orientation meetings up to half a day without question and, in some cases, a full day. Adjuncts would welcome written manuals or memoranda discussing the nature of their assigned responsibilities and the procedures to be followed. In addition to the mechanics of the program, procedures to be followed, and the amount of time and effort expected of the average adjunct, the orientation should include explicit discussion of the issues of judicial ethics and conflicts of interest. Many of the judicial adjuncts interviewed in the evaluation sites were sensitive to questions of conflicts of interest and judicial ethics, but many also felt they would have benefited from explicit discussions or written materials on these matters prior to undertaking their service.

## Operating the Program

The court's responsibility for the program does not end with its initiation. Very few programs are self-executing, particularly programs using many adjuncts, such as settlement and arbitration programs. Beyond the usual daily administrative responsibilities associated with the program, a court should consider the following items.

### Monitoring

Even if a formal evaluation procedure is not established, the court should keep key statistics on the program's impact and review them periodically. As pointed out, monitoring the program has several positive effects. It helps the court to identify problems early. It provides information indicating success or failure, progress or slippage in the program. It enables the court to assess whether the program is meeting its goals, not only at the end but while it is proceeding; it may identify not only what needs to be adjusted but the type of adjustments that are appropriate.

### Provide Caseload Feedback to Judges and Judicial Adjuncts

It is important that the judges and adjuncts be aware of how the program is progressing, whether the results are positive or indicate developing problems. Positive results build support in the dubious and sustain enthusiasm in advocates. If problems are identified, steps can be taken to address them or to terminate the program early. The sharing of information is an important element of some of the more successful programs we have observed.

### Provide Performance Feedback to Judicial Adjuncts

Beyond data, one of the most often-expressed concerns of adjuncts in the six evaluation sites is the absence of any feedback on how they individually are performing their assigned tasks. Even if a lawyer is very confident of his or her ability as a lawyer, he or she appreciates suggestions on how to perform judicial duties better, or confirmation from a judge that the adjunct is doing the assigned job well. Personal expressions of thanks, sharing suggestions for improvement, and confirmation of a job well done can be very important elements in maintaining a successful program.

**Hold Follow-up Meetings**

A few evaluation sites scheduled follow-up meetings with judicial adjuncts after their programs had been operating for a while. These proved to be very successful. It gave the court an opportunity to answer unexpected or uncovered questions from the judicial adjuncts, it allowed the adjuncts to share among themselves problems they had encountered and their responses to them, and it allowed the court to learn of any potential or actual problems that occurred in the early stages. The courts that held these meetings have included adjuncts who had already served and adjuncts about to serve; both groups have found these meetings to be very useful.

**Revise Procedures and Manuals**

It may be necessary to change some of the original procedures after the program has operated for a few months. Monitoring the program helps the court to identify these needs and, as indicated, sometimes to identify necessary adjustments. Probably in the second or third quarter of a program's life, the original procedures and manuals should be reexamined and revised as needed.

## Guidelines for the Use of Lawyers to Supplement Judicial Resources

The items discussed in this chapter draw not only on our observations in the six evaluation sites but also on the *Guidelines for the Use of Lawyers to Supplement Judicial Resources* developed by the project advisory board in 1984. We note that none of the results in the six evaluations detracts from or suggests the need for amending the guidelines. If anything, the value of the guidelines has been reinforced by our experience in the six sites.

The text of the *Guidelines* is reproduced below. Supporting commentary can be found in the *Guidelines* publication itself.

**Guideline 1: The Use of Lawyers to Supplement Judicial Resources**

Court systems should consider using lawyers in a variety of capacities as supplemental resources when full-time judicial resources are inadequate to meet the demands made of them. Such use should not be a permanent alternative to the creation of needed full-time judicial positions. Lawyers temporarily serving the courts in any capacity are referred to in these guidelines as judicial adjuncts.

### Guideline 2: Establishing a Judicial Adjunct Program
The development of any judicial adjunct program should include the following:

*Program Objectives.* Programs should be developed to meet identified needs. Objectives for each program should be related to the identified needs and should be stated prior to the start of each program. These objectives should be explicit and, to the extent feasible, expressed in measurable terms.

*Court Involvement and Control.* Responsibility for administration of the program should reside with the court. Judges and other personnel of the court to be served should be involved in its planning.

*Bar Involvement.* The support and cooperation of the local legal community is necessary to the success of any judicial adjunct program. Lawyers should be involved in program planning from the outset.

*Other Support.* The court should solicit the advice and cooperation of others who will play a role in the program.

*Evaluation and Monitoring Procedures.* To the extent possible, programs should be planned to permit sound evaluation of their effectiveness. Evaluation procedures should be in place before a program is commenced. Continuing programs should be monitored periodically for sustained effectiveness.

### Guideline 3: Scope of Judicial Adjunct Programs
Except for serious criminal trials and child custody proceedings, most types of cases are appropriate for assignment to judicial adjuncts.

### Guideline 4: Selection of Judicial Adjuncts
Those eligible to serve as judicial adjuncts should be selected by the appropriate judicial authority. Criteria should be established to ensure that participants in the program are highly qualified. As required by the nature of the duties to be performed, emphasis should be placed on reputation, demeanor, knowledge of the law, and specific experience in trial, appellate, or other relevant practice.

### Guideline 5: Orientation and Training of Judicial Adjuncts
Orientation and training programs should be provided for new judicial adjuncts. Their scope, format, and length should vary with the complexity and formality of proceedings over which the judicial adjunct will preside.

### Guideline 6: Party Consent to Appearance Before a Judicial Adjunct
Assignment of cases to judicial adjunct programs should not be subject to the consent of the parties or their counsel. Appropriate mechanisms should be established to provide parties an option concerning the particular judicial adjunct before whom they will appear, without permitting a party to delay the resolution of the case.

### Guideline 7: Ethical Considerations
Judicial adjuncts should be bound by the Code of Professional Responsibility and by appropriate provisions of the Code of Judicial Conduct. The judicial adjunct and the litigating attorneys should share responsibility for identifying conflicts and possible conflicts that preclude the judicial adjunct from hearing a particular matter.

**Guideline 8: Compensation**

Courts establishing programs of limited duration or programs that require limited time from judicial adjuncts should solicit service on a *pro bono* basis. Other programs should compensate judicial adjuncts in the amount necessary to recruit and retain an adequate number of qualified lawyers.

**Guideline 9: Facilities and Other Resources**

The type of judicial function to be performed and the availability of public facilities and other resources should be considered in determining the facilities and other services furnished to judicial adjuncts.

# Notes to Chapter Five

1. Cf. *Guidelines*, Appendix A.
2. *Guidelines*, p. 15.

CHAPTER SIX

# Conclusion

Judicial adjunct programs, particularly those using judges *pro tem* and lawyers as trial referees, have a positive impact on the number of dispositions and the time to disposition in courts. In two programs the impact seemed to involve, also, a "Hawthorne effect," with the adjunct program a key element of a more total court commitment to change. The number of additional dispositions achieved by adjuncts may represent the equivalent of adding several judicial positions.

Not only were there quantitative gains from using judicial adjuncts, but also adjunct programs appear to result in improved relations between the court and the bar, particularly members serving as judicial adjuncts, and an improved understanding among adjuncts—and indirectly more broadly within the bar—of the judicial role and the problems experienced by judges in dealing with ill-prepared and inarticulate attorneys. Adjunct programs also produce a knowledgeable group of people able to speak out on matters of concern to the judiciary. Even when quantitative, caseload-related results were not as great as originally hoped, all courts experienced this indirect qualitative gain.

Finally, the use of judicial adjuncts may, in appropriate circumstances, be evidence of a court's efforts to do all it can to address temporary or continuing problems of calendar management without adding permanent judicial resources. There is no evidence in the six evaluation sites, or in the sites studied as background for development of the guidelines in Phase I of this study, that the use of judicial adjuncts, even as judges *pro tem* or trial referees, adversely affects a court's ability to obtain needed judicial positions.[1] The possibility of such an adverse effect remains a concern in some sites, however.

The use of adjuncts appears to involve some additional out-of-pocket expenses and to impose some administrative burdens on a court's staff, but those costs and the burdens were viewed by both judges and staff in five of the six evaluation sites as justified by the benefits achieved by the programs; the exception was found in Seattle, where the absence of a clear reduction in the trial rate led the judges to discontinue that court's settlement conference program. Even in this latter instance, the court's out-of-pocket and indirect staff costs were not an expressed concern.

The most significant concerns about the use of judicial adjuncts—that the use of practicing lawyers in judicial or quasi-judicial roles creates inevitable and undesirable problems of conflicts of interest and creates the appearance that justice is being adversely affected—were not deemed to be problems in the six sites evaluated. No doubt the sensitivity of the judges in each of these sites to the potential for problems caused them to design and monitor the programs to avoid these problems. The organized bar associations also were sensitive to potential problems and worked with the courts to avoid or minimize them. It will remain important for courts instituting adjunct programs to be sensitive to these issues and for adjuncts to be sensitive to them, as well. We also were advised of no instance of an adjunct's trying to gain financially from his or her affiliation with the court.

Evidence of problems arising from two other concerns about adjunct programs—that they depreciate the importance of a full-time judiciary and that they may complicate or preclude the addition to a court of needed judges—is lacking in all sites. Some people in each site remain concerned about these possibilities, but they were not manifest during the project.

When the guidelines were being developed during Phase I of this study, the courts studied reported many positive results and few negative consequences from their programs. These courts, however, seldom were able to document the impact of their adjunct programs. The six evaluation efforts over the past 30 months have confirmed the positive, anecdotal statements from the courts originally visited. The use of judicial adjuncts may not always produce results as positive as desired, as happened in Seattle, or may not have the indirect consequences desired, as in Tuscon, but it appears that courts can achieve significant improvements in case management through the use of judicial adjuncts. Sometimes the improvement is traceable to the use of adjuncts and sometimes the use of adjuncts is part of a new commitment by the bench to reduce delay and cure backlogs, but in all cases improvement is discernible.

As demonstrated in five of the six sites, a significant proportion of the bar, for various reasons that include a general commitment to the legal system, is willing to commit significant amounts of time to the courts without compensation. In times of restricted budgets, the bar's willingness to donate its services makes the potential positive impact of judicial adjuncts on a court's dispositions even more attractive.

All six evaluations demonstrate with encouraging consistency that courts can benefit, sometimes appreciably but in all cases positively, from the use of lawyers as supplemental judicial resources.

## Notes to Chapter Six

1. We note, again, that since the program started in Connecticut six additional judgeships have been created and six more were recommended in the governor's budget for 1987.

PART TWO

# Evaluation Reports for Six Sites

The following six chapters present a detailed description of each program, the results of the quantitative, qualitative, and administrative evaluations, and the authors' suggestions for adjustments to the program in each site to improve its operation or impact.

In each of the site reports, background descriptions are of the situation as it existed when the program was initiated and of the program as originally designed. If the situation or program changed significantly during the evaluation, the changes are noted. A program that remains in effect at the time this report is being written, September 1986, is described generally in the present tense. If the program or situation terminated during the evaluation, it is described in the past tense.

CHAPTER SEVEN

# The Tucson Pro Tem Judge Program

The Pima County Superior Court serves Tucson, Arizona, the second largest city in the state. It is a trial court of general jurisdiction, handling civil cases with a demand for money damages over $500 or for equitable relief, felonies and misdemeanors, and civil and criminal appeals from lower courts. It is divided into four divisions: civil, criminal, probate, and domestic relations. During the period of the study, there were five judges primarily assigned to civil cases, although all seventeen judges heard some civil trials. The court uses a master calendar system for civil case assignment.

The City of Tucson is growing much faster than the capacity of the court has grown. The court wanted to take some steps to improve its caseload management in order to head off some of the problems the rapid growth has created. The problems for a court faced with rapid growth in the jurisdiction's population are apparent from some of the data produced during the evaluation.

## Description of the Program

The Pima County Superior Court has used *pro tem* judges in several capacities for several years.[1] In 1982 the court instituted a civil delay reduction program in which *pro tem* judges were used to help assure firm trial dates and to fill in when judges were ill or on vacation. *Pro tem* judges continued to be used for these purposes on a limited, *ad hoc* basis until February 1984, when the court began a new phase in its use of *pro tem* judges.

Because of some problems in calendaring cases for trial, in late 1983 the court recognized that many more civil cases had been scheduled for court and jury trials in the first quarter of 1984 than the court could possibly try. To alleviate this situation the court decided to assign approximately 300 civil court-trial cases—all the court trials pending at the time—to its panel of *pro tem* judges.

The presiding judge and assistant presiding judge selected new *pro tem* judges from attorneys who had practiced at least five years and whom they believed to be good trial lawyers. They then recommended these attorneys to the Chief Justice of Arizona for appointment by him for the statutorily defined six-month terms. Originally, only the judges of the court selected *pro tem* judges, but starting in 1984, selected attorneys' names were reviewed by a committee of the local bar, also. Since 1984, *pro tem* judges have been added to the panel as needed. Some are used only in domestic relations cases. (By early 1985 the panel of attorneys appointed by the chief justice had grown to approximately 70.)

In February 1984 each of approximately 50 *pro tem* judges was assigned a block of six court-trial civil cases for disposition. It was hoped the court then would be able to calendar and try the remaining jury-trial cases on their assigned (sometimes newly assigned) trial dates. *Pro tem* judges were told to schedule their block of six cases as they saw fit.

After assignment, each *pro tem* judge reviewed the cases for possible conflicts of interest. If a case presented a conflict of interest, the *pro tem* judge informed the court and the case was reassigned, either to another *pro tem* judge or to a regular judge for trial. Similarly, if one of the parties exercised the right to remove a *pro tem* judge from a case without cause after assignment, the case was reassigned by staff either to another *pro tem* judge or to a regular judge, depending upon the circumstances.

It was anticipated that *pro tem* judges would schedule settlement conferences before trials were held and dispose of some of their assigned cases without trial. It was thought each *pro tem* might have to try only two of the six cases. The court undertook to provide courtrooms, if possible, for needed trials and to provide the *pro tem* judges with clerical and court reporting support. An attempt was made to hold as many as possible of the trials conducted by *pro tem* judges in regular courtrooms in order to assure an appropriate setting. This was not always possible, however, so some trials were conducted in the library of the courthouse or in the conference facilities of the *pro tem* judges' law offices. Trials in the courtrooms tended to be more formal than those conducted elsewhere. When sitting in a courtroom, most *pro tem* judges chose to wear a robe, but no matter what the setting all *pro tem* judges were addressed as "Your Honor." When a *pro tem* judge achieved disposition of an assigned case, the disposition was reported to the court.

Judgments of *pro tem* judges have all the force and authority of judgments of regular judges of the court. Appeals of their rulings are handled as are appeals of cases disposed by regular judges.

While this special program was in effect, the court continued to use *pro tem* judges for other matters, including civil and criminal jury trials.

For the first six months of 1984 the court used selected *pro tem* judges to conduct civil mental commitment hearings at the local state mental hospital. The number of lawyers on the list for these hearings was much more limited than the general *pro tem* panel and their use was more sparing, since the judge responsible for disposition of civil mental commitment cases wanted to assure expertise in the area and to provide litigants with a regular judge to the greatest degree possible. A graduate student from the University of Arizona conducted a separate evaluation of this program under contract with the National Center for State Courts. Her report is Appendix A. For the balance of this chapter, only the civil court-trial *pro tem* judge program will be discussed.

Two adjustments were made in the design of the program after it was implemented. Some *pro tem* judges recused themselves from selected cases; others were challenged and removed by the litigating parties. Rather than reassigning these cases to different *pro tem* judges for trial as originally planned, these cases were reassigned to regular judges of the court. In addition, some court-trial cases were assigned directly to regular judges for trial after the *pro tem* program began. These adjustments meant that the civil court-trial list was divided between regular judges of the court and *pro tem* judges.

## Program Goals

The *pro tem* judge program was implemented to achieve the following four goals:

- Dispose of the 300 civil court-trial cases originally assigned to the program, thereby reducing the civil pending caseload.
- Reduce the number of civil and criminal jury trials not reached because a judge was not available.
- Reduce over the long term the time from filing of the motion-to-set to disposition for civil and criminal cases.
- By improving case currency, enhance the reputation of the court in the local legal community.

## Quantitative Evaluation

Data were collected by the court on all civil court-trial-list cases disposed between January 1984 and March 1985. These data were analyzed to determine the impact of *pro tem* judges on the caseload of the court during the first year of the special program. A majority of the 346 civil court-trial cases disposed during the period had been assigned to a *pro tem* judge in early 1984, more than two-thirds during February 1984. Almost three-quarters of the 346 cases were disposed by *pro tem* judges; the remainder were disposed by regular judges of the court.

Cases disposed by *pro tem* judges and regular judges were similar. Table 1 compares the two groups of cases by type. Contracts made up over half of the court-trial cases assigned to *pro tem* judges and regular judges. Appeals made up a similar proportion of the caseloads of both *pro tem* and regular judges, although the proportion of arbitration appeals was higher

**TABLE 1**

**Types of civil court-trial and jury cases disposed by *pro tem* judges and regular judges, January 1984 to March 1985**

|  | \multicolumn{6}{c}{Court-trial cases} | \multicolumn{2}{c}{Jury-trial cases} |
|---|---|---|---|---|---|---|---|---|
|  | \multicolumn{2}{c}{Pro tem judges} | \multicolumn{2}{c}{Regular judges} | \multicolumn{2}{c}{Total} |  |  |
| Type of case | No. | Percent | No. | Percent | No. | Percent | No. | Percent |
| Motor vehicle tort | 18 | 8 | 7 | 8 | 25 | 8 | 78 | 49 |
| Nonmotor vehicle tort | 24 | 11 | 4 | 5 | 28 | 9 | 36 | 22 |
| Contract | 131 | 60 | 53 | 64 | 184 | 61 | 30 | 19 |
| Malpractice | 0 |  | 0 |  | 0 |  | 4 | 2 |
| Fraud | 1 | <1 | 2 | 2 | 3 | 1 | 0 |  |
| Eminent domain | 0 |  | 1 | 1 | 1 | <1 | 0 |  |
| Quiet title | 2 | 1 | 0 |  | 2 | 1 | 0 |  |
| Declaratory judgment | 2 | 1 | 2 | 2 | 4 | 1 | 0 |  |
| Foreclosure | 5 | 2 | 1 | 1 | 6 | 2 | 2 | 1 |
| Interpleader | 1 | <1 | 1 | 1 | 2 | 1 | 0 |  |
| Real property | 0 |  | 0 |  | 0 |  | 1 | <1 |
| Other/unclassified | 34 | 16 | 12 | 14 | 46 | 15 | 9 | 6 |
| TOTAL | 218 | 100 | 83 | 100 | 301 | 100 | 160 | 100 |
| **Appeals** |  |  |  |  |  |  |  |  |
| Arbitration appeal | 12 |  | 8 |  | 20 |  | 3 |  |
| Justice of the Peace appeal | 20 |  | 5 |  | 25 |  | 0 |  |
| TOTAL APPEALS | 32 |  | 13 |  | 45 |  | 3 |  |

for regular judges, and justice of the peace appeals were a larger proportion of *pro tem* judges' caseloads.

Because of the design of the program *pro tem* and regular judges had very different types of contact with cases assigned to them. Those assigned to *pro tem* judges in blocks of six in early 1984 already had had one or more scheduled trial dates, but upon the new assignment *pro tem* judges were expected to assume control over these cases, schedule a new trial date for each, and conduct any pretrial proceedings—settlement conferences, pretrial hearings, etc.—necessary. Once the new trial date was set by the *pro tem* judge, it was expected to be firm.

*Pro tem* judges found that many of the cases assigned to them had already been disposed or could be disposed without trial. Table 2 shows how and at what point in the proceedings cases assigned to *pro tem* and regular judges were disposed.

**TABLE 2**
**Point when court-trial cases assigned to *pro tem* and regular judges were disposed, January 1984 to March 1985**

|  | Court-trial cases | | | |
|---|---|---|---|---|
|  | *Pro tem* judges | | Regular judges | |
| When disposed | No. | Percent | No. | Percent |
| Before assignment | 6 | 3 | — | — |
| Between assignment and pretrial | 97 | 44 | 4 | 5 |
| After pretrial hearing (including trials) | 90 | 41 | 75 | 90 |
| Unknown | 25 | 11 | 4 | 5 |
| TOTAL | 218 | 100 | 83 | 100 |

Because the court uses a master calendar system to assign civil cases to its regular judges on the date scheduled for court trial, cases assigned to regular judges for trial already have been through all the preparatory processes designed to dispose of them without resorting to a trial. After assignment to a regular judge almost all dispositions are by trial. The difference in assignment practices for regular and *pro tem* judges has an effect, shown in Table 3, on caseload figures. Half the civil court-trial cases assigned to *pro tem* judges were settled and only 30 percent were tried; almost all these cases assigned to regular judges were tried.

## TABLE 3
### How cases assigned to *pro tem* and regular judges were disposed, January 1984 to March 1985

|  | Court-trial cases |  |  |  | Jury-trial cases |  |
|---|---|---|---|---|---|---|
|  | *Pro tem* judges |  | Regular judges |  |  |  |
| How disposed | No. | Percent | No. | Percent | No. | Percent |
| Settlement/stipulation | 108 | 50 | 5 | 6 | 100 | 62 |
| Change of venue | 0 | 0 | 0 | 0 | 1 | <1 |
| Summary judgment | 6 | 3 | 0 | 0 | 1 | <1 |
| Transferred to arbitration | 0 | 0 | 0 | 0 | 2 | 1 |
| Dismissed by court | 38 | 17 | 4 | 5 | 46 | 29 |
| Court trial to judgment | 66 | 30 | 74 | 89 | 6 | 4 |
| Jury verdict | 0 | 0 | 0 | 0 | 5 | 3 |
| TOTAL | 218 | 100 | 83 | 100 | 161 | 100 |

During 1984 fifty-three *pro tem* judges conducted 85 civil court trials and 22 civil and criminal jury trials. The 17 regular judges completed 83 civil court trials and 455 other trials during that same period. In 1985, the use of *pro tem* judges to conduct civil court trials declined almost by one half, and they were assigned no criminal trials. Their use dropped from 107 trials in 1984 to 66 trials in 1985. At the same time, the number of trials conducted by regular judges of the court rose. Regular judges conducted 183 civil court trials, more than twice the number they conducted in 1984, and 419 other trials. Overall, the number of trials conducted by regular judges increased 12 percent between 1984 and 1985 (see Table 4). Regular judges, even those serving only as trial judges, have responsibilities beyond presiding at trials. There is no unequivocal way to equate the trial dispositions of the *pro tem* judges with an equivalence of regular judges. But if we use trials disposed per judge as a rough measure of judicial workload, all 50 of the *pro tem* judges collectively disposed of as many cases by trial as 3.4 regular judges did during 1984.

Even with the addition of a large number of cases disposed by *pro tem* judges during 1984, the civil pending caseload continued to increase, as it had in every year since 1980 (see Figure 1). And the 1984 dispositions still were below the peak reached in 1979. They increased dramatically in 1984, owing in part to improved case counting procedures enacted when the court began using a new computer system to monitor its caseload. A program that was carved out during the year to dispose of inactive cases

## TABLE 4
### Trials concluded in the Pima County Superior Court, 1984 and 1985

|  | By *pro tem* judges 1984 | By *pro tem* judges 1985 | By regular judges 1984 | By regular judges 1985 | TOTAL 1984 | TOTAL 1985 |
|---|---|---|---|---|---|---|
| **Civil** | | | | | | |
| Jury trials concluded | 17 | 18 | 146 | 126 | 163 | 144 |
| Court trials concluded | 85 | 48 | 83 | 183* | 168 | 231 |
| TOTAL TRIALS CONCLUDED | 102 | 66 | 229 | 309 | 331 | 375 |
| TOTAL CASES DISPOSED | | | | | 6,294 | 8,314 |
| Trial rate** | | | | | 5.3% | 4.5% |
| **Criminal** | | | | | | |
| Jury trials concluded | 5 | 0 | 296 | 271 | 301 | 271 |
| Court trials concluded | 0 | 0 | 13 | 22 | 13 | 22 |
| TOTAL TRIALS CONCLUDED | 5*** | 0 | 309*** | 293 | 314*** | 293 |
| TOTAL CASES DISPOSED | | | | | 2,242 | 2,100 |
| Trial rate** | | | | | 14.0% | 14.0% |

\* Figure includes five trials conducted by out-of-county judges.

\*\* Total trials concluded divided by total cases disposed.

\*\*\* Does not include 100 lower court appeals (trial de novo).

from the pending caseload also contributed to the increase in the number of cases disposed. But, as had happened in the five preceding years, more cases were filed than were disposed, so the civil pending caseload grew once again. The court was able to dispose of the 300 cases originally assigned to the *pro tem* judge program by early in the program's second year, but it has not yet been able to meet its first goal, reducing the size of the civil pending caseload.

The data on civil court-trial cases highlight a continuing problem in this court. Most cases had more than one trial date assigned before being disposed. The average number of trial dates scheduled for cases disposed by *pro tem* judges was 2.7; the average for cases disposed by regular judges was 3.3. Many of the cases assigned to *pro tem* judges had already had one or more trial dates scheduled at the time of assignment. The *pro tem* judge would then take over scheduling responsibility and assign another firm date for the start of the trial. If the case was not disposed as a result of pretrial proceedings, the trial began on the new date assigned by the *pro tem* judge. Cases assigned to regular judges are not given a firm trial date. For cases with more than one trial date, the average length of time between the first and last dates was approximately ten months for cases assigned both to *pro tem* and to regular judges.

The median time from the filing of the motion-to-set[2] to disposition for cases assigned to *pro tem* judges was approximately one month shorter than for cases assigned to regular judges. The trend in time-to-

**FIGURE 1**
**Civil caseload history**
**1978 through 1985, Pima County Superior Court**

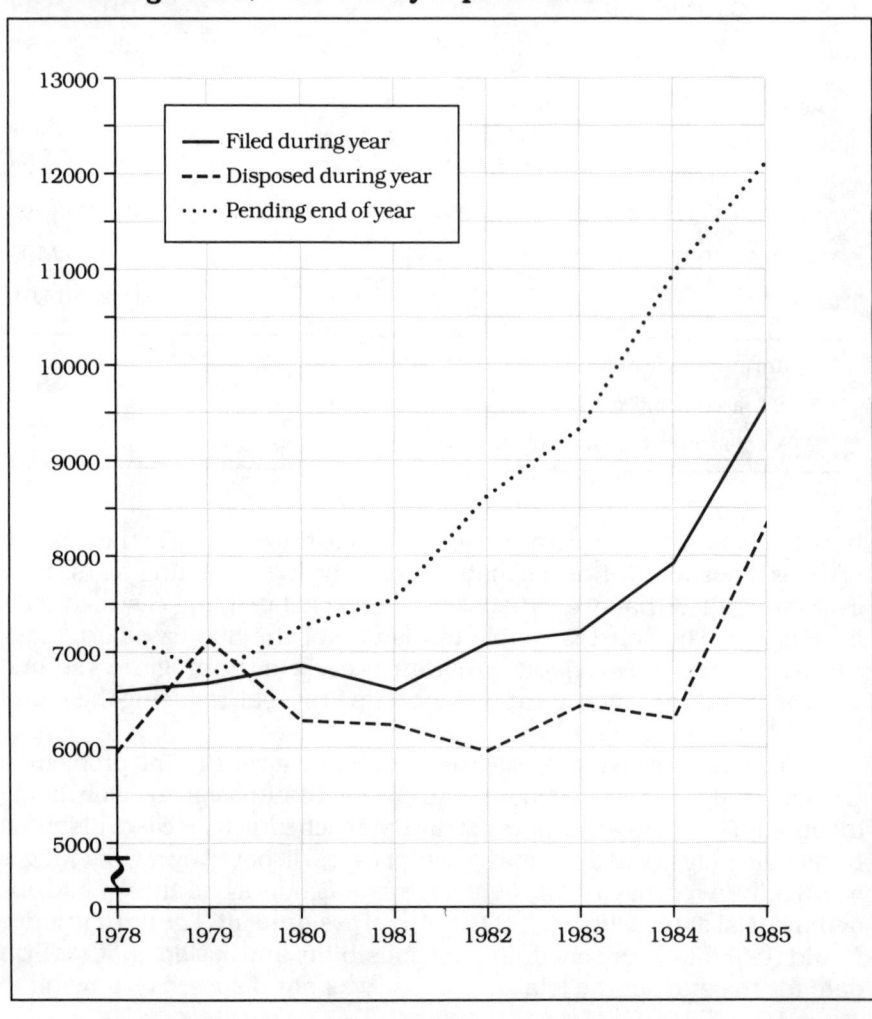

disposition figures for *pro tem* and regular judge cases is shown in Figure 2. Cases are grouped in three-month intervals by the date of disposition. The segment of the bar below the line represents median time from filing of the complaint to motion-to-set; the segment above the line represents median time from motion-to-set to disposition.[3] Median time from motion-to-set to disposition grew steadily over the 15 months of the evaluation for cases disposed by *pro tem* judges. This pattern appears to reflect nothing more than that the cases disposed of last by the *pro tems* were older than the cases disposed of shortly after the *pro tems* received the cases. The cases disposed of in a short time fall largely into two categories: (1) some of the assigned cases had already been settled without the court's having been advised; and (2) some *pro tem* judges tried to settle all their cases first; only when settlement efforts failed was a trial date discussed and selected. The additional time to trial for this latter group appears as increased time between at-issue and disposition.

Apart from an almost eight-month increase in time-to disposition during the second three-month period, time from motion-to-set to disposition remained fairly constant for regular judges. Regular judges of

**FIGURE 2**
**Median time-to-disposition for civil court-trial cases disposed by regular and *pro tem* judges, January 1984 through March 1985 (days), Pima County Superior Court**

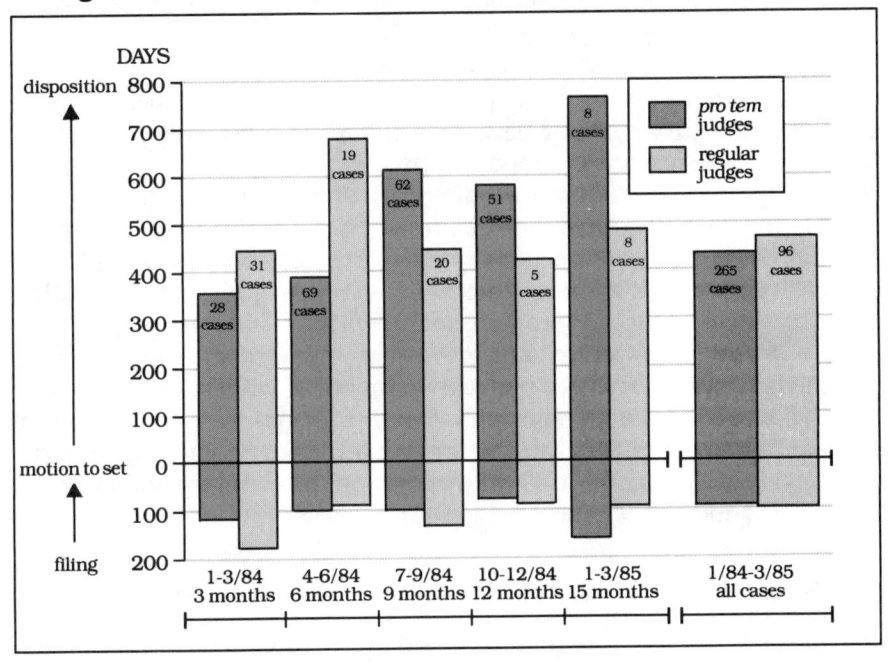

the court had cases assigned to them gradually. The small variation in the length of time from at-issue to disposition may be an indication that the court-trial list is beginning to be brought under control, since regular judges were assigned civil court-trial cases in which a *pro tem* judge had been removed or that were assigned a trial date after the start of the program. On the other hand, the flat pattern of the regular judges' bars in Figure 2 also suggests a failure, during the evaluation, to reduce the court's general pace of litigation.

The court may be able to begin to reduce the time from motion-to-set to disposition if it continues to use *pro tem* judges to handle the overflow of civil court trials. Civil disposition volume in 1983 represented 90 percent of filing volume; in 1984 it sank to 87 percent. Many in Tucson believe this percentage would have been even lower if the *pro tem* program had not been operating.

Data were collected on a sample of cases disposed from the civil jury-trial list (civil cases requesting a jury trial) between January 1984 and June 1985. The first 50 cases disposed each quarter were selected as representative of all cases disposed from the jury-trial list during the interval. These cases were concentrated in the tort categories (see Table 1). Most were being heard in the first instance; only 2 percent were appeals, all from arbitration awards.

Most of these jury-list cases were resolved without trial. Sixty-two percent were settled or disposed by stipulation; another 28 percent were dismissed by the court. Three percent were disposed by jury verdict and four percent by court-trial judgment. (It is interesting that the jury-trial list yielded more court trials than jury trials (see Table 3).)

Time-to-disposition information was available for cases disposed from the civil jury-trial list between September 1984 and June 1985. These cases also were grouped in three-month intervals. During the 9-month period studied the median length of time from motion-to-set to disposition increased five months, from 10.5 months to 15.5 months. Most of these cases were not disposed by trial, but there still were increasing delays during a time when *pro tem* judges were adding resources to the court. (There were some civil jury trials heard by *pro tem* judges during this period, but none was included among the cases sampled.) Although it is not known whether or to what extent the use of *pro tem* judges for civil and criminal *jury* trials reduced the number of cases that had to be continued for trial (Goal 2), it is clear that the court's third goal—reducing the time to disposition for civil jury and criminal cases—has not yet been met.[4]

## Qualitative Evaluation

Participants in the *pro tem* program were interviewed twice. Staff interviewed attorneys serving as *pro tem* judges, litigating attorneys, judges of the court, including the presiding judge and the administrative judge of the civil division, and court administrative personnel. The results of these interviews are summarized below.

**Overall Acceptance**
The *pro tem* judge program has been well received by the legal community of Pima County. Most of the attorneys selected to serve as *pro tem* judges are well respected and are thought to have the ability, experience, and reputation necessary to serve in a program of this kind. Litigating attorneys interviewed did not think that all the *pro tem* judges were of uniformly high ability, but they knew that they could use a "peremptory" challenge if their case were assigned to a less well-respected *pro tem* judge.

**Selection of *Pro Tem* Judges and Reasons for Acceptance**
When *pro tem* judges were first used by the court, the procedure for their selection was rather informal; volunteers were screened only by the judges. In 1984, a provision for review of proposed *pro tem* judges by a committee appointed by the local bar association was added to the process and should serve to further enhance acceptance of the program.

When asked why they had agreed to serve as *pro tem* judges, most mentioned altruistic reasons—they thought that after years of having the court serve their needs, it was time for them to contribute something to the court. Some said that they were willing to help the court because speeding the trials of other cases would mean that their own cases further back in line would be reached sooner. A few attorneys who volunteered because they were interested in investigating the possibility of becoming a judge were no longer interested in a judgeship; but a few others had become interested as a result of their service.

**Benefits to *Pro Tem* Judges**
Almost uniformly, attorneys who had served as *pro tem* judges stated that the experience had given them a deeper appreciation for the judges of the court. They were made aware of the problems and frustrations inherent to the position. Several said they were surprised and dismayed at the quality of presentations made by other attorneys. (This sentiment was echoed at a number of other sites studied.) This increased understanding and appreciation may serve to foster increasingly good relations between attorneys who serve as *pro tem* judges and the regular judges of the court.

**Conduct of the Trials**
*Pro tem* judges and the litigating attorneys were satisfied with the tone and conduct of the trials and hearings. Because of limitations on the amount of space available, some of the trials and many of the hearings were conducted in facilities in the courthouse other than courtrooms (the court law library, for example) or outside the courthouse entirely, in the

conference facilities at the *pro tem* judge's law office. There was a perception that trials conducted away from the courthouse had been less formal. *Pro tem* judges had not worn robes outside the courthouse and some may have used less strict rules of evidence. There is a strong preference among the litigating attorneys that, when possible, proceedings be conducted in the courthouse in regular courtrooms.

*Pro tem* judges sat on a great variety of cases.[5] Given the potential extent of the program, interviewees were asked whether there were any types of cases that should not be assigned to *pro tem* judges for trial. Custody and felony cases were mentioned by many of those interviewed as being inappropriate for *pro tem* judges to try.[6] It is felt that *pro tem* judges should not be expected to sentence defendants to prison, and they should not be asked to make decisions on issues as sensitive as child custody. Others thought they should not be asked to sit on high-visibility or highly controversial cases since these might have an adverse economic effect on their law practices. *Pro tem* judges were thought by all those interviewed to be equally appropriate for court or jury trials, within the specific limitations on the types of cases mentioned.

**Conflicts of Interest**

Prior to the increase in the use of *pro tem* judges by the court in 1984, there was a concern expressed that expanding the program might cause insurmountable problems with conflicts of interest. This concern was not borne out. *Pro tem* judges were quick to recuse themselves from cases assigned to them where they had an outside relationship with one of the attorneys or parties to the suit. Litigating attorneys felt free to use their "peremptory" challenge to remove a *pro tem* judge they did not want to hear their case. Some litigating attorneys believed that if they challenged a *pro tem* judge, their case would automatically be assigned to a regular judge of the court. Court administrative staff say that this is not the case. Some of these cases have been assigned to other *pro tem* judges for disposition; others have been assigned to regular judges of the court. Extending to the *pro tem* program the lawyers' right to remove one regular judge from a case without stating a reason helped to fit the program into the normal proceedings of the court, while also providing an alternative for those who may not have been fully supportive of the program at its start.[7]

**Compensation for *Pro Tem* Judges**

*Pro tem* judges serving this court are not paid for their service, and most of them think that compensation would not be appropriate. So long as the time demands do not become excessive, the *pro tem* judges interviewed said they are willing to continue to serve without compensation when called upon.

Pro tem judges were asked to indicate the amount of time they spent per case as a part of the caseload data collection effort discussed above. They reported that almost one-quarter of the cases assigned to them had not required any of their time to reach disposition. They guessed that they spent an average of approximately eight hours per case on the remaining three-quarters of the cases assigned to them. Most of these cases were resolved without trial, but the *pro tem*s still had to review the files, hold hearings, and, in many instances, prepare for a trial, whether or not it was completed. For each block of six cases assigned, we estimate that a *pro tem* judge spent an average of 36 hours.

**Temporary or Permanent Program?**
When the court increased the use of *pro tem* judges in 1984, the increase was looked upon as a temporary measure by most of the attorneys. Since that time, people's perceptions of the program have shifted; now everyone anticipates the continued use of *pro tem* judges at a high level, at least until the court is able to reduce its large and still growing backlog. When the backlog is under control, the attorneys think the heavy use of *pro tem* judges should be reduced, but believe the court still will need *pro tem*s to fill in for regular judges when they are sick, on vacation, or during other authorized absences.

Most of those interviewed did not think that the continued use of *pro tem* judges would keep the county board of supervisors from approving additional needed judges for the court. A few of the interviewees had fundamental philosophical objections to the program—they did not like the idea of a "part-time" anything—but most were very supportive of the program.

# Costs and Administrative Issues

**Costs**
Attorneys serving as *pro tem* judges serve without compensation. This removes one potential source of major expense for the program, but other substantial costs remain.

The program is administered by one employee, who spent 160 hours the first month setting up the program and 15 hours per month thereafter administering it. The salary and fringe benefits for this amount of time, representing indirect costs, and not out-of-pocket cash outlays, are estimated to have totaled $6,600. Another $750 was spent duplicating the files for the *pro tem* judges to use, bringing the total estimated cost to the court for implementing and running the program to $7,350 for the period from January 1984 through June 1985 (see Table 5). Hereafter it would cost an additional $2.50 to duplicate the file for each

## TABLE 5
**Estimated costs of *pro tem* judge program, January 1984 through June 1985**

| Cost element | Estimated hours | Estimated cost |
|---|---|---|
| Project administrator | 225 per year | $ 6,600 |
| Student intern | 132 per year | 1,150 |
| Secretary | 60 per year | 660 |
| Copying files | — | 750 |
| TOTAL | | 9,160 |

case assigned to the program and $265 per month for the salary and fringe benefits of the employee administering it.

The court also estimated the amount of money spent collecting the data for the program evaluation. During the first 17 months of the program, a secretary spent five hours per month completing data collection forms for the National Center for State Courts, at a total cost of $660, and a student intern spent 11 hours per month collecting data, counting files, and doing other tasks as needed. The student intern was not paid for his time, but the court estimates that if he had been paid, the total cost during the 17-month evaluation would have been approximately $1,150.

The total cost for implementing, conducting, and supporting the evaluation of the program for its first 17 months of operation was estimated to be approximately $8,010 ($9,160 if the student intern's estimated fee is included), excluding the time the caseload manager, the court administrator, the administrative judge of the civil division, and the presiding judge spent in designing the program and coordinating its introduction with the local bar association. And it does not include any fees or reimbursement for expenses to the attorneys who served as *pro tem* judges. There were approximately 300 cases disposed by *pro tem* judges during the first 17 months of the program, resulting in an estimated per case cost of $26.67 not including the student intern and $30.53 including the intern. No comparable cost figures for cases disposed by regular judges are available.

### Administrative Issues
By the time we began to evaluate the use of *pro tem* judges to hear civil court trials in this court, there was an established plan for how the program would be designed. The court had been using some *pro tem* judges in this capacity for a number of years, and also had the example of

the superior court in Phoenix, where *pro tem* judges have been used to conduct civil trials since the late 1970s.

At the start of the expanded program in the court, no training or orientation was offered by the court to new *pro tem* judges. Most of the *pro tem* judges interviewed stated that they were experienced trial attorneys and did not need any training to prepare for their service. A few indicated that some review of the "nuts and bolts" of conducting a trial would have been helpful. There were some portions of a judge's duties that, because of their own responsibilities as litigators, they had been too preoccupied during trials to observe. Several mentioned that the judges' benchbook was very helpful when they were called upon to conduct a jury trial.

The *pro tem* program put a considerable burden on the clerical support staff of the court. Adding *pro tem* judges to the complement of regular judges had the effect of requiring the clerical support staff to stretch scarce resources even further. Frequently there was a scramble before the start of a *pro tem*-conducted trial to gather up the necessary courtroom staff. Courtroom staff had to be supplied for trials conducted outside the courthouse, also. For these cases, the staff person in the court administrative office who coordinated the program contacted the *pro tem* judge a week before the scheduled trial date to determine whether support staff were needed. If they were, she contacted the heads of each group of employees affected—such as courtroom clerks and court reporters—to make the arrangements. Court reporters used most frequently for such trials were either floaters or the reporters assigned to vacationing judges. Travel to trials conducted outside the courthouse was an added burden to the normal workload of the court administrative staff.

The staff remain willing to continue their support of the program, with the extra work it entails, so long as the program is needed by the court.

## Overall Assessment

The *pro tem* judge program in the Pima County Superior Court has focused the attention of the local legal community on the need for bringing the caseload under control. The civil pending caseload has been increasing steadily for a number of years; unless steps are taken to bring dispositions into balance with filings, it will continue to grow. When the court announced its need for qualified attorneys to volunteer to conduct civil court trials, many attorneys agreed to donate their time to help. They appear to have enjoyed and benefited from their experience. The scheduling crisis the court feared in early 1984 was averted, but the pending caseload problem has not yet been resolved.

The court has begun to meet two of the four goals it set for the program: the initial group of civil court-trial cases have been disposed, most without undue delay, and the local legal community has taken note of its actions aimed at resolving its caseload problems. But its efforts must be continued if real improvement is to be made. The program was introduced in early 1984 as a temporary measure to deal with a perceived crisis. As soon as the original group of civil court-trial cases were disposed, the court anticipated that it would be able to return to its former practice of using *pro tem* judges to fill in during emergency situations when a case would otherwise be set over. The number of civil cases disposed during 1984 was greater than in 1983, but filings increased even more. The court has not yet solved its civil court-trial caseload problem.

There has not been any discernible effect on the civil jury-trial caseload, either. The time to jury trial continues to increase. Some members of the local legal community think that the jury-trial situation would have been much worse if the *pro tem* program had not been implemented, but, as with the civil court-trial caseload, the court has not yet caught up with the current demand for jury trials.

The program has not yet met its caseload goals, at least in part as a result of its design. Most cases were assigned in a block at one time. More gradual and continuous assignment would have permitted the program to take better hold and establish a pattern of practice that the court could build on. In removing the 300 civil court-trial cases from its calendar and assigning them to *pro tem* judges, the court lost most of its scheduling flexibility. These civil trials were the small matters that the court previously was able to fit in around other, larger civil and criminal jury trials. When the regular judges were not occupied with a civil or criminal jury trial, there were no civil court trials waiting for them to hear. At the same time, *pro tem* judges were using the empty courtrooms to conduct civil court trials. Some of the regular judges of the court began to resent the presence of the *pro tem* judges, as they feared that an outsider unfamiliar with the judge *pro tempore* program would believe the *pro tem* judges were doing the work of the idle regular judges. It was in response to this developing problem that adjustments were made to the assignment policy and some civil court-trial cases were once again assigned to regular judges. This problem also led the court to abandon the block-assignment approach in favor of using *pro tem* judges to assist with trials as they come up on the regular master calendar.

The court should continue to be careful to use as *pro tem* judges only those attorneys who are qualified and have the respect and acceptance of the legal community. The more formal selection procedures developed shortly after the expanded *pro tem* program was implemented in 1984 should be continued. In order to keep *pro tem* judges in the program for the long term, the court should continue to be careful not to overburden the *pro tem* judges. Many *pro tem* judges indicated that if they found that serving the court was having too negative an impact on their law practices, they would withdraw.

The court has become aware of a few factors that need to be changed if the *pro tem* judge program is to continue.
- Change the mix of case assignments. Rather than limiting most of the *pro tem* judge assignments to civil court-trial cases, the court plans to assign them both civil court and jury trials. This should help to introduce flexibility in scheduling back into both the regular judges' and *pro tem* judges' calendars.
- Establish time standards for cases assigned to *pro tem* judges. Some cases originally assigned to *pro tem* judges in February 1984 were not disposed for a full year. The court thinks that dispositions would be achieved more promptly if the *pro tem* judges had an indication from the court of the time frame for disposition expected of them.
- Review whether more space in the courthouse can be provided for *pro tem*-conducted trials. It was acceptable to hold trials at the *pro tem* judges' law offices when everyone thought that this situation was only going to last a few months. It may now continue for a number of years, so the practice of holding proceedings outside the courthouse should be reexamined.

Even though the court has not yet begun to meet most of its caseload-related goals, the implementation of this program has served to improve the already good relations between the bench and the local bar. The court has received the attention and support of the local legal community. With some adjustments to the design of the program it should be able to begin to meet its caseload goals as well.

## Notes to Chapter Seven

1. Statutory authority for the judge *pro tempore* program is in Arizona Rev. Stat. §12-141.
2. Lawyers file a motion-to-set in order to request assignment of a date for trial.
3. In this setting the median is the length of time at which half the cases reached the end point specified for the interval.
4. If the court were concentrating on disposition of older cases its median time-to-disposition figures would get higher, but there was no special effort during the evaluation to focus the court's resources on older cases.
5. As indicated in Table 3, *pro tem* judges presided over five criminal jury trials. One *pro tem* judge interviewed had presided over a felony drunk driving trial.
6. *Guidelines*, p. 13.
7. *Guidelines*, p. 18.

CHAPTER EIGHT

# The Portland Pro Tem Judge Program

The Multnomah County Circuit Court (Portland, Oregon) is the largest general jurisdiction court in the State of Oregon, serving one of the state's 20 judicial districts. The circuit court has general jurisdiction over civil and criminal matters not granted exclusively to other courts, as well as jurisdiction in probate and juvenile matters. The court processes approximately a third of all state court trial work at the general jurisdiction level.

Twenty judges serve the Multnomah County Circuit Court. The presiding judge is appointed by the chief justice. The incumbent during our study had served as presiding judge for eight years. Eighteen judges serve in a general trial pool and one judge is assigned exclusively to probate matters.

Administrative responsibility for the circuit court rests with the presiding judge (who is also the chief civil judge) and the Judges General Committee, which consists of five sitting judges. The court uses a master calendar system. The presiding judge is responsible for the assignment of cases to judges, for the disposition of all pretrial civil matters, and for "Rule 4" hearings to decide whether to dismiss or continue cases that have been pending for more than six months without apparent activity. The chief criminal judge has jurisdiction over all criminal matters prior to trial. Judges of the general trial court preside over trials in civil, criminal, and domestic relations cases. Domestic relations judges are aided by family consultants who help to conciliate family disputes.

Since July 1, 1982, the court has had a mandatory arbitration program for all civil cases with complaints seeking money damages less than or equal to $15,000 and for domestic relations cases in which child custody or spouse support are not an issue. Parties appear before a single arbitrator. The arbitrators are paid a fee by the parties for the service.

In 1985, there were 22,958 cases filed in the Multnomah County Circuit Court. With 20 authorized judicial positions, this equals 1,148 filings per judge. The court terminated 22,515 cases, or 1,126 per judge during 1984. At the close of the year there were 750 cases (about 7.7 months of inventory) pending per judge.

As shown in Table 6, both case filings and case terminations decreased from 1983 to 1985, but the court continued to terminate more cases than were filed.

More civil cases are tried in the Multnomah County Circuit Court than any other case type; the mean age to trial for civil cases tried was less than 17.5 months in 1984. During that year the court received 20 days of help from visiting circuit court judges, four days from district court judges, and 267 days from *pro tempore* judges.

**TABLE 6**
**Multnomah County Circuit Court filings and terminations**

|  | 1983 | 1984 | 1985 | Percentage difference |
|---|---|---|---|---|
| Filings | 23,075 | 22,471 | 22,958 | -2.6 |
| Terminations | 24,337 | 22,515 | 23,586 | -7.4 |

**1984 filings and terminations by case type**

|  | Civil | Dissolution | Criminal | Guardianship | Decedent's estate | TOTAL |
|---|---|---|---|---|---|---|
| Filings | 8,028 | 8,404 | 4,417 | 506 | 1,603 | 22,958 |
| Terminations | 8,115 | 8,926 | 4,506 | 524 | 1,515 | 23,586 |
| Terminations as percentage of filings | 105% | 106% | 102% | 88% | 99% | 100.3% |

# Problems That Led to Creation of the Adjunct Program

Oregon civil procedure did not allow motions for summary judgment until 1975.[1] In 1976, the *Willamette Law Journal* commented:

> The Oregon summary judgment statute borrows directly from Fed.R.Civ.P. 56 which, since its promulgation in 1938, has served as a model for numerous state summary judgment statutes. Rule 56 has proved successful in streamlining federal practice by providing a method for an early

disposition of cases involving no triable issues of fact. With enactment of OR 18.105, Oregon litigants now also may achieve a quick and economic resolution of many cases formerly forced to trial by formalistic pleading technicalities.[2]

Five years after the adoption of the summary judgment procedure, it was providing neither early nor economic disposition of cases in Portland. By late 1980 and early 1981 a case could be given a trial date before the summary judgment hearing date because of a backlog in scheduling summary judgment motions; it was taking up to a year to get a summary judgment motion scheduled. Because scheduled trial days were reached before the motion date, trials would begin with a summary judgment hearing and then go on to trial if the motion were denied. The court was understandably concerned about this scheduling anomaly. The court turned to the local bar for assistance and began using *pro tempore* judges to hear summary judgment motions.

The court has used attorneys as judicial adjuncts for many years, as authorized by Oregon Revised Statutes § 1.635. In the 1960s and 1970s courts in Oregon were able to compensate attorneys sitting as *pro tempore* judges through state funds. State funds for this purpose terminated in 1980; the use of *pro tem* judges diminished but did not end.

The use of *pro tem* judges hearing summary judgment motions has increased and evolved into a program where all summary judgment motions and many domestic relations motions, plus a few individually referred cases, are heard by attorneys sitting as *pro tem* judges.

# The Program

### Summary Judgment Motions

The Multnomah County Bar Association Committee on Judicial Qualification proposes names of local attorneys for *pro tempore* service to the court. The presiding judge selects attorneys from this list for appointment as *pro tempore* judges by the Oregon Supreme Court. The court must obtain supreme court appointment for its proposed *pro tempore* judges, but the supreme court has never rejected a proposed candidate. Initially, the supreme court would appoint attorneys as *pro tempore* judges for a specific date upon which the attorney could hear summary judgment motions. The supreme court has since decided to give standing appointments for attorneys to serve as *pro tempore* judges. Thirty-two attorneys served as summary judgment *pro tems* from January 1983 to September 1984. Circuit court judges continued to hear some summary judgment motions until March 1984, when the court began scheduling all summary judgment motions before *pro tems*. *Pro tem* judges hearing summary judgment motions are not compensated for their time.

All civil motions filed in the circuit court are scheduled through the presiding judge's office. To have a summary judgment motion set on the calendar, an attorney must prepare a motion *praecipe*. This document includes identification of the attorney, his or her telephone and bar numbers; case number, name, case type, type of motion, and approximate time needed.

Until September 1985, the scheduling of motions was done by the presiding judge's administrative assistant and law clerk. Currently scheduling is done by the court's calendaring office.[3] On average, one day a week is scheduled for civil summary judgment motions. The clerk telephones *pro tem* judges to ascertain their availability and to schedule them for future hearing dates; a conference room in the courthouse also is scheduled. As summary judgment motions and *praecipes* are filed, the clerk assigns the case to the next available date and time. Motions are usually scheduled at ten-minute intervals, with a maximum of 25 motions scheduled per day for one *pro tem* judge who works very quickly.

When scheduled, attorneys are given the *pro tempore* judge's name. Each attorney is allowed a peremptory challenge of the *pro tempore* judge;[4] challenges for conflict are also considered at this time. For a variety of other reasons, e.g., settlement, continuances, and stipulations, some cases are either temporarily or permanently removed from the calendar.

Two to three days before the scheduled hearing, the *pro tempore* judge is given the case files for review. Last-minute review of filings is required because opposing parties are allowed to file affidavits until the day before the hearing.[5]

The day before the hearings a formal typed calendar is prepared listing all summary judgment motions scheduled before the *pro tem*. The *pro tem* is given a copy of the calendar and asked to make a brief notation of the ruling on the calendar itself. (The *pro tem* judges serve as their own court clerks; court staff are not present during hearings on summary judgment motions.) In the majority of cases the *pro tem* rules immediately and asks prevailing counsel to prepare an order. Cases taken under advisement, cases that are granted in part, and cases with other complications require additional work and the preparation of a memorandum.

When a summary judgment motion is filed, the case remains on the normal calendar track to trial. If the summary judgment motion is not dispositive of all issues, the case continues in line for assignment by the presiding judge to a trial judge.

## Domestic Relations *Pro Tem* Program

The court also uses *pro tempore* judges to aid judges hearing domestic relations matters. In domestic relations cases, *pro tem*s hear all types of motions, support enforcement cases, and "district attorney" cases (for child support orders).

Domestic relations short motions are calendared by the calendar clerks and heard by either the domestic relations trial judges or *pro tempore* judges. Short motions may be *pendente lite* motions involving support, costs, child custody, or restraint, or motions in adoption, name change, dissolution default, filiation, support enforcement, contempt matters, and modification of decrees. A short motion is one estimated to require a hearing of less than 30 minutes. Longer motions are calendared before regular judges on the regular "call" docket if a motion *praecipe* has been filed.

*Pro tem* judges assist occasionally on regular domestic relations motions set for Mondays. They also hear support enforcement cases on Tuesdays and Thursdays. For the period July 2 to November 13, 1984, seven attorneys served as domestic relations *pro tempore* judges. One domestic relations *pro tem* also heard a summary judgment motion. A total of 36 pro-tem days were served, with one attorney serving 14 days during this 4½-month period.

**Reference Judge Program**
Chapter 704 Oregon Laws 1983 authorizes reference judge panels of senior judges and not more than 30 other *pro tempore* judges. The reference-judge program allows litigants to request the assignment of a full-power reference judge to hear their case in lieu of a regular judge. Reference judges are compensated by the parties at a daily rate equivalent to that of a circuit court judge. The parties may request a reference judge by name or ask the court to appoint one. Such a request can be made at any time before trial. The conduct of the trial by a reference judge is the same as that of any circuit court nonjury trial. After trial, the reference judge files a written report with the court administrator, at which time the referral of the action terminates and the presiding judge orders the judgment contained in the report entered as the judgment of the court. This judgment may be appealed in the same manner as any final judgment of the circuit court in a civil action.

The original legislation authorizing the reference-judge panel included a sunset clause. The Oregon legislature has subsequently withdrawn the sunset clause and made the program permanent. In spite of this legislative approval, the reference-judge panel has been used in very few cases. Fewer than 25 cases were referred to reference judges during the National Center's evaluation. Therefore, use of reference judges will not be analyzed in this report. Future circumstances may increase the use of the reference-judge panel, which could have a significant impact on the court's caseflow, but to date this has not been the case.[6]

The circuit court in Portland does not use its attorney *pro tem* judges for jury trials because it interprets section 1.655(3) of the Oregon Revised

Statutes to preclude *pro tem* judges *and members of their firm* from appearing before a jury panel during its term after the *pro tem* judge has presided before the jurors. The trial bar in Portland is relatively small; rather than risk eliminating several lawyers from availability for trial after a *pro tem* judge sits and incurring the administrative burden of tracking availability and nonavailability, the court has chosen to use its attorney *pro tem* judges only on nontrial matters.[7]

## Goals

The frequency with which attorneys file motions for summary judgment caused considerable concern among judges of the Multnomah County Circuit Court. The presiding judge and special assignment judges had to devote more and more time to summary judgment hearings. Calendaring of the hearings became backlogged. Relief from these conditions was seen as the major contribution that could be made by the use of *pro tempore* judges. The master calendar used by the court is a system of interdependencies—removal of summary judgment motions from the workload of the regular bench affects the entire court. Several results would follow from the use of *pro tem* judges for summary judgment hearings.

- The presiding judge's responsibility to assign and oversee summary judgment motions would be lessened and he could spend that time improving other assignment areas.
- Those judges who previously heard summary judgment motions would be able to allocate that time to other duties.
- The litigants would have swifter and more economic resolution of their cases through the use of *pro tems*.

The court never formalized the use of *pro tempore* judges hearing summary judgment motions into a program with stated goals. There were no projections of judge time to be saved, increased dispositions, or improvement in case processing times.

The two major unstated goals were to provide relief to the bench from the increasing and backlogged summary judgment motions and to provide litigants with an opportunity to benefit from the procedure, something that was unavailable for the most part when summary judgment motions could not be heard until the start of the trial.

## Quantitative Evaluation

Between January 1983 and December 1985, 2,512 summary judgment motions were scheduled in the Multnomah County Circuit Court before *pro tem* judges (see Table 7). This is an average of 837 cases per year. To add perspective to this figure, in Multnomah County there were 7,501

## TABLE 7
## Number of cases listed for summary judgment motion hearing

|  | TOTAL | Pro Tem Judges No. | Pro Tem Judges Percent | Regular Judges No. | Regular Judges Percent |
|---|---|---|---|---|---|
| January, 1983 | 104 | 70 | 67 | 34 | 33 |
| February | 175 | 137 | 88 | 38 | 22 |
| March | 123 | 72 | 59 | 51 | 41 |
| April | 117 | 89 | 76 | 28 | 24 |
| May | 118 | 71 | 60 | 47 | 40 |
| June | 65 | 24 | 37 | 41 | 63 |
| July | 51 | 0 | 0 | 51 | 100 |
| August | 123 | 65 | 53 | 58 | 47 |
| September | 81 | 51 | 63 | 30 | 37 |
| October | 85 | 41 | 48 | 44 | 52 |
| November | 125 | 48 | 38 | 77 | 62 |
| December | 106 | 77 | 73 | 29 | 27 |
| TOTAL | 1,273 | 745 | 59 | 528 | 41 |
| January, 1984 | 36 | 36 | 100 | 0 | 0 |
| February | 116 | 113 | 97 | 3 | 3 |
| March | 107 | 103 | 96 | 4 | 4 |
| April | 112 | 112 | 100 | 0 | 0 |
| May | 139 | 139 |  | 0 |  |
| June | 105 | 105 |  | 0 |  |
| July | 88 | 88 |  | 0 |  |
| August | 57 | 57 |  | 0 |  |
| September | 106 | 106 |  | 0 |  |
| October | 84 | 84 |  | 0 |  |
| November | 45 | 45 |  | 0 |  |
| December | 52 | 52 |  | 0 |  |
| TOTAL | 1,047 | 1,040 | 99 | 7 | 1 |
| January, 1985 | 82 | 82 |  | 0 |  |
| February | 71 | 71 |  | 0 |  |
| March | 61 | 61 |  | 0 |  |
| April | 80 | 80 |  | 0 |  |
| May | 63 | 63 |  | 0 |  |
| June | 71 | 71 |  | 0 |  |
| July | 27 | 27 |  | 0 |  |
| August | 31 | 31 |  | 0 |  |
| September | 57 | 57 |  | 0 |  |
| October | 85 | 85 |  | 0 |  |
| November | 64 | 64 |  | 0 |  |
| December | 35 | 35 |  | 0 |  |
| TOTAL | 727 | 727 | 100 | 0 |  |
| GRAND TOTAL | 3047 | 2512 | 82 | 535 | 18 |

civil cases filed in 1984; thus the *pro tems* heard more than one summary judgment motion for every nine cases filed.

The National Center selected approximately ten percent of the cases with motions for summary judgment heard by regular judges and by *pro tem* judges to identify the party who filed the motion and the outcome of the hearing. The *pro-tem*-judge sample is larger than the regular-judge sample because the *pro tem* judges handle many more of these cases than regular judges. Outcomes were classified as follows:

Motion granted in full

Motion granted in part or against some parties only

Motion denied

Motion dismissed

Case disposed with no resolution to the motion or unknown

For cases in which a cross-motion was filed, the outcome of the hearing was coded only with respect to the first motion filed. Results of the analysis are given in Table 8. If no distinction is made between which side filed the original motion, the analysis shows no difference in results between *pro tem* and regular judges. However, if the side filing the case is included in the analysis, differences emerge.[8]

*Pro tem* judges were more likely to grant or grant in part motions than were regular judges when comparisons are based on which side originally filed the motion. Similarly, they denied smaller portions of motions than did the regular judges when the side filing the motion is controlled. Both groups of judges were more likely to deny motions filed by the defense, but *pro tem* judges denied fewer defense motions than did the regular judges. Regular judges denied more plaintiffs' motions than did *pro tem* judges.

**TABLE 8**
**Results of summary judgment motion hearings**

|  | *Pro tem* judges ||||  Regular judges ||||
| --- | --- | --- | --- | --- | --- | --- | --- | --- |
|  | \multicolumn{8}{c}{Motion filed by} ||||||||
|  | Plaintiff || Defense || Plaintiff || Defense ||
|  | No. | Percent | No. | Percent | No. | Percent | No. | Percent |
| Granted | 52 | 39 | 43 | 39 | 4 | 22 | 17 | 40 |
| Granted in part | 18 | 13 | 12 | 11 | 3 | 17 | 0 | 0 |
| Denied | 29 | 21 | 39 | 36 | 5 | 28 | 19 | 44 |
| Dismissed | 12 | 9 | 6 | 6 | 2 | 11 | 0 | 0 |
| Unresolved before disposition or unknown | 24 | 18 | 9 | 8 | 4 | 22 | 7 | 16 |
| TOTAL | 135 | 100 | 109 | 100 | 18 | 100 | 43 | 100 |

Plaintiff-filed motions were more likely to be either dismissed, left unresolved, or unknown at the disposition of the case than were those filed by the defense. The difference in outcomes between plaintiff- and defense-filed motions was greater for regular judges than it was for *pro tem* judges.[9]

## Qualitative Evaluation

### Overview
It is difficult to assess statistically the impact of the use of *pro tempore* judges hearing summary judgment motions. Quantitatively, there are no similar programs against which the Multnomah County Circuit Court experience can be measured. Where statistical measures do not exist, general opinions and observations become more important in the process of determining how well a program operates. Realizing that the opinions of those involved would probably be the most reliable indicator of program success, the project staff conducted 21 interviews, 17 of which were with *pro tem* judges. Almost all *pro tem* judges also had been litigating attorneys before other *pro tem* judges.

In general, most of those interviewed thought that the program worked well and provided a significant service to the court. The *pro tempore* judges were pleased to be able to serve the court.

In the following qualitative discussion, the total number of responses to a given question does not always equal the number of persons interviewed. For most questions there were a few people who, for one reason or another, did not have an opinion. In some instances, also, the question was not asked in a particular interview or more than one equally weighted response was given to a question.

### The *Pro Tempore* Judge Panel
The make-up of the *pro tempore* judge panel was rated very highly. Of those interviewed, half thought the panel could be called "blue ribbon," five considered it more representative of a good cross-section of the bar, and six indicated that they did not know enough of the panel members to pass judgment.

There was no need to conduct large-scale recruitment of *pro tem*s as there are only 32 attorneys on the panel. Of the 17 *pro tem*s interviewed, eight offered their services in response to an appeal by the court, six accepted appointment upon direct appeal from the presiding judge, and three were recruited in some other fashion. Without doubt, the presiding judge played a key role in this process; the respect with which he is held within the legal community enabled him to enlist the most capable attorneys to serve as *pro tempore* judges.

As in other evaluation sites, there was a strong sense of public service among the *pro tems*. Eleven viewed their service as fulfilling an obligation to perform *pro bono* work as a member of the Oregon bar. Two additional *pro tems* saw their service as a public service to the court, but one that also would enable them to get their own cases to summary judgment hearing much more quickly than they could before the *pro tem* program. Eight of the *pro tems* said gaining an understanding of what a judge goes through in making decisions from the bench was an additional motivating factor. Five of the *pro tems* said candidly that they desired to be a judge and thought that by serving as *pro tems* they might improve their chances.

### Frequency of Service and Compensation

The *pro tems* interviewed represented a wide range of experience in serving the court. Some had been serving as *pro tems* for up to three years, while two had only served one time. The frequency with which the *pro tems* served ranged from once every six months to once every few weeks for *pro tems* hearing summary judgment motions and once a week for *pro tems* hearing domestic relations matters. The frequency of service thought most appropriate for hearing summary judgment motions was once every three months, although two said they would sit once a month if they were paid for their time.

The majority of the *pro tems*, 12 of the 17 interviewed, thought that *pro tem* service should be without compensation. One of the persons who indicated that the *pro tems* should receive compensation was hearing domestic relations matters and thought that a paid *pro tem* might have more authority than someone serving *pro bono*.

### Conflicts of Interest

A conflict of interest had been a problem for only two of the 17 *pro tems* interviewed, even though all have active practices in Multnomah County. The majority of the *pro tems* indicate that conflicts are no problem because whenever there is a possibility of conflict the *pro tem* recuses him- or herself.

### Training and Orientation

There was little enthusiasm for training among the *pro tems*. Four *pro tems* said they had reread the continuing legal education chapter on summary judgment motions, but thought there was no need for the court to include this chapter as part of an orientation or training packet.

The area that was most in need of some sort of explanation or training was the question of how to handle paperwork. Do the judge's notes go into the file? Where and how do they record the disposition? Are future calendar events reported? Beyond these mechanics, two *pro tems* suggested that it would assist new adjuncts if they were given the names of a couple of experienced *pro tems* to call and ask for a general overview of service, what problems might be expected, and what they would need to know.

**Time Commitments**

At least one of the adjuncts reported that he had staff within his firm do research for him. The median time spent in preparation for one day's hearings was between seven and eight hours. The hearings themselves were scheduled in a range from ten to fifteen minutes apart to two every five minutes, depending on the preference of the *pro tem* judge.

There was a great variety of attitudes and responses when the adjuncts were asked about taking motions under advisement. One *pro tem* had taken only one of his 40 cases under advisement. Another took 75 percent of his calendar under advisement. Most *pro tems* prefer to do this in as few cases as possible; five commented that motions taken under advisement create a lot of extra work.

Two *pro tems* who had taken cases under advisement indicated they were somewhat concerned because the Oregon Supreme Court had appointed them to serve for one day. One might assume that *pro tems* have power to take cases under advisement and rule at a later date, but whether or not their appointment extends to setting a subsequent time for further argument or further filing was unclear when these situations arose. The current indefinite appointments remove this concern.

**Attorneys' Fees**

A significant number of interviewees are uncertain whether they can rule on attorneys' fees and costs. There are a variety of solutions used: some *pro tems* refer the case to the presiding judge for consideration of this matter; others do rule on attorneys' fees and costs, but if there is any objection they refer the question to the presiding judge for decision; a third group rules without referring cases to the presiding judge.

# Costs and Administrative Issues

### Costs

Virtually all costs for the program have been absorbed by existing staff and resources. The presiding judge and court administrator have devoted considerable amounts of time in the development of the systems for recruiting, scheduling, and overseeing the use of *pro tems*. As noted, the presiding judge employed his considerable stature to develop the program. Since the use of *pro tems* has become more and more institutionalized, the efforts of the presiding judge and court administrator have been reduced, but one should not discount the time initially required.

The major support for the *pro tems* hearing summary judgment motions was provided during the evaluation period by the presiding judge's administrative assistant and law clerk. It is estimated that they devoted up to 20 percent of their time to the *pro tem* program. These two staff members are officially classified, respectively, as Judicial Assistant and Court Operations Specialist II. Twenty percent of their annual salaries plus a 35 percent fringe benefit rate totals $9,878. This is the indirect cost of the program, since no extra budget funds are committed to it. The *pro tems* serve without compensation, and courthouse facilities are used for the hearings.

As stated previously, 1,040 cases were scheduled in 1984 for summary judgment motions (see Table 7). Of those cases analyzed by the National Center, 58 percent (603) were heard on the original day scheduled. The median review time per case was 30 minutes, plus ten minutes for the actual motion. Time spent posthearing varied greatly for the various *pro tems*, but estimating an additional 20 minutes per case totals one hour of *pro tem* time per case. Multiplying the time per case by the number of cases heard suggests a savings of 603 hours of judge time through the use of *pro tem* judges. This is approximately one-third of a full-time judge's hours annually.

**Administrative Issues**
There was one mechanical element of the summary judgment motion procedure that was a problem for ten of the interviewees. Most *pro tems* like to pick up their files a couple of days in advance of the hearing, so they will have adequate time to prepare without cutting too much into their normal business day. The problem with preparing in advance is that the Oregon Rules of Civil Procedure previously allowed the opposing party to file his or her affidavit as late as the day before the hearing. Therefore, the *pro tem* often did not receive the response until late the day before, or sometimes not at all. With a change in the rules as of January 1, 1986, this problem should be eliminated.

Other problems with the mechanics of the program were singled out:
- Initially, there was a problem with attorneys knowing that they had to send copies of their filings to the *pro tems*' offices. This problem seems to be under control and attorneys are receiving filings at their offices.
- Papers that should have been in a case file had not found their way into the case file when the *pro tems* received it.
- There was a problem with communication: when a case had been taken off the calendar or reset, the *pro tem* often was not informed.
- Some felt the court should call *pro tems* further in advance so that they could block out time from their trial schedules.

- One *pro tem* expressed the opinion that an actual courtroom is not necessary, that a conference room in the courthouse could be used, or the *pro tem*s might be able to hear motions at their own offices. Another objected to using a conference room, however, because he felt it did not give a proper impression to clients who might be present.
- A couple of *pro tem*s suggested having a checklist in the file indicating the disposition and any issues that might remain regarding attorneys fees, costs, the right to replead, and other issues. The *pro tem* would keep one of the copies of this form and the other would stay in the file.
- One attorney said resetting cases turned his one day of service into two or three. He feels cases should be reset to be heard by whichever *pro tem* is sitting for the new date.

## Overall Assessment

The *pro tempore* judges provide a service to the court and the litigants. About 600 hours of circuit judge time were saved in one year just through the use of *pro tempore* judges to hear summary judgment motions. In the sample of cases studied, 51 percent of the motions heard by *pro tem* judges were granted either in full or in part. It is not possible to determine cost savings in time and expenditure realized by the litigants, but it is not insignificant.

### Judge Time Saved

Summary judgment motions are viewed by the circuit judges as particularly time consuming. They also present a difficult scheduling problem. In theory, for each judge-hour saved, a judge should be able to devote an hour to trial-related work. One might expect, therefore, that the trial disposition rate would have increased after *pro tempore* judges began hearing all summary judgment motions. In fact, the equation is not so simple. Circuit court judges may not have spent as much time per case as the *pro tem*s have been able to. Also, when there are small blocks of time freed that previously had been consumed by one event, e.g., summary judgment motions, there is a tendency for extraneous matters to fill up that time. In fact, there was a slight decrease in the number of trials conducted per judge between 1983 and 1984. There are three possible reasons for this: the court was not able to schedule as much judge time to civil trials as it has in the past;[10] the trials themselves were of longer duration; or judges were required to spend more time on other nontrial duties.

Another unmeasurable is the quality of time available to circuit judges. Without the necessity of hearing summary judgment motions the judges can devote the energy that was used preparing for, hearing, and deciding summary judgment motions to other matters. The trial rate or the number of dispositions may not increase proportionate to the time served by the *pro tem*s, but there may be an increase in the quality of justice.

**Benefit to Litigants**
Since *pro tem*s began assisting the court, resolution of summary judgment motions has occurred at a much earlier date. This is a great benefit to litigants who get their "day in court" much earlier than if *pro tem*s were not available. There is a possibility that the quality of decisions may be better from *pro tem*s than from circuit judges. Many judges did not have much or any experience with summary judgment motions when they practiced, since the procedure has only been allowed in Oregon since 1975. There may have been a natural tendency for judges to deny or avoid summary judgment motions. Lawyers practicing now have had ten years' experience with this procedure, so summary judgment motions are more accepted by them and, possibly, granted more readily by them.

With the pressures of increasing caseloads, circuit judges do not have the freedom to spend as much time as they might want on each case. Within the limitations of their practices, *pro tem*s do. For circuit court judges, a summary judgment motion is one step in the overall judicial process and the tendency may be to prefer to resolve disputes at trial; attorneys do not have the same concerns. The judge hearing the motion is not the judge who will try the case. Therefore, when the case is a close call, the circuit judge may tend to let the decision go to the trial judge. In addition, it is often said that judges in general are concerned about the rate at which they are overturned at the appellate level. This concern might influence their rulings on summary judgment motions.

Both bench and bar have grown into the use of summary judgment motions in the last ten years. Appellate courts have had time to interpret and refine the rule authorizing the procedure. A consequence of this maturation may be better prepared and better presented motions.

All of these factors tend to foster a slightly better atmosphere for the *pro tem*s to make decisions on summary judgment motions. The statistical analysis of summary judgment proceedings reinforces this possibility.

**Bench-Bar Relations**
Compared with other *pro tem* programs, the use of *pro tem*s in the Multnomah County Circuit Court is quite limited. There are only 32 attorneys on the *pro tem* panel and they hear only motions. Nevertheless, the benefit to bench-bar relations should not be overlooked. The attorneys are proud to serve, do so without compensation, and can see the benefit of their service. Attorneys who argue their motions before the *pro tem*s also appreciate the aid the bar is providing the court. In turn, the court is grateful for the relief the *pro tem*s provide.

### Problems with the Program
The presiding judge's administrative assistant and law clerk initially and now the court's calendaring office have been able to deal effectively with the administrative aspects of the program, but the court has not developed an effective monitoring process.

In our opinion, the court should make a commitment to develop information about the program similar to that presented here. Such information would provide a picture of how the program is working and also would help identify problem areas before they become exacerbated. Areas that might be monitored are the following: the type of decision, the number and delay of cases taken under advisement, tracking of cases denied summary judgment through trial, tracking of appeal rate for cases granted summary judgment, continuances, cases withdrawn, challenges of *pro tem*s, and other significant characteristics. Monitoring of individual *pro tem* performance also could be developed.

With a limited number of *pro tem*s serving and with general knowledge of how the calendaring system operates, there is the possibility of *pro tem* shopping by the litigating attorneys. It was suggested in interviews that this is occurring. The court should investigate this possible practice and develop calendaring methods that do not allow *pro tem* judge shopping.

### Issues to Be Addressed and Items to Be Changed if Program Is Continued
There have been a few additions to and deletions from the list of 32 *pro tem*s over the past two years but the list remains relatively constant. The court should decide how long attorneys should be asked to serve, the frequency of their service, and how additional attorneys should be recruited.

Inviting *pro tem*s to meet to discuss the program could be very worthwhile. It not only would help the court chart the future use of *pro tem*s, but would allow the *pro tem*s to discuss problems they might be having.

If the program is to continue indefinitely, the court should also consider a combination of training and evaluation of individual *pro tem*s. A sitting or retired judge could be enlisted to sit in on a critique of each *pro tem*. This would help the *pro tem* judges improve their demeanor or style, if necessary, and provide positive reinforcement to those doing well.

The Oregon Bar Association is considering requiring *pro bono* public service of its members. If this requirement is adopted, the court should encourage the bar to accept *pro tem* service as meeting this requirement.

# Notes to Chapter Eight

1. A motion for summary judgment argues that there is no genuine issue of material fact in the case and contends that as a matter of law the facts require a final judgment in favor of the moving party.

2. "Summary Judgment Procedure in Oregon: The Impact of Oregon's Adoption of FR 56," 13 *Willamette L.J.* 73 (1976).

3. Approximately one-half the time of a full-time-equivalent employee is assigned to this task.

4. Oregon Revised Stat. §§ 14.250-14.270 allow filing an affidavit of prejudice against two assigned judges. In no event has the presiding judge allowed this device to result in assignment to a regular judge.

5. Oregon Revised Stat. §18.105. On January 1, 1986 this statute was amended to provide that the summary judgment *praecipe* must be filed 45 days before the date set for trial, with all papers pertinent to the motion filed within 21 days of the *praecipe*.

6. Reference judge cases are limited to nonjury cases. It has been the court's policy to encourage the use of reference judges only in cases projecting very long trials.

7. When the court had funds to pay *pro tem* judges (before 1980), attorney *pro tem* judges from other counties were used to preside over jury trials, since they normally would not practice in Portland and the court could reimburse them for their expenses as well as their time. When funds for *pro tempore* judges were eliminated, the practice of importing *pro tem* judges from other counties ended.

8. The data were analyzed using $x^2$ goodness-of-fit tests. This statistic is not dependent on the type of underlying distribution, so may be used to compare the distributions for variables about which few specifics are known, such as the data analyzed here.

The $x^2$ value computed for each set of data was converted into a probability value (p-value) using a table of computed values. The number of categories of data are used to calculate the "degrees of freedom" of the $x^2$. In general, larger computed $x^2$ values lead to smaller p-values, meaning that the differences observed in the data are unlikely to be due to chance. The p-values are commonly expressed as a range because the calculated $x^2$ values usually fall between the figures reported on an $x^2$ table.

The $x^2$ values computed for different combinations of data are as follows:

| | | |
|---|---|---|
| 1. Entire table | $x^2_{12} = 7.89$ | $.90 > p .75$ |
| 2. Regular judges alone | $x^2_4 = 14.37$ | $.01 > p .005$ |
| 3. *Pro tem* judges alone | $x^2_4 = 9.68$ | $.05 > p .025$ |

The first $x^2$ value above is converted to a p-value of between .90 and .75; we expect a $p^2$ value this large between 75 and 90 percent of the time and therefore it is unlikely that there are any real differences when the entire table is analyzed. But because the table is actually "nested," that is, it is really two sets of two columns rather than four individual columns, we can proceed further and analyze each pair of columns separately. When this is done, the analysis shows there are significant differences in the way that regular judges and *pro tem* judges treated plaintiffs and defendants.

9. See also "Benefits to Litigants," p. 81.

10. When the new Multnomah County Justice Center was opened in 1983, an additional judge was assigned to criminal cases, for example.

CHAPTER NINE

# The Arizona Court of Appeals Pro Tem Judge Program

The Arizona Court of Appeals was created in 1965. The court has two divisions: Division One in Phoenix with a chief judge and eleven associate judges, and Division Two in Tucson with a chief judge and five associate judges. The 18 judges serve six-year terms. Division One has four panels with rotating membership consisting of one presiding judge and two associate judges each (Departments A, B, C, & D).

## Background

The Arizona Court of Appeals has appellate jurisdiction in all actions and proceedings originating in or permitted by law to be appealed from the general jurisdiction courts except criminal cases in which the death penalty or life imprisonment has been imposed. In 1965, fewer than 500 cases were filed. By 1975 filings had tripled. In the next ten years, filings almost doubled over 1975. In 1984, the two divisions of the Arizona Court of Appeals had 2,803 filings. Division One in Phoenix accounted for 1,904 of those filings, with 858 criminal, 605 civil, and 441 other appeals.

Between 1983 and 1984, Division One filings rose 6.7 percent, from 1,784 in 1983 to 1,904 (see Table 9). Most case categories recorded increases in filings during the year. Civil filings increased from 553 in 1983 to 605 in 1984, a 9.4 percent increase. The court had a record number of terminations in 1984, increasing from the previous record of 1,833 in 1983 to 1,907 in 1984.

The pattern of growth continued in 1985, although at a slower pace (see Table 9). Civil filings rose to 636, while total filings rose 2.7 percent to

1,955. Total terminations again set a record, at 1,951 terminations by the court plus 64 additional cases transferred to other courts. Although civil terminations increased in 1985 over 1984, for the first time since 1983 total civil terminations were less than total civil filings (626 to 636).

The Arizona Court of Appeals has actively sought ways to process its increasing caseload efficiently. Although the court has expanded to two divisions with 18 judges, increasing the number of judges has not been the only way the court has responded to its increased caseload.

In 1975 and 1976 Division One (Phoenix) participated in an experimental study to improve its productivity. New procedures were tested, modified, and adopted by the court. Some of these procedures have been discontinued, others remain available today but are not used often by attorneys. The court tried more new procedures in 1985. These attempts to stem the increasing backlog and delay in Division One were able to slow, at best, the increasing case inventory. Nevertheless, the court's willingness to test new procedures continues today.

Because of these efforts plus the addition in mid-1982 of three more judges to Division One, in 1983, for the first time in ten years, more cases were terminated than filed in Division One. Over the last ten years both the number of cases filed and those terminated have increased dramatically, but they have remained relatively close. Over this same period, the pending caseload has grown until it is almost equivalent to the number of cases filed and terminated annually. If at the beginning of a year the court has a pending caseload equal to the number of cases it can terminate that

**TABLE 9**
**Filings and terminations, Division One, 1983 through 1985**

|  | 1983 No. | 1983 Percent change | 1984 No. | 1984 Percent change | 1985 No. | 1985 Percent change |
|---|---|---|---|---|---|---|
| **Civil only** | | | | | | |
| Filings | 553 | 4.1 | 605 | 9.4 | 636 | 5.1 |
| Terminations | 651 | 34.0 | 616 | -5.4 | 626 | 1.6 |
| **All cases** | | | | | | |
| Filings | 1,784 | -.03 | 1,904 | 6.7 | 1,955 | 2.7 |
| Terminations | 1,833 | 18.2 | 1,907 | 4.0 | 1,951* | 2.3 |

*Plus 64 cases transferred out of the court.

year, there is a built-in one-year delay for the typical case. This built-in one-year delay for *all* types of cases is dwarfed by the delay experienced in the court's *civil* caseload.

## Developing the Program

Despite its efforts to improve its case processing and reduce the time to disposition, civil cases requiring oral argument were taking approximately two years from at issue to argument in Division One in 1984. Further efforts to improve civil appeals case processing without adding more judges were perceived to be critically needed by the judges of Division One.[1] Consequently, the court decided to form the Ad Hoc Committee on Judges *Pro Tem* in Appellate Courts to discuss the possibility of using *pro tempore* judges.

Arizona is the only state that currently authorizes the general use of judges *pro tem* in an intermediate appellate court.[2] The general jurisdiction court in Phoenix, the Superior Court of Maricopa County, has used *pro tempore* judges for a number of years to assist its judges with their "fast track" civil delay reduction program.[3] The program in Maricopa County has been very successful in reducing case processing times and assuring firm trial dates. Because of this success and similar use of *pro tems* in Tucson (see Chapter 7) there is widespread support within the community for the use of *pro tem* judges. Therefore, it was considered particularly viable to develop a *pro tem* program for the court of appeals.

On February 24, 1984, the Ad Hoc Committee met to discuss the case processing delay problems facing Division One, the experience with *pro tems* in the appellate courts of Oklahoma, and the possible use of *pro tems* in the Arizona Court of Appeals. The committee was composed of one Arizona Supreme Court justice, two Court of Appeals judges, one trial judge, three practicing attorneys, one law professor, one staff attorney for the Arizona House of Representatives, and a National Center for State Courts representative.

Following the February 24 meeting, the committee members pursued the task of developing a *pro tem* program. On March 21, 1984, Division One of the Court of Appeals unanimously approved the idea of using *pro tempore* judges. The committee then began to draft an outline of the contemplated program.

At the request of Division One, the Supreme Court approved the establishment of the judge *pro tem* program in April 1984. (See Appendix B.) By administrative order Division One created a new department of the court, Department E, consisting of panels of one regular judge and two *pro tem* judges. The administrative order was filed on May 7, 1984 (see Appendix B). It provides that the regular judge of the court is the presiding judge of the panel and that the panels will hear only civil appeals in which oral argument has been requested. All cases assigned to Department E are disposed of by a memorandum decision that is unpublished and does not have precedential value.

The court has an internal grading system for cases. Cases are marked from *one*, indicating the least degree of difficulty and amount of new material, to *ten*, indicating the most complex and novel cases. Cases assigned to Department E are supposed to be cases with a grade between *three* and *seven* that do not appear to involve an issue requiring publication.[4] The judges of the court agreed that even if a case turned out to be one in which the opinion should be published, the opinion from Department E would remain an unpublished memorandum opinion. This decision was made to enlarge the appearance of justice and minimize feelings of conflicts of interest among litigants based on practicing attorneys' possibly creating law useful in their practice.

## The Program

Division One adopted a set of "Internal Operating Guidelines" (see Appendix B) that established the following timetable for development of the *pro tem* judge program by September 1984:

| Activity | Completion Date |
|---|---|
| Each Division One judge recommends 20 names to Chief Judge | April 1, 1984 |
| Invitations sent by Chief Judge | May 1 |
| Invitations to serve as judges *pro tempore* accepted | May 15 |
| Chief justice appoints judges *pro tempore* | July 1 |
| Cases for Department E identified (to be heard Sept.-Dec. 1984) | July 1 |
| List of cases and counsel sent to judges *pro tempore* to identify conflicts | July 1 |
| List of *pro tempore* judges sent to parties for disqualifications | July 1 |
| Panels set and cases for Department E calendared internally | July 15 |

The process repeated itself for cases heard in later periods.

When attorneys were invited to serve as *pro tem* judges they were asked to agree to the following conditions of service. First, they would sit on one calendar containing three cases. Second, they would read all the briefs and be prepared to rule on the issues presented upon the conclusion of oral argument. Third, they would attend a preargument conference, oral argument, and a postargument conference. Fourth, they would write a proposed memorandum opinion in one of the cases and distribute a draft of that memorandum to the other panel members within 30 days of the argument. Fifth, they would serve without compensation. Sixth, they would observe the relevant provisions of the Code of Judicial Conduct during their term of service. (See Appendix B for the court's letter.)

The chief judge of Division One maintains the master list of *pro tem* judges. The list was established from nominations of each of the judges on the court. The goal was to obtain highly qualified, respected members of the bar. All judges *pro tem* must have at least the minimum requirements established by the Judicial Qualifications Commission.[5]

Judges *pro tem* were provided with a list of all cases being assigned to Department E. The list showed the parties, the attorneys, and the trial judges. Judges *pro tem* identified those cases in which they had conflicts of interest. The parties were sent a list of all 50 judges *pro tem* and allowed to strike up to five names from the list. Judges *pro tem* and cases then were matched based on the absence of conflicts and strikes, three cases for each three-member panel. The chief judge, an additional judge, and the clerk of the court checked on and marked conflicts on a chart and assigned cases. In a few instances after cases were assigned, *pro tem*s identified conflicts from the briefs, which required further juggling of panels.

There was an unexpected and potentially disruptive development regarding the initial list of 50 lawyers. The original list of names submitted by the court's 12 judges was fairly evenly balanced between plaintiff and defense lawyers. The 50 names, which were selected at random from those submitted, turned out to be unbalanced toward defense lawyers; there were five lawyers from one insurance defense firm and two lawyers from the same corporation's law department. The Trial Lawyers Association wrote the court a letter expressing concern.

The court had two meetings and agreed that the next time lawyers were selected the judges would check the balance between plaintiff and defense lawyers more carefully. They also agreed not to have two lawyers from the same firm on the same panel, but they decided, further, not to start the process over again. Subsequent lists were screened by the entire court to avoid this problem thereafter.

Three cases are scheduled for argument before a new panel of Department E each week. The first panel sat on September 13, 1984; a panel sat each week thereafter and except for Christmas and New Year's weeks continued to do so through June 1985. Department E resumed operations in September 1985 and continued through June 1986, at which time the use of *pro tem* judges was terminated.

The actual operation of Department E went very much as planned. The process of matching cases to *pro tem* judges used 28 of the 50 lawyers for cases heard from September 13 to December 13, 1984. The 28 finally selected represented a better balance between plaintiff and defense lawyers than the original fifty.

Oral argument in Department E is conducted as in any other department in Division One. A calendar is prepared listing the cases set for oral argument and the judges hearing the oral argument. There is no mention on the calendar that two of the three judges on the panel are *pro tem* judges, except that the Division One judge is designated as the panel's presiding judge.

The panel meets about an hour before arguments are to start to discuss the cases. (The panel often is provided a bench memorandum prepared by the presiding judge's law clerk.) At the argument, usually the presiding judge introduces him-/herself and the other judges and briefly describes the delay reduction goal of the *pro tem* program. In those panels observed by project staff, all three judges shared equally in questioning the attorneys.[6]

The presiding judge's clerk attends the argument and the proceedings are recorded electronically. The presiding judge tells the arguing attorneys what their time allotments are and keeps track of the time limitations for each case.

Following oral argument the judges retire to conference, make final decisions on each appeal, if possible, and make writing assignments. Although project staff did not attend actual conferences, in joint interviews with *pro tem* and court of appeals judges, we observed a very collegial attitude.

# Goals

The November 1984 case aging study indicated that the median time from at-issue to decision was twenty-five months for civil cases. The Division One judges who helped develop the *pro tem* program set the goal of the program at bringing at-issue-to-argument time down to twelve months for all cases requiring oral argument. After the first eight months of the program, the court decided to extend the program for one year to June 1986 with a goal of reducing to six months the time from at-issue to argument.

Some involved with the program were less concerned about exact goals and were not as optimistic, indicating that the program would be beneficial if it did no more than assist the court to avoid falling further behind.

To other judges the major project goal was a qualitative one: to maintain a work environment in which judges could devote appropriate time to the decision-making process while statistically improving case processing times. A litigant who has to wait well over two years in the appellate process to reach a final disposition of his or her dispute may be understandably critical, but speed of resolution is not the primary concern of these judges. If appellate judges have pending caseloads so burdensome that they adopt shortcuts solely to increase dispositions, some appeals may not be given the attention they deserve. Department E's goal for this group, therefore, was to reduce the time to final disposition without reducing the amount of "quality time" the Division One judges have to apply to the decision-making process.

## Quantitative Evaluation

The National Center initially collected data on all civil memoranda cases with and without oral argument disposed between July 1983 and June 1984 to provide a baseline against which any improvements in case processing time attributable to Department E could be measured. The dates of five possible case processing events were collected: filing of the record, at-issue, under advisement, decision, and mandate.

Table 10 provides a complete review of time intervals between all the above events for cases that resulted in memorandum decisions. The median time from filing of the record to mandate was 798 days (26.2 months).[7] The 90th percentile was 1,071 days (35.1 months), meaning that one in every 10 of these civil cases did not reach mandate until almost three years after the notice of appeal was filed.

From September 1984 to June 1985, 146 cases were scheduled in Department E. In general terms, if Department E sits 40 weeks a year, and three cases a week are assigned, it should be able to hear and dispose of 120 cases per year. Actual scheduling is somewhat greater, as seen by the 146 total cases for the first nine months. Since Department E panels have one judge, and preparation of memorandum opinions is distributed equally, two-thirds, or 97 of the 146 dispositions for the first group of cases, can be assigned to the *pro tems'* participation.

On average, in calendar year 1984 each Division One judge was responsible for about 51 civil terminations. In 1985 this increased slightly to an average of 52 civil terminations per judge. (In 1984 and 1985, the division produced an average of about 160 *total* terminations per judge each year.) If the *pro tem* judge positions in Department E represent almost 100 of that department's civil terminations, they together produced very close to the average number of civil terminations of two regular judges in 1984 and 1985 (approximately 50 per judge per year). Of course, each of the regular judges had to participate in the cases

## TABLE 10
### Time interval statistics for memoranda cases disposed, July 1983 to June 1984

|  | Number of cases | Median (in days) | 90th Percentile (in days) |
|---|---|---|---|
| **Filed to** | | | |
| At-issue | 191 | 123.5 | 258.0 |
| Under advisement | 175 | 665.0 | 885.5 |
| Decision | 193 | 737.0 | 983.0 |
| Reconsideration | 3 | 825.5 | — |
| Review | 69 | 848.0 | 1,148.0 |
| Mandate | 192 | 798.0 | 1,071.0 |
| **At-issue to** | | | |
| Under advisement | 173 | 573.5 | 680.0 |
| Decision | 190 | 627.5 | 764.0 |
| Reconsideration | 3 | 728.0 | — |
| Review | 67 | 750.0 | 904.0 |
| Mandate | 189 | 678.0 | 872.0 |
| **Under advisement to** | | | |
| Decision | 175 | 41.5 | 205.5 |
| Reconsideration | 3 | 76.5 | — |
| Review | 65 | 169.5 | 331.0 |
| Mandate | 173 | 132.0 | 335.0 |

— = No value is reported for the 90th percentile for intervals with too few values (three or fewer for 90th percentile).

assigned to his or her regular department in addition to the Department E work, but this one rough measure of productivity indicates the court gained about two full-time-equivalent positions to address civil cases. The number of cases included in the evaluation of the Department E program is shown in Table 11, classified by their method of disposition and whether they belonged to the comparison group (cases argued before the start of the Department E program) or the study group.

Countering this very positive view of the effect of the *pro tem* judges are two perspectives on the bottom line, total civil terminations: (1) in 1985, when Department E operated all year, there were only 10 more civil terminations than in 1984; and (2) 1985's 626 civil case terminations do not equal the court's record of 651 in 1983, which was the first full calendar year of a fourth department in Division One (Department D started operation in July 1982). Some of 1983's record terminations may

**TABLE 11**
**Number of civil appeals disposed by court, July 1983 through September 1985**

|  | Comparison period (argued before 9/13/84) | Study period (argued after 9/13/84) |
|---|---|---|
| **1. By opinion** | | |
| Without oral argument | 33 | 16 |
| With oral argument | 107 | 34 |
| **2. By memo** | | |
| Without oral argument | 119 | 67 |
| With oral argument | 187 | 160 |
| Department E only | — | 117 |
| **3. By order/stipulation/ supplemental memo** | | |
| Without oral argument | 8 | 3 |
| With oral argument | 2 | 5 |
| Department E only | — | 1 |

**Note:** Cases were identified as belonging to either the comparison group or the study group according to when the case was argued or placed under submission. Dispositions for some of the cases in the comparison group occurred after September 13, 1984. Data collection for Department E cases continued through June 1986. All other data given for cases in the study period groups run through October 1985 only, since after that date it could not be determined which disposed cases had been argued.

have been "housecleaning" terminations, but in 1983 the division was able to produce 281 memorandum opinions, compared with the 1985 total with Department E of 274 memorandum opinions. It appears that the gains in *time* to argument and to termination did not translate into equally dramatic improvements in the *number* of dispositions. The effect of sitting in Department E on the regular judges seems to have been to lessen the output they could achieve in their regularly assigned departments, so that the net impact of the extra department using *pro tem* judges is quite small.[8]

Slightly more Department E cases were reversed and remanded than were cases in the comparison group; slightly fewer were affirmed. Neither of these differences is statistically significant. More Department E cases were decided by unanimous vote.[9] Except for these minor differences (see Tables 12 and 13), Department E cases and similar cases handled during the previous year by panels made up only of judges were disposed in similar patterns.

## TABLE 12
## Disposition of civil appeals with oral argument, by percent

|  | Percent by memo ||| Percent by opinion ||
|---|---|---|---|---|---|
|  | Comparison | Study | Dept. E only | Comparison | Study |
| **1. Vote** | | | | | |
| Unanimous | | | | | |
| 2-0 | 0 | 0 | 0 | 1 | 0 |
| 3-0 | 89 | 97 | 93 | 86 | 94 |
| Dissent | | | | | |
| 2-1 | 2 | 1 | 7 | 12 | 6 |
| Other | 1 | 0 | 0 | 1 | 0 |
| Per curiam | 9 | 2 | 0 | 0 | 0 |
| **2. Result** | | | | | |
| Affirmed | 64 | 65 | 61 | 51 | 53 |
| Reversed | 11 | 5 | 10 | 14 | 12 |
| Reversed & remanded | 21 | 21 | 27 | 31 | 35 |
| Remanded | 1 | 3 | 17 | 0 | 0 |
| Dismissed | 2 | 1 | 17 | 2 | 0 |
| Other | 1 | 5 | 0 | 2 | 0 |
| **3. Reconsideration** | | | | | |
| Requested | 36 | 24 | 37 | 35 | 21 |
| Granted | 2 | 0 | 0 | 3 | 0 |
| **4. Review** | | | | | |
| Requested | 51 | 21 | 23 | 64 | 24 |
| Granted | 3 | 0 | 4 | 10 | 3 |

**Note:** See note on Table 11 for a description of cases included in each category.

The rate at which requests for review were filed was cut in half for cases disposed by memo, and by two-thirds for cases disposed by opinion. This change between the comparison and study time periods can be attributed to a change in court procedures and is not directly related to the implementation of Department E panels. Some cases decided by Department E panels requested reconsideration and review, but not at a rate that was higher than before the implementation of the Department E program.

How do these same groups of cases compare in the length of time needed for disposition? The median times for four major intervals for

94  FRIENDS OF THE COURT

these cases are shown in Figure 3. The associated data are contained in Table 14. The zero line in Figure 3 was chosen to enable the reader to compare the time intervals before and after submission of cases to the court. The bars in Figure 3 are grouped by whether or not the case had an oral argument and how it was decided, i.e., by opinion or by memo. Within these four groups are two or three bars, one for the comparison period, a second for the study period, and a third—in the with-oral-argument-by-memo group—for Department E cases.

## TABLE 13
### Disposition of civil appeals without oral argument, by percent

|  | Percent by memo | | Percent by opinion | |
|---|---|---|---|---|
|  | Comparison | Study | Comparison | Study |
| **1. Vote** | | | | |
| Unanimous | | | | |
|   1-0 | 0 | 0 | 3 | 0 |
|   2-0 | 1 | 0 | 0 | 0 |
|   3-0 | 76 | 97 | 76 | 100 |
| Dissent | | | | |
|   2-1 | 2 | 1 | 18 | 0 |
|   Other | 0 | 0 | 3 | 0 |
| Per curiam | 21 | 1 | 0 | 0 |
| **2. Result** | | | | |
| Affirmed | 69 | 78 | 58 | 50 |
| Reversed | 16 | 9 | 6 | 6 |
| Reversed & remanded | 8 | 13 | 33 | 31 |
| Remanded | 5 | 0 | 0 | 0 |
| Dismissed | 2 | 0 | 3 | 6 |
| Other | 0 | 0 | 0 | 6 |
| **3. Reconsideration** | | | | |
| Requested | 36 | 17 | 33 | 31 |
| Granted | 0 | 0 | 0 | 0 |
| **4. Review** | | | | |
| Requested | 29 | 18 | 45 | 31 |
| Granted | 5 | 0 | 13 | 25 |

**Note:** See note on Table 11 for a description of cases included in each category.

**FIGURE 3**
**Median time-to-disposition for civil appeals, Court of Appeals, Division One, Arizona (days), July 1983 through September 1985**

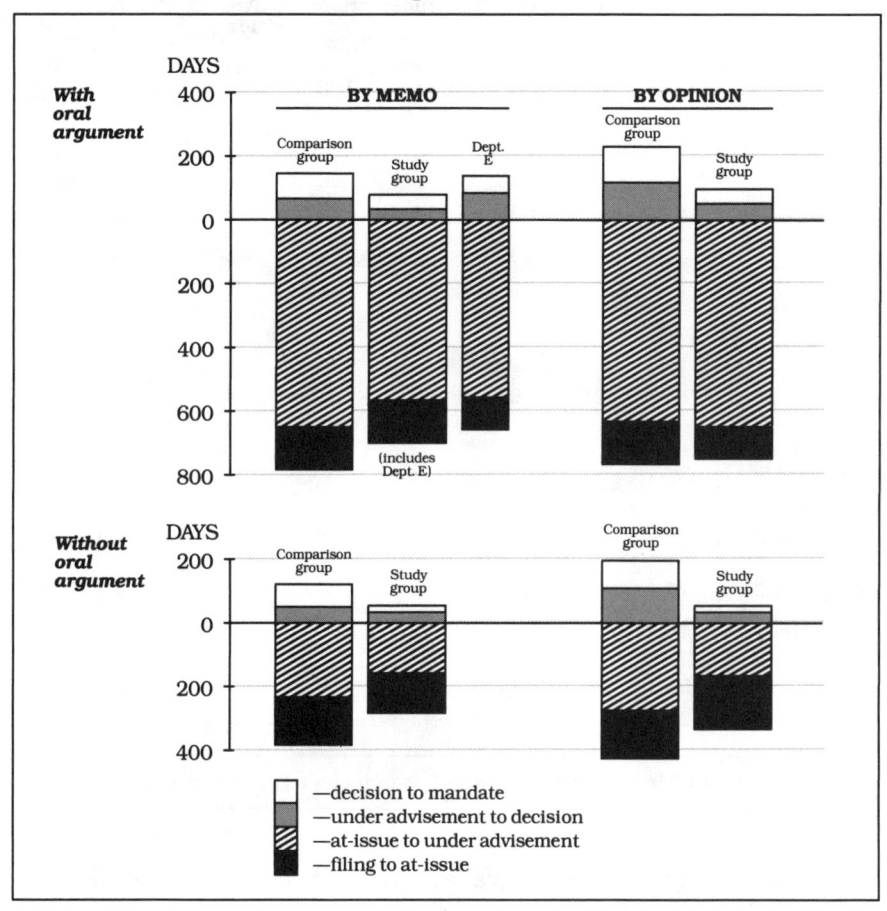

Cases with oral argument have much longer median times to disposition than those submitted without. Most of this difference is accounted for by the longer interval from at-issue to oral argument. Almost none of the difference in time to disposition appears to be the result of the distinction between the manner of disposition—by opinion or by memo. Cases disposed during the study period were processed faster than similar cases disposed during the previous year for all four major case groupings. The interval that was reduced proportionately the most during the study period was the time from decision to mandate, primarily because of the rule change that made motions for reconsidera-

## TABLE 14
### Change in time-to-disposition for civil appeals (median days)

|  | Filing of record to at-issue |  | At-issue to oral argument/under advisement |  | Oral argument/ under advisement to decision |  | Filing of record to decision |  |
|---|---|---|---|---|---|---|---|---|
|  | Days | Percent change | Days | Percent change | Days | Percent change | Days | Percent change |
| **With oral argument** |  |  |  |  |  |  |  |  |
| **By memo** |  |  |  |  |  |  |  |  |
| Comparison cases | 140 |  | 640 |  | 86 |  | 964 |  |
| Study cases | 128 | −9 | 548 | −14 | 62 | −28 | 842 | −11 |
| Department E cases | 123 | −12 | 512 | −20 | 106 | +23 | 755 | −22 |
| **By opinion** |  |  |  |  |  |  |  |  |
| Comparison cases | 146 |  | 609 |  | 148 |  | 1,034 |  |
| Study cases | 115 | −21 | 608 | 0 | 84 | −43 | 864 | −15 |
| **Without oral argument** |  |  |  |  |  |  |  |  |
| **By memo** |  |  |  |  |  |  |  |  |
| Comparison cases | 124 |  | 244 |  | 41 |  | 532 |  |
| Study cases | 110 | −11 | 162 | −34 | 28 | −32 | 374 | −34 |
| **By opinion** |  |  |  |  |  |  |  |  |
| Comparison cases | 108 |  | 274 |  | 119 |  | 614 |  |
| Study cases | 122 | +13 | 158 | −42 | 44 | −63 | 341 | −42 |

**Note:** See note on Table 11 for a description of cases included in each category.

tion and for review less attractive rather than because of any differences between Department E and the court's other departments.

The largest reductions in the number of days occurred in the time from at-issue to oral argument/under advisement. The median time for this interval for Department E cases was more than four months shorter than for similar cases processed the preceding year. All cases with oral argument decided by memo (this includes the Department E cases as well as cases decided by panels made up of three regular judges) had a median time for this interval that was three months shorter than that for the comparison group. The difference was large also for cases submitted without oral argument. It was almost three months shorter for cases decided by memo and almost four months shorter for cases decided by opinion.

The time interval from at-issue to oral argument for cases decided by memo was reduced during the study period because of increased capacity; Department E had the same effect as opening up a new service line: all the lines get shorter. When the Department E program was proposed, there was some concern that requiring each judge to sit on some additional panels would delay the work of regular departments of the court. Contrary to this fear, cases processed in the other civil departments are reaching disposition more rapidly than those processed during the comparison period. The median time from at-issue to under advisement for cases decided without oral argument was between three and four months *shorter* during the study period. The court has been able to speed the processing of all four major groups of civil appeals, not just Department E cases.

The impact of the "Hawthorne effect" is most apparent from these data. Parts of the process independent of Department E showed reduced processing time. The time from filing of the record to at-issue—a period entirely controlled by attorneys—went down for each category except cases decided by opinion but without oral argument. One Phoenix attorney ascribes at least part of this improvement to the court's tightening up on time extensions granted to lawyers to conclude their work. The time from argument to decision for cases before the four regular departments of the court went down dramatically, especially for cases without oral argument decided by opinion. The reduction in time for this category of cases more than offset the extra time the attorneys took to prepare their briefs, so overall there was a 42 percent reduction of time for this category, the highest of the groups of cases evaluated. All the no-argument cases stayed in Departments A-D. The extra work of the regular judges is apparent from the data shown in Table 14 and charted in Figure 3; the *pro tem* judge program may have been an important catalyst in spurring the court to achieve these gains, but Department E alone cannot be given all the credit for the court's improvements. The interval from oral argument to decision for Department E cases was longer than in the comparison group (see Table 15). It also was longer from decision to reconsideration. The longer interval for oral argument to decision indicates that Department E cases as a group required more time in the decision writing process. Judges and *pro tems* interviewed indicated that some *pro tem* judges took substantially longer than expected to complete their draft opinions. Each adjunct's invitation to serve on Department E explicitly stated that the adjunct would be "required to write a proposed disposition in one of the civil cases heard, and distribute that proposed draft within 30 days of the argument." There should not have been any misunderstanding of the writing time requirements. In a few cases the adjuncts ignored the court's deadline. In some cases the pressure of earning a living squeezed out the adjunct's "free" time to write an opinion; writing and reviewing opinions is not quite as glamorous or compelling as hearing arguments.

**TABLE 15**
**Change in time-to-disposition for civil appeals with oral argument disposed by memo (median days)**

|  | Comparison | Study | Percent change | Dept. E only | Percent change |
|---|---|---|---|---|---|
| **Filing to** | | | | | |
| At-issue | 140 | 128 | − 9 | 123 | −12 |
| Oral argument | 774 | 705 | − 9 | 704 | − 9 |
| Decision | 862 | 786 | − 9 | 755 | −12 |
| Mandate | 964 | 841 | −13 | 841 | −13 |
| **At-issue to** | | | | | |
| Oral argument | 640 | 548 | −14 | 512 | −20 |
| Decision | 720 | 632 | −12 | 620 | −14 |
| Mandate | 816 | 704 | −14 | 723 | −11 |
| **Oral argument to** | | | | | |
| Decision | 86 | 62 | −28 | 106 | +23 |
| Mandate | 198 | 130 | −34 | 158 | −20 |
| **Decision to** | | | | | |
| Reconsideration | 47 | 55 | +17 | 61 | +30 |
| Review | 104 | 108 | + 4 | 118 | +13 |
| Mandate | 88 | 42 | −52 | 79 | −10 |

**Note:** See note on Table 11 for a description of cases included in each category.

A third explanation for the increased decision-writing time may be that it is more difficult, and therefore more time consuming, for the regular judge and the *pro tem* judges on a Department E panel to discuss and revise the drafts of the memos written for the cases they heard and to discuss the action to be taken on motions for reconsideration. Regular judges of the court are all located in the same building and can usually communicate with one another without difficulty. It is relatively easy for all-judge panels to meet to review draft opinions or resolve differences among themselves as to how a motion for reconsideration should be disposed. The coordination involved in maintaining contact between the *pro tem* judges and the regular judge on each panel should not produce significantly slower times for completion of memoranda, but it may contribute a few days of extra time.

Even with these longer time intervals included, however, the median time from filing of the record to mandate for Department E cases was still 13 percent (123 days) shorter than that for similar cases that were disposed during the comparison period. Had the court's original schedule for completing memorandum opinions been adhered to, the reduction in time might have been even more dramatic.

Cases disposed between January and June 1986 showed continued improvement. Cases disposed by opinion had a median time from filing to decision of 577 days; cases disposed by memorandum had a median time of 586 days. These are both shorter than the medians measured for these same groups of cases over the entire study period. The ninetieth percentile from filing to decision for cases decided by memo was 794 days, considerably shorter than the 983 days for this same interval for cases disposed during the comparison period (see Table 10).

## Qualitative Evaluation

A qualitative evaluation of the Division One *pro tem* program was conducted through on-site interviews with six of the twelve judges of the court, fourteen *pro tem* judges, and thirteen attorneys who argued cases before Department E. The latter group was included in an effort to obtain the perspective of litigants and the general bar on the program.

In general, the judges, *pro tem* judges, and litigating attorneys had a very positive response to the program. With the exceptions noted below, almost all of those interviewed praised the court for undertaking the program and believe that the effort has been and will continue to be of benefit to the court and to litigants.

### Quality of the List and Qualities that *Pro Tem* Judges Should Have

Views on the lawyers appointed as *pro tem* judges are fairly closely divided between those who think everyone on the list is of high quality and those who feel that the list contains "by and large" high-quality lawyers. Among the regular judges of Division One, the majority view is that some lawyers on the list do not possess the skills and quality the judges would desire. Perhaps not unexpectedly, however, some of those on the list who were mentioned explicitly as not being the "best" lawyers were viewed as having performed well as *pro tem*s. One litigating attorney had very favorable comments to make about a *pro tem* judge who was identified by another *pro tem* as being less qualified to be on the list than he would have expected. Perhaps the *pro tem* judges thought to be not highly qualified rose to the occasion or others' opinions of these lawyers are not fully informed.

Despite this division about the lawyers selected, there is virtual unanimity that lawyers who serve as *pro tem* judges should be regarded as highly qualified by both judges and the bar. This perception of quality is thought to be needed to assure acceptance of the program by the litigating bar and clients. Some argued that a lawyer highly qualified to be a *pro tem* judge in a trial court is not necessarily going to be a good appellate judge and that the criteria for the two should be different, but everyone agreed that quality should be the first criterion. Several lawyers mentioned indicia of quality to be the number of years lawyers have practiced and their trial or appellate experience.

### Selection and Screening of *Pro Tem* Judges

The quality of the list is determined by the selection and screening process used. The judges seem to be the only ones capable of commenting on this aspect of the process, as no *pro tem* knew how he or she had come to be invited. Several of the judges feel that the court needs to improve its selection and screening process, with one judge proposing that active, respected members of the bar join two or three Court of Appeals judges on a screening committee. Except for a minimum requirement of years at the bar, none of the judges proposed specific criteria for selection.

### Why Lawyers Agree to Serve as *Pro Tem* Judges

There was substantial agreement among the *pro tem* judges on why they agreed to serve. The foremost explanation was a sense of professional responsibility to the court and the community at large, associated with an effort to help the court reduce its backlog of cases. Several *pro tem*s said they were flattered and pleased to be invited to join a list they regarded as relatively exclusive. A few lawyers thought that it would be a useful opportunity to learn more about the appellate process, although about the same number indicated they had no expectation of gaining any useful experience. Only three lawyers indicated they were interested in being an appellate judge.

The reaction among the *pro tem* judges to their service has been very positive. Three of the *pro tem*s used the word "fun." Another said it was "real enjoyable." Another said that it had refreshed his interest in law; he wished he could have had the experience earlier in his career.

### Time Spent by *Pro Tem* Judges

Quite a wide range of hours spent on the program was estimated by the *pro tem* judges. One *pro tem* estimated he spent as few as 9 hours. Two said they were unable to estimate their hours but thought they spent more than a judge would have spent. One *pro tem* estimated he spent between 11 and 15 hours, three estimated between 16 and 20 hours, two estimated between 26 and 30 hours, three estimated between 31 and 40 hours, and two estimated they will have spent about 100 hours before they are finished. The latter clearly are unusual. In one of the 100-hour cases, the *pro tem* judge felt he had to review all of the seven volumes of the case record and analyze it carefully in order to provide guidance to the trial judge for the next trial. In the other case, the *pro tem* judge indicated that he had taken his service very seriously. He predicted his case would go to the Supreme Court, and thus he was being extraordinarily conscientious in preparing his opinion.

**Lawyers as Appellate Judges**
No one interviewed questions the propriety of using lawyers on an appellate court to address a significant delay problem. Some *pro tem* judges and litigating lawyers feel that if the backlog problem is resolved, the public is entitled to have only regular judges determine their appeals, but no one questioned either the current effort or the underlying concept of using lawyers to help the court. All but one of the judges interviewed also thought that the program was sufficiently positive—even with its additional administrative burdens and problems—that other appellate courts should consider adopting the program.

As indicated above, judges, *pro tem* judges, and litigating attorneys all were pleased with and sometimes very impressed with the level of attorney participation during oral argument. Only two litigating attorneys said the *pro tem* judges on their cases did not ask any questions. In most cases, the litigating attorneys indicated that the *pro tem* judges went directly to the important and difficult issues and asked challenging questions. One attorney said the questions were a little like law school, but he did not think they were inappropriate.

Several suggestions were made for modifying the composition of panels. A few lawyers suggested that three-lawyer panels would be as effective as two-lawyer-and-one-judge panels and would save the judges the time needed to sit on those panels. Another liked the composition in the present program but suggested that only two cases be assigned to the panels so that the regular judge would not have to take the time to write an opinion. One judge and one *pro tem* suggested that a panel of two judges and one *pro tem* would resolve the problem of conflicts of interest and lawyers making law.

The import of these alternative suggestions may be that the bar is sufficiently pleased with the addition of lawyers to the appellate bench that they are trying to identify ways to preserve attorney participation while relieving the court of some of the burden of having the extra panel.

**Compensating *Pro Tem* Judges**
None of the *pro tem* judges interviewed thinks that compensation is necessary. Several said they would have been insulted had the court

offered compensation. Several said that compensation, if offered, would be minimal (especially compared to their usual billing rates) and therefore was inappropriate.

One litigating attorney felt that it was important for the system to pay for lawyers' services, but he had no inherent problem with attorneys volunteering. His concern about attorneys not being compensated was tied to his concern that too few lawyers do *pro bono* work for the system and that not paying lawyers causes the court to draw from the same relatively limited pool of lawyers who already volunteer their time.

**Orientation and Training of *Pro Tem* Judges**
When the *pro tem* judges were asked if the orientation or training provided by the court was sufficient, almost all said it was. In response to more specific questions, however, some of the *pro tem*s had some suggestions to offer about additional information that would have been useful.

The principal area of uncertainty appears to be what resources of the court are available to the *pro tem* judges. For instance, several *pro tem*s mentioned that they did not know whether they could use the regular judges' law clerks. Several were not aware that the judges' law clerks would be preparing bench memoranda prior to argument. Five *pro tem* judges mentioned that they were not clear in advance what would go on in the preargument meeting or that a preliminary decision would be reached during this meeting.

The court's style sheet on opinions was made available to all *pro tem*s, but according to some of the judges, some of the *pro tem*s followed the court's style and some did not. Some of the regular judges told the *pro tem* judges on their panels that they would prepare the final draft of the opinion and that their law clerks would do the final cite checking. Other judges apparently did not, since some of the *pro tem*s expressed uncertainty about who would do the final cite checking.

It appears that the interest in orientation of the *pro tem* judges focuses on the "nitty-gritty" procedural aspects of their service. They feel comfortable with the preargument discussions and writing opinions, but might have felt a little more comfortable if some of the above items had been discussed or covered in a memorandum prior to their appearance at court.

**What Lawyers Tell Their Clients and the
Litigating Attorneys' Reactions to the Program**
One of the key concerns of the court has been how litigants react to the use of *pro tem* judges at the appellate level. In most cases the litigating attorneys did not feel compelled to advise their clients that the appellate panel would include *pro tem* judges. When the clients *were* advised, it

appears that they were given a relatively *pro forma* description without the type of "sales pitch" for the program that seems to occur regularly at the trial level. This could be considered a tribute to the lawyers selected and attorney confidence in the system operating properly. It also may reflect a different attitude among lawyers about appellate practice or about the degree of client involvement appropriate in appellate cases. None of the respondents was able to offer any insight into why this apparent confidence is greater at the appellate level than at the trial level.

## Costs and Administrative Issues

### Costs

It is often very difficult to estimate costs of a program because most costs are personnel costs and most court employees are not employed exclusively for a particular program. There were many employees who assisted in the operation of the *pro tem* judge program. The clerk of the court was involved with the program from its inception; one staff attorney screened cases for assignment to Department E; judges' law clerks in some instances wrote briefing memoranda; all levels of clerical employees were involved in the processing of Department E cases. Two of the judges of Division One gave considerable time and effort to the development and operation of the *pro tem* program. Without their continued participation, the program certainly would not have run as smoothly as it has.

The selection of *pro tem* judges, selection of cases for Department E, and assignment of cases to particular panels consumed considerable clerical time. Table 16 lists the tasks required during the *pro tem* program and the number of hours devoted to each task for the development period September 1984 through June 1985.

The total amount of time spent by clerical employees in program support was 1624.5 hours, or 203 person-days. A work-year for clerical employees averages around 230 days, so 203 person-days represents 88 percent of a full-time-equivalent position.

Assuming the average employee involved with the program, excluding the judges, earns $23,000 a year and that the fringe benefit rate is 30 percent of salary, plus general overhead at 60 percent of salary and fringe, the clerical cost of the program is estimated to be about $42,100.

| | | |
|---|---|---|
| Salary | 88% of $23,000 | $20,240 |
| Fringe benefits | 30% of $20,240 | $ 6,072 |
| Overhead | 60% of $26,312 | $15,787 |
| | TOTAL | $42,099 |

## TABLE 16
## Department E program personnel requirements in start-up year*

### A. Special *Pro Tem* Program Processes

| DESCRIPTION | TIME (hours) |
|---|---|
| 1. Staff attorney review | 275.0 |
| 2. Initial preparation and devising set-up procedures | 38.5 |
| 3. Invitation to serve (1st & 2nd panels) | 22.0 |
| 4. Thank you's and requests to check conflicts (1st & 2nd panels) | 20.0 |
| 5. Creating *pro tem* attorney strike form (Document #11—never used) | 28.0 |
| 6. Letters to case attorneys *re* disqualification (1st & 2nd panels) | 49.0 |
| 7. Letter *re* selection and request to extend participation | 30.0 |
| 8. Preparation of case list by month | 18.0 |
| 9. Preparation January/June 1985 maililng list | 2.5 |
| 10. Time and evaluation letter to *pro tem* judges | 24.0 |
| 11. Preparation of monthly calendar | 60.0 |
| 12. Review database | 15.0 |
| 13. Preparation of oral argument notice notifications | 75.0 |
| 14. Preparation of weekly motion calendar | 55.5 |
| 15. Preparation of petition for review for transfer to Supreme Court (approximately 10 cases) | 25.0 |
| 16. Preparation of Department E time use report | 6.0 |
| Subtotal | 743.5 |

### B. Daily Processing

| DESCRIPTION | TIME (hours) |
|---|---|
| 1. Receipts for records by *pro tem* judges | 150.0 |
| 2. Docketing (each item) | 60.0 |
| 3. Process an order | 110.0 |
| 4. Process a decision | 120.0 |
| 5. Mandates & distribution | 60.0 |
| 6. Processing, handling, and maintenance of appeal file | 381.0 |
| Subtotal | 881.0 |
| TOTAL | 1624.5 |

*Time estimates provided by the Arizona Court of Appeals Clerk of the Court.

To calculate the expenditure of judge time for Department E, it is estimated that the Division One judges spent the same hours per case as did the *pro tems*, who estimated an average of 11.2 hours per case. For the 146 cases, therefore, it took approximately 1,635 hours of judge time or 204 days (97 percent of a 210-day work-year). Arizona Court of Appeals judges' annual salary was approximately $60,000 in 1984. Calculating judges' costs in the same manner as clerical costs results in the following total:

| | | |
|---|---|---|
| Salary | 97% of $60,000 | $58,200 |
| Fringe benefits | 30% of $58,200 | $17,460 |
| Overhead | 60% of $75,660 | $45,396 |
| | | TOTAL $121,056 |

The combined clerical and judge costs total $163,155.

During the period that the personnel hours for program support were recorded, some 146 cases were scheduled. In this very rough cost analysis, each appeal cost about $1,100 to complete. Costs should have been considerably less in the second year of the program, as some of the costs would not be repeated and some of the start-up time should be greatly reduced for subsequent panels. It also is important to acknowledge that none of these "costs" involve cash expenditures by the court. Staff and judges devoted the hours indicated and were paid, but the program was implemented by everyone working harder; additional budget-item expenditures were incurred only for postage and copying (see Table 16).

The cost-per-case for all Arizona Court of Appeals cases can be averaged by taking fiscal year 1983-84 expenditures of $3,297,545 and dividing by 1,869 terminations (the average of calendar-year terminations for 1983 and 1984). The average expenditure-per-case for all court of appeals cases was $1,764.

Two major factors are not taken into account in this analysis. First and foremost, the development time of the chief judge and other judges of Division One is not considered in the cost-per-case for the *pro tem* judge program. Second, of all the appeals handled by the court, the civil memorandum decision cases are probably considerably above the average in time required. To the extent that civil cases are more time consuming than the average court of appeals case, the *pro tem* program appears to be even more cost-effective.

The above analysis points out two facts to be kept in mind. First, even if a program uses *pro tem* judges who donate their services, there will be considerable indirect (i.e., noncash) costs. Second, it is nonetheless possible to develop and implement an innovative and comprehensive new program without incurring costs that are out of proportion.

### Administrative Matters

During the interviews the administrative concerns discussed related to the court's handling of the provision of robes, the availability of court files, and courtroom and office space. The interviews revealed another area that might be considered administrative, however: the timely production of opinions by *pro tem* judges. Both areas are discussed in this section.

The *pro tem* judges indicated that the administrative aspects of the program were handled very well. Judges reported some delay initially in having case files ready for the *pro tem* judges to take with them following argument, but that matter appears to have been dealt with satisfactorily and without much difficulty. It appears that the time and care the court took prior to September 1984 to plan for the administrative aspects of the program were well spent.

As stated previously, the court advised the *pro tem* judges in writing that draft opinions were to be produced within 30 days of the argument. Some *pro tems* apparently have overlooked this. It was apparent during interviews that at least some have not been as diligent in producing opinions as they or the judges would desire. Even some of the litigating attorneys noted that they were surprised at how long it took to get their decisions from Department E, since they assumed that one of the advantages of using attorneys in Department E would be that the attorneys would produce their decisions more quickly than the regular judges are able to. One *pro tem* judge suggested that the court did not have a clear perception of how long *pro tem* judges would be allowed to take to produce memoranda and what procedures would be followed if a *pro tem* judge exceeded the limits. The expectation was that the presiding judge of each panel would remind *pro tem* judges that their decisions were still outstanding after 30 or 60 days. But even when this happened, some *pro tem* judges did not respond by producing a decision. It has been suggested that the *pro tems* take additional time preparing their decisions because they lack experience in writing appellate opinions or as a result of the demands of their practices. To the extent that this is a factor, it can be said that if *pro tems* serve another time in Department E, they may be able to complete their decisions in a shorter period of time.

## Overall Assessment

### Positive Aspects of and Gains from the Program

The most obvious way to assess a court program is to observe whether the program has met its clearly stated and realistic goals. When Department E was established, the Arizona Court of Appeals stated that Division One was "currently facing a substantial delay in the disposition of civil appeals where oral argument has been requested."[10] The court set as its goal reducing the time to oral argument to 12 months. As of January 1986, civil cases being orally argued were at-issue 8 to 10 months earlier. The court, therefore, has not only met but surpassed its goal. By June 1986 the time from at-issue to oral argument had been reduced to 4 months. In addition, the program has been operated cost-effectively, with considerable support and approval from the legal community and without any apparent diminution in the quality of justice.

There was a broad range of comments regarding the use of *pro tem* judges in the court of appeals in interviews conducted by National Center staff. Even with this range of views, the most common response by far to the *pro tem* program in Division One is very positive. It is the belief of almost all that the number of cases decided by the *pro tem* panel has to have a beneficial effect upon the civil caseload of the court. The following two paraphrased comments describe the range of thought about the Division One program:

- The benefits of the program are dramatic in assisting the court to reduce its backlog.
- This program adulterates the court's function to declare the law. The court operates as an institution and it should remain as such.

Those who have served as *pro tems*, those who have litigated before Department E and, indeed, some of the judges on the court of appeals do not know the exact impact of the program, but it is clearly understood that the *pro tem* judges are disposing of cases that the regular judges would not have heard and decided for a significant period of time. It was noted by some of those interviewed that this impact might not be discernible in the caseload data, because the court's caseload is continually increasing.

Several litigating attorneys felt that their Department E cases had been argued and decided more quickly than other cases that were before regular departments of the court. The quantitative analysis contradicts this belief; it indicates that the cases before the regular judges were being decided more rapidly than the Department E cases. The litigating attorneys were probably comparing Department E case processing times with the amount of time it used to take to reach decision in one of the other departments prior to the start of the *pro tem* program.

A number of those involved with the *pro tem* program thought that the impact of the program on the court's backlog and whether the court achieved its goals with the program would determine their final view of whether the program should be temporary or permanent. Some thought that if the court is unable to achieve its goal of reducing the time from at-issue to mandate to one year during the designated trial period, the program should continue until the court has lowered the time to one year. Others believed that if the court is unable to achieve its goals through the *pro tem* program, the court should use the extra time and energy the regular judges are committing to the program on other caseload experiments. As the quantitative analysis illustrates, the court is reducing the time to process civil appeals. The statistics, however, tend to reinforce an opinion expressed by one person who described the *pro tem* program as "whittling away at a piece of granite, not demolishing the granite; the court will have a continuing need to whittle at the granite."

The delay in civil appeal processing time has been reduced and this reduction has had a beneficial effect on both litigating attorneys and the judges of Division One. Litigating attorneys now feel that their cases can be argued before a panel and decided in a much more timely fashion. The general attitude of the litigating bar has improved greatly, even though there was no indication that before the start of the program the judges of the court of appeals were held in anything but the highest regard.

It is often difficult to maintain an atmosphere within a court where the judges are willing to try new and innovative procedures for dealing with increased and complex caseloads. The judges of Division One who have reviewed reports containing data on case processing times have been able to see the success of the *pro tem* program in reducing the civil backlog. This success has fostered a cooperative and innovative spirit within Division One.

As we have pointed out several times, the data show more mixed results from using *pro tem* judges than is reflected in participants' opinions. The data also suggest that greater effort by the regular judges contributed as much or more to the gains as the use of judicial adjuncts. Yet it also seems clear that even with the court's interest in and commitment to reducing case processing times and its backlog, the *pro tem* judge program provided both a specific impetus and a focus for the effort expended. The court may have made gains without Department E, but Department E generally is credited as being the catalyst within the court. It also was viewed very positively by the bar. Department E was a highly visible symbol of the court's commitment. The fact that the court chose to extend the program's life six months beyond its projected end reflects the court's understanding of the impetus Department E provided. So despite the mixed statistical results, Department E is seen as a worthwhile endeavor by the court.

### Problems with the Program

The decision that all of the Department E opinions would be memorandum opinions was tied directly to concern about possible conflicts of interest and attorneys "making" law that might affect their practices. Some of the regular judges and the court's advisory committee believed that litigants would be concerned about the appearance of justice in these circumstances.

There was some division between the judges and attorneys on this question. The judges thought that even though the screening process is not foolproof and that some of the cases assigned to Department E might warrant published opinions, the appearance of justice issues are substantial enough that the court should not change its mind on any of the cases. They believed that if publication really was important, the supreme court could accept the case and see that the decision is published. In at least one instance, the supreme court has accepted a case and adopted the memorandum decision of Department E.

The general consistency of judges' opinions about nonpublication is not found among attorneys. The *pro tem* judges appear to understand the court's reasoning and to accept it more generally than litigating attorneys. This may reflect the effect of *pro tem* judges' informal exchanges with the regular judges or a different quality of understanding among the attorneys selected to be *pro tem* judges. Whatever the basis for the difference, even the *pro tem* judges are not uniform in their view about whether the potential for appearance-of-justice problems justifies the decision that all cases will result in unpublished memorandum opinions.

Some of the reactions regarding the decision not to publish were institutional and some personal. The institutional perspective is reflected by three attorneys who felt that the screening process of the court was not perfect and thus some cases appropriate for publication might be assigned to Department E. The personal perspective was expressed by four *pro tem* judges who expressed in varying degrees their disappointment that their opinions will not be published. One of these four attorneys indicated that he might not have been so eager to volunteer had he known in advance that none of the cases assigned his panel would be published.[11] Another said he had lost his "zest" for writing his opinion (he had not yet written that opinion when interviewed approximately five months after argument).

Litigating attorneys for the most part did not have significant concern about opinions from Department E being published. One litigating attorney, upon being told that the opinion for which he was still waiting would be a memorandum opinion rather than a published opinion, said that he could understand the court's reasoning behind the decision but nonetheless was disappointed that publication would not even be considered. Another litigator, who also understood the court's reasoning, thought that the court was being overly cautious, since either two attorneys or an attorney and a judge would have to agree before a lawyer could write an opinion establishing law. He thought the parties would not have an appearance-of-justice problem and that the need for agreement by at least two people lessens the risk of one attorney trying to "create" law that would benefit his or her practice.

The initial reaction of most litigating attorneys was that they had no problem with Department E cases being published. Those lawyers who were upset that the cases would not be published agreed with or accepted the court's decision after being told the reason.

If the *pro tem* program were to be reactivated and the pool of *pro tem*s renewed, the court should remember the experience when the first pool of *pro tem*s was selected. The plaintiff's bar was upset at the perceived defense orientation of the pool. The major concern that the court has to consider is that high-quality attorneys continue to be selected to serve as *pro tem*s. This does not mean that only the best-known attorneys should be chosen, but the principal consideration should be the ability to serve as a *pro tem* judge in an appellate court. The court need not assume a reactive position to criticism by the bar when selecting attorneys for its pool. Nevertheless, the criteria used must be well chosen and stated clearly.

The court also might consider expanding the information provided to *pro tem* judges about the mechanics of the program (use of judges' law clerks, the purpose of the preargument conference, and whether lawyers should or should not use associates in their firms, among others). The information could be provided during a meeting with the *pro tem* judges, in written form, or both.

## Notes to Chapter Nine

1. It was not until November 1984 (well after Division One had begun its *pro tem* program to reduce delay) that delay in Division One was documented in a case aging study conducted by the court with the assistance of the Arizona administrative office of the courts. The median time from filing of the record to decision for all civil cases without oral argument requiring a decision was 13 months; for cases requiring oral argument the median time was 31.5 months.

2. The Arizona Court of Appeals *pro tempore* judges are authorized by Arizona Rev. Stat. §12-146. Between 1981 and 1983, Oklahoma allowed its Supreme Court to make temporary assignments of lawyers to additional divisions of the Court of Appeals under §30.14 of Title 20 of the Oklahoma Statutes. The provisions of that section terminated on December 31, 1983. Mississippi, Tennessee, and Texas allow their governors, upon notification of the disqualification of appellate judges, to make temporary appointments of "like," "competent lawyer," and "learned in the law" persons, respectively, to the appellate court bench. (Mississippi Code 1972 Ann. § 9-1-13; Tennessee Code Ann. §17-2-102; Civil Statutes of the State of Texas, Title 39, Article 1815.) This use of attorneys is more limited than Arizona allows and Oklahoma used to allow.

3. See L. Sipes *et al., Managing to Reduce Delay* (Williamsburg, Va.: National Center for State Courts, 1984), pp. 41-61.

4. Department E did not receive all the mid-difficulty cases in the court, but the effect of this transfer of cases to Department E was to change the general mix of cases left for the regular departments of the courts. The cases remaining for Departments A-D generally were the "easiest" and "hardest."

5. The *pro tem* must be a United States citizen, have a law degree, have been a state resident for ten years, be over 30 years of age, and have ten years legal experience (even though Arizona Rev. Stat. § 12-146 only requires five years of legal experience).

6. There were discernible differences in the degree to which each judge participated, but this was attributed more to individual style than to a judge's being a *pro tem* or not. Interview results confirmed staff's observations.

7. Half the cases are faster and half slower than the median case. The National Center's figure differs by 3.8 months (30 months to 26.2 months) from that calculated by the Arizona administrative office of the courts. The AOC sample included all civil cases, not just those concluded by memorandum opinions.

8. This result may reinforce the argument of some that appellate courts have much less flexibility in judicial productivity than trial courts and that adding judges may have to be a response to delay and growing backlogs more often at the appellate level than at the trial level. *Cf.* P. Carrington, D. Meador, & M. Rosenberg, *Justice on Appeal* (St. Paul, Minn: West Publishing Co., 1976).

9. Time interval figures and type of disposition figures for this study were calculated from data supplied by the court of appeals. As a result of a computer problem during the course of this study, the court was not able to indicate which cases disposed after October 1985 had oral argument. As a result, figures reported for the study groups were calculated from cases that were argued or submitted after September 13, 1984, and disposed before November 1, 1985. Data were available for all Department E cases that were disposed through June 1986.

10. Arizona Court of Appeals, Administrative Order, May 7, 1984.

11. The Administrative Order establishing Department E states that all cases will be disposed of by memorandum decisions as provided for in Rule 28, Arizona Rules of Civil Appellate Procedure.

CHAPTER TEN

# The Connecticut Trial Referee Program

The trial courts of Connecticut are highly unified. All cases except those involving estate matters are heard in the Superior Court. The portion of the Superior Court's caseload that is comparable to that of a general jurisdiction court in other states is heard in the "judicial district" (JD) locations of the court. The state is divided into 12 judicial districts, with at least one JD court location in each. There were 125 judges at JD locations when the program began; six more were approved by the legislature during its course.[1]

In the early 1980s the growing backlog of civil cases awaiting trial in the JD courts, causing waits of 5 to 6 years for jury trials in some courts, was generating concern both inside and outside the legal community. In an effort to reduce the backlog and delay in the court, the then Chief Justice, John A. Speziale, announced a program to use attorneys as trial referees to conduct nonjury trials. A trial referee program was proposed rather than a judge *pro tem* program because of state constitutional limitations on the exercise of judicial power. Referees conduct civil, nonjury trials in cases seeking damages in excess of $15,000. The current Chief Justice, Ellen Ash Peters, has continued and vigorously pursued the program.

Experienced lawyers were encouraged to participate in the program. They were divided into two groups, depending in part on how much time they were expected to be willing to devote to the program. Retired lawyers were asked to participate up to full-time as trial referees. Active lawyers were asked to serve as cases arose that involved their legal specialty (for example, medical malpractice). The lawyers were to supplement the judges already hearing nonjury civil cases.

Refereed trials are conducted in a manner similar to regular court trials. Referees are called "your Honor" or "Mr. Referee" by the litigating attorneys. Following trial, the referee decides the case, writes a memorandum of decision, and the judgment is rendered accordingly by a superior court judge. There are provisions in the enabling rules for litigating attorneys to file motions with the referee to correct the memorandum and also to present objections or exceptions to a superior court judge at a "short calendar" hearing. The judge then reviews the memorandum of decision and the objections or exceptions filed and makes his or her decision whether to accept the memorandum and enter judgment on the case. Those few cases in which the memoranda of decision are not accepted initially may be referred back to the same or another referee or to another judge for additional proceedings. Once judgment is entered on a case, any further objections are handled as appeals in the appellate courts. (See Appendix C for the rules of the program.)

## Goals

The program was implemented with the following goals in mind:

1. Reduce the size of the civil court-trial list[2] by using trial referees to conduct additional nonjury trials.
2. Once the nonjury trial list has been reduced to an acceptable size, reduce the size of the civil jury-trial list by transferring judges to the jury side of the court from the nonjury side.
3. Accomplish the above at no greater cost to the judicial system than processing the cases with judges.

Each goal is quantitative in nature, and progress in meeting it can be measured using caseload management and court financial data. Speedier dispositions were expected to follow from achieving these goals, but there were no explicit goals regarding a reduction in the time to trial.

The program also had some qualitative goals that were understood but not explicitly stated:

1. The quality of decisions on the cases heard by referees should not be perceived to be less than that of decisions in cases tried by judges.
2. The program should enhance the already good relations between bench and bar.

At the beginning, the program was recognized as having certain risks:

1. The provisions for objections and exceptions might be used by litigating attorneys in a large number of cases, resulting in large delays between the end of the refereed trial and final disposition.

2. Delay had the potential for eliminating any gains made by the program in shortening the interval between being placed on the trial list and the start of trial.
3. Attorneys might try to avoid the program by requesting a jury trial more often.

## Operation of the Program

The program was announced on October 25, 1983, and implemented soon after. Trial referees were nominated by the administrative judge of each JD location and appointed by the chief justice. The first group of lawyers selected to be trial referees were sworn in for a one-year term on February 1, 1984. The program was established in all twelve JD courts across the state at the same time, with general guidance from the state court administrative office as to how it was to be implemented. Each JD court was allowed to operate its own version of the program to fit with its already established procedures.

In order to obtain a broad view of program operations while confining the time and cost of the evaluation to reasonable limits, it was decided to conduct the project evaluation at three sites, two large courts (New Haven and Bridgeport) and one medium-sized court (Waterbury). Because of the nature of the program and available data, the quantitative evaluation used a "before-and-after" model in which the situation before implementation of the program was compared with the situation during and after the program's start.

Bridgeport uses a master calendar system for its civil cases. Cases are assigned by the presiding judge to a trial referee at the calendar call on the morning of the scheduled trial date. The referee takes all the time he or she needs to review the file, in part to determine that there is no conflict of interest, and then the trial begins. The distribution of the types of cases disposed by refereed trial in Bridgeport and the two other study sites during FY 1985 is given in Table 17. Ninety-five percent of all cases assigned to trial referees in each of the study sites involve either tort or contract disputes.

In Waterbury, the litigating attorneys in each case participate in the selection of the trial referee. Once a referee is assigned, the litigating attorneys work with the referee to schedule the trial when all are available.

The presiding judge in New Haven personally assigns all cases to trial referees. Once assigned, the judge's court clerk works with the referee and the litigating attorneys to select a trial date.

The program has been used in differing degrees by the three sites. The presiding judge in Bridgeport assigns all court-trial cases either to a trial referee or to a factfinder; thus he can assign all judges to hear jury trials. The factfinder program is another judicial adjunct program, implemented in Bridgeport, New Haven, Hartford, and Stamford in July

## TABLE 17
### Distribution of types of cases disposed by refereed trial, with state totals, fiscal year 1985

|  | Bridgeport | New Haven | Waterbury | TOTAL STATE |
|---|---|---|---|---|
| Contracts | 35 | 13 | 10 | 154 |
| Torts | 21 | 4 | 12 | 72 |
| Property | 1 | 0 | 0 | 18 |
| Eminent domain | 0 | 0 | 0 | 2 |
| Wills | 0 | 0 | 1 | 2 |
| Miscellaneous | 2 | 1 | 0 | 21 |
| TOTAL CASES | 59 | 18 | 23 | 269 |

## TABLE 18
### Changes in the court-trial list, 1983 to 1986

| Court-trial list | Bridgeport | New Haven | Waterbury |
|---|---|---|---|
| July 1983 | 1,237 | 2,164 | 664 |
| July 1984 | 1,104 | 1,530 | 414 |
| July 1985 | 495 | 909 | 306 |
| July 1986 | 355 | 275 | 169 |
| Percentage change from July 1983 to July 1986 | –71% | –87% | –75% |
| *Number of cases disposed by* | | | |
| **Referees** | | | |
| January 1984 to July 1985 | 120 | 52 | 45 |
| **Refereed trials** | | | |
| January 1984 to July 1985 | 58 | 24 | 29 |
| **Factfinders** | | | |
| After full hearing, July 1984 to July 1985 | 54 | 50 | 16 |

1983, to dispose of civil cases with a demand of $15,000 or less. Through the use of the two judicial adjunct programs, Bridgeport has been able to reduce by more than one-half the size of its court-trial list in two and a half years, from 1,315 cases in January 1984 to 355 cases in July 1986. Table 18 shows the impact the two judicial adjunct programs have had on the court-trial list at all three study sites.

In New Haven the presiding judge assigned cases to trial referees through early 1985, but then temporarily discontinued the use of referees. When we visited the court in the summer of 1985 there were indications that he once again was assigning cases to trial referees. Only longer court trials (estimated to last two days or longer) are assigned to referees. No judges were reassigned from court to jury trials in New Haven during the course of the study.

The court in Waterbury assigns a few court-trial cases each month to referees. Its court-trial list was considerably smaller than either Bridgeport's or New Haven's when the program started, so the need to use referees was not so great.

## Quantitative Evaluation

Despite the differences in implementation of the program at each JD court and the extent to which it has been used in each of the three sites evaluated, the caseload data from each court are quite similar.

From January 1984 through June 1985, from one-quarter to almost one-half of all cases referred to referees were disposed before the start of trial (see Table 19).[3] Of those disposed before trial, most were disposed by settlement or stipulated judgment. Most cases that continued to trial were disposed by judgment. Only in Waterbury did the number of cases

**TABLE 19**
**Manner of disposition of cases assigned to trial referees, January 1984 through June 1985**

|  | Bridgeport | | New Haven | | Waterbury | |
| --- | --- | --- | --- | --- | --- | --- |
| **Disposed before trial** | No. | Percent | No. | Percent | No. | Percent |
| Default | 0 | 0 | 2 | 4 | 0 | 0 |
| Settled/stipulated judgment | 37 | 31 | 9 | 17 | 5 | 11 |
| Dismissed | 0 | 0 | 8 | 15 | 0 | 9 |
| Withdrawn | 8 | 7 | 4 | 8 | 6 | 13 |
| Subtotal | 45 | 38 | 23 | 44 | 11 | 24 |
| **Disposed after start of trial** | | | | | | |
| Judgment | 58 | 48 | 24 | 46 | 29 | 64 |
| Stipulated judgment | 6 | 5 | 1 | 2 | 0 | 0 |
| Settled/withdrawn/dismissed | 11 | 9 | 4 | 8 | 5 | 11 |
| Subtotal | 75 | 62 | 29 | 56 | 34 | 76 |
| TOTAL | 120 | 100 | 52 | 100 | 45 | 100 |

disposed by judgment make up over half (64 percent) of the cases originally referred to trial referees.

The program was used more in Bridgeport and Waterbury than in New Haven. During FY 1985 refereed trials accounted for 4.7 percent of all cases removed from the court-trial list in Bridgeport. In Waterbury, 5.5 percent of the court-trial list removals were by refereed trial. The comparable figure for New Haven was 1.3 percent.

The discussion that follows focuses on data from Bridgeport, unless otherwise indicated, as Bridgeport of the three courts studied best demonstrates the impact a program of this type can have on case processing. We understand that Bridgeport is representative of what happened in a number of other JD courts that were not included in our study.

Figure 4 shows the size of the court-trial list and the jury-trial list from July 1978 to July 1986. There has been a gradual decline in the number of cases awaiting court trials since mid-1980, before the implementation of either the factfinder or the trial-referee program. The decline was much steeper after the start of the trial referee program. The jury-trial list caseload increased slightly until mid-1983, but it has been headed down since.

Figure 5 shows the number of cases added to and removed from the court- and jury-trial lists. The number of cases added to the court-trial list has been declining gradually in Bridgeport since early 1979. Dispositions from the court-trial list peaked in 1981, seesawed for the next three years, but increased dramatically, far surpassing the number of cases filed, in late 1984, after the start of the trial referee program. This graph suggests that there is a six-month lag before the benefits of a new program become visible in the caseload data. Dispositions from the court-trial list increased in the period that began six months after the start of the factfinders program and again in the period that began six months after the trial referee program began. Dispositions from the court-trial list exceeded additions to it from January 1984 at least through July 1986. The effect of this increase in disposed cases is seen in the dramatic decline in the court's pending caseload between January and July 1986.

Figure 6 shows the median age of all cases on the court-trial list for all three study sites. The median age has been decreasing gradually since before the start of the program in all study sites and for the entire state.[4] Because of the prior introduction of the factfinder program, the impact of the trial referee program on the decreasing time to disposition is uncertain, but it appears that the referee program contributed to an acceleration in the rate of decline in time to disposition. Without question, the combination of the two programs was powerful.[5]

The number of cases added to the jury-trial list in Bridgeport has been increasing gradually since 1981, closely shadowed by the number of

**FIGURE 4**
**Pending trial list history, 1979-1986**
**Bridgeport Superior Court**

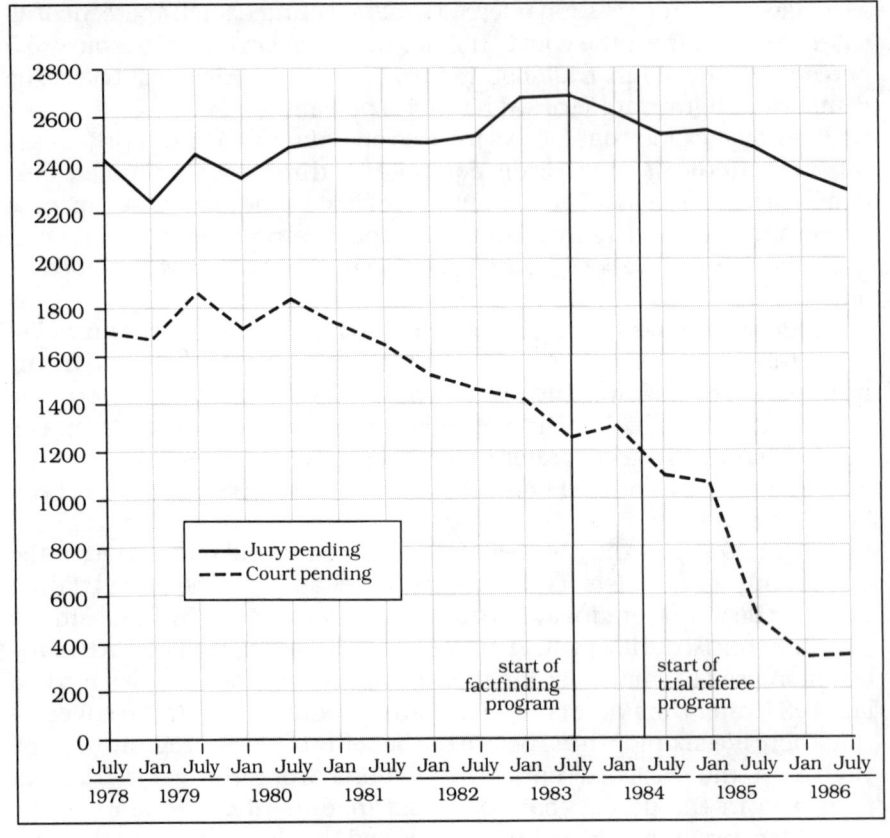

cases disposed from it. The net result of these two factors has been a slight decrease in the number of cases awaiting jury trials (seen in Figure 4). It is the view of the litigating attorneys interviewed that the referee program is not causing any demonstrable additions to the jury-trial list.

The bars in Figure 7 represent the median case processing times for major types of cases disposed by judges and trial referees. (So few eminent domain and wills cases were disposed by them that these case types were not included in this graph.) The portion of the bar below the zero-line represents the median time from case filing to being placed on the trial list; the portion above the zero-line represents the median time from being placed on the trial list to disposition—the portion of time during which the case is under the active control of the court. As indicated previously, 95 percent of the cases assigned to attorney trial referees in Bridgeport were either torts or contracts; the sets of bars for these cases

CONNECTICUT TRIAL REFEREE PROGRAM    119

**FIGURE 5**

**Cases added to and disposed from trial lists,
1979 through 1986, Bridgeport Superior Court**

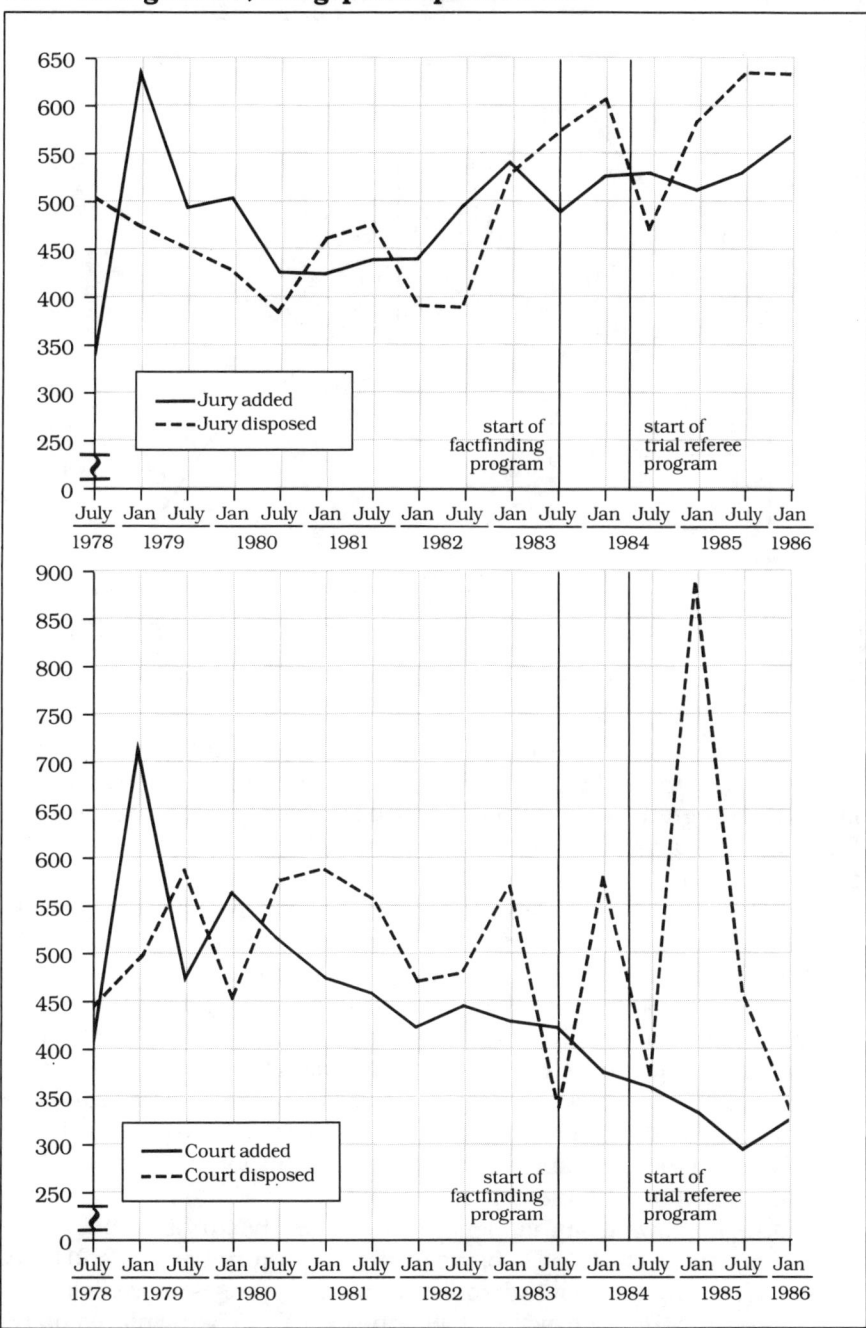

**FIGURE 6**

**Court-trial list median age of pending cases (months), Connecticut Superior Court**

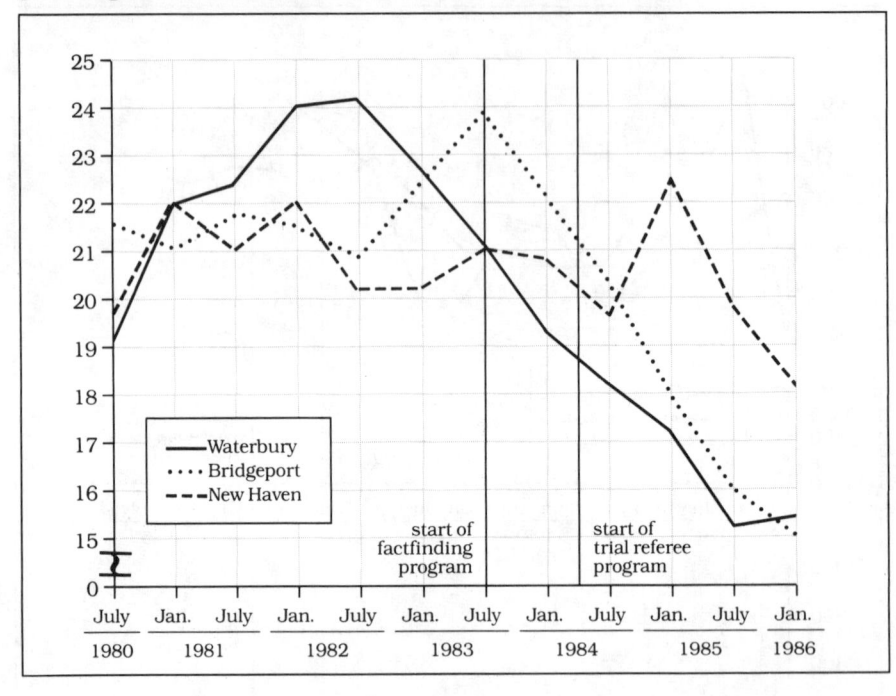

[Chart showing three lines — Waterbury, Bridgeport, New Haven — with median age in months on the y-axis (15–25) and dates from July 1980 to Jan 1986 on the x-axis. Vertical markers indicate "start of factfinding program" and "start of trial referee program."]

show that the median time from being placed on the trial list to disposition decreased from 1983 to 1985. (It should be added that the factfinder program deals exclusively with contract cases, so the decrease for contract cases represents a combination of the effects of the two programs.)

The bars for contract and tort cases demonstrate another change that is occurring in the court. At the same time that the portion of the bars above the zero-line (time from trial request to disposition) is decreasing, the portion of the bars below the zero-line is increasing, although not by as much. This suggests that in 1984 attorneys waited longer before requesting that a case be placed on the court-trial list than they did in 1983, and that the same result followed in later years. One explanation for this shift is that the attorneys were adjusting to the quicker trial dates each successive year by waiting longer (possibly until discovery was more complete) to request a trial.[6]

Figure 8 shows what happened to cases on the jury-trial list for the same time intervals—filing to being placed on the jury-trial list and being placed on the jury-trial list to disposition. Most jury cases are vehicle torts, other torts, or contract cases. In 1984, the time from being placed on the

**FIGURE 7**

**Court-trial list cases disposed FY 1983 through FY 1986*, Bridgeport median time-to-disposition (days)**

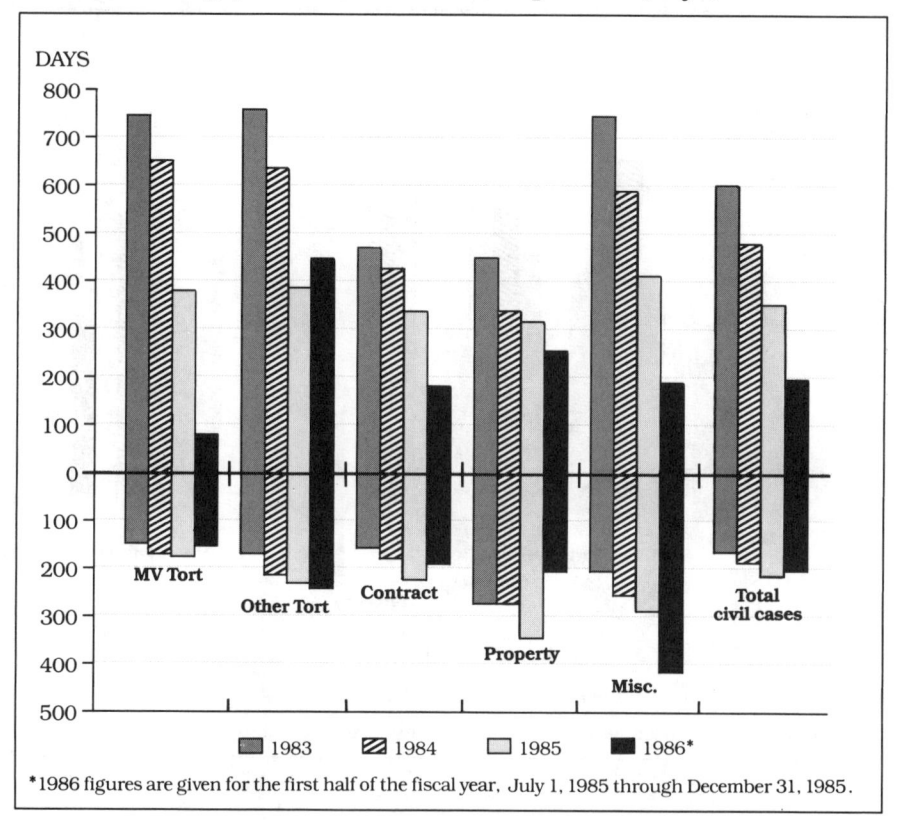

*1986 figures are given for the first half of the fiscal year, July 1, 1985 through December 31, 1985.

jury-trial list to disposition increased for all types of cases except "miscellaneous." It decreased for torts and "miscellaneous" cases in 1985, but increased again for contracts. By January 1986 the time from being placed on the jury-trial list to disposition was lower for all but "miscellaneous" cases. If the courts continue to use trial referees and more judges continue to hear jury trials, the jury-trial list should soon be brought under control (Goal 2, above).

Very little use was made by attorneys of the provisions in the rules to file motions to correct, objections, or exceptions in any of the three sites studied (see Table 20). Motions to correct (filed with the referee) ranged from a low of 3 percent of all cases disposed by judgment in Bridgeport to a high of 20 percent in New Haven. But only one case in New Haven followed up the motion to correct with exceptions that had to be resolved by a judge at the short calendar hearing. Objections to the referees' memoranda of

## FIGURE 8
**Jury-trial list cases disposed FY 1983 through FY 1986\*, Bridgeport median time-to-disposition (days)**

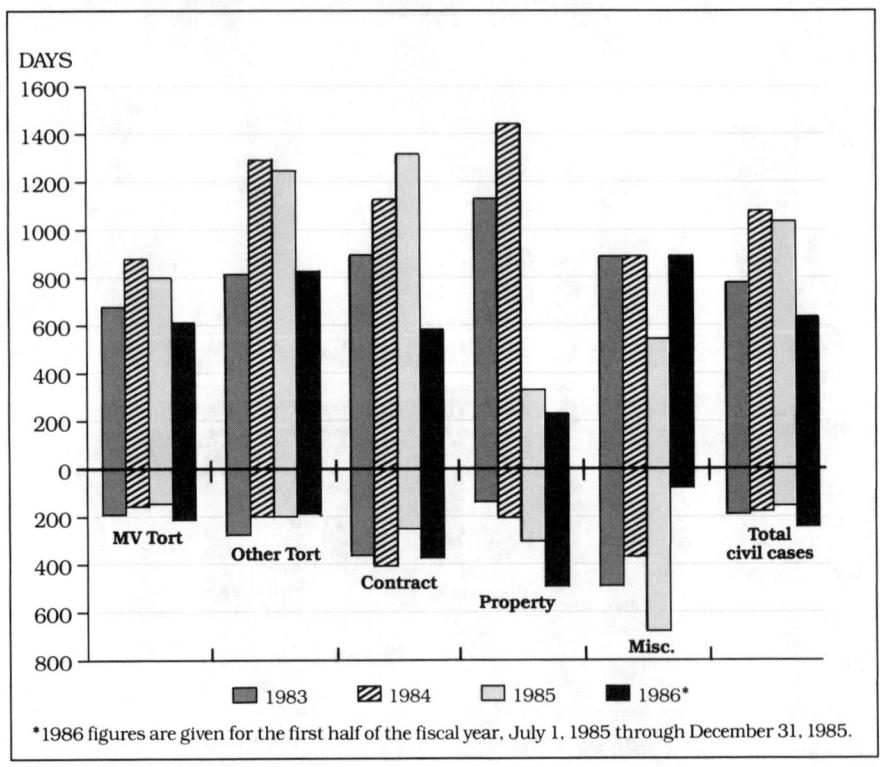

*1986 figures are given for the first half of the fiscal year, July 1, 1985 through December 31, 1985.

decision were filed somewhat more often than were motions to correct, ranging from 9 percent of all cases disposed by judgment in Bridgeport to 25 percent in Waterbury. No memoranda of decision were rejected at the short calendar hearing at any of the study sites, so the "double trial" problem that was a concern at the start of the program did not develop. Two cases disposed by trial referees were appealed to the supreme court challenging the constitutionality of the trial referee program, however. The Supreme Court has upheld the constitutionality of the program but has required consent of the parties to conduct refereed trials.[7]

Some of the differences between the way the program was implemented at the three study sites are reflected in their time-interval data. In Bridgeport, where the case is assigned to the referee at the calendar call on the morning of the scheduled trial date, trials start normally on the day they are assigned. In New Haven, where the trial date is scheduled only

## TABLE 20
## Motions to correct, exceptions, and objections filed at the three study sites, January 1984 to June 1985

|  | Bridgeport | New Haven | Waterbury |
|---|---|---|---|
| TOTAL CASES DISPOSED BY REFEREES | 120 | 52 | 45 |
| TOTAL DISPOSED BY TRIAL JUDGMENT | 58 | 24 | 29 |
| Cases with motions to correct | 2 | 5 | 2 |
| Cases with exceptions filed | 0 | 1 | 0 |
| Cases with objections filed | 6 | 5 | 6 |
| Cases in which memoranda of decision were rejected | 0 | 0 | 0 |

after the case has been assigned to a referee, the average time from assignment to start of trial is 19 days. As mentioned above, the court in New Haven has made it a policy to assign cases with longer expected trials to referees. Average referee trial length in New Haven is approximately one-half day longer than in either Bridgeport or Waterbury, and a lower percentage of New Haven's trials lasted one day or less (48 percent, versus 58 percent in Bridgeport and 67 percent in Waterbury).

The entire process from assignment to short calendar hearing is much faster in Bridgeport than in either New Haven or Waterbury. Part of this is due to the faster start cases get in Bridgeport, but most of the time savings in Bridgeport comes after the hearing starts.

Table 21 shows the amount of time referees devoted to the program per case at each of the three study sites. Referees in New Haven report that they spend almost twice as much time on specific tasks related to the trial-referee program as referees in either Bridgeport or Waterbury. Again, this may be a result of the stated New Haven policy of assigning cases with longer expected trials to referees. It may also be an indication of a difference in the way lawyers practice law in the three sites.

In all three sites the presiding judge of the court handled all of the referee program short calendar hearings. Most short calendar hearings were reported to have lasted one minute or less. The longest reported in each site lasted less than thirty minutes.

At the beginning of the second year of the program the number of cases disposed from the jury-trial list for the whole state was larger than the number of cases added to it. The court still needs the extra judicial

## TABLE 21
### Distribution of time referees spend disposing of one case

|  | Bridgeport | New Haven | Waterbury |
|---|---|---|---|
| **Reviewing record** | | | |
| Mean | 1.5 hours | 2.2 hours | 1.1 hours |
| Median | 1.0 | 2.0 | 1.0 |
| Range | 0-10 | .3-8 | 0-4 |
| **Preparing findings** | | | |
| Mean | 2.0 | 5.2 | 2.0 |
| Median | 1.0 | 3.0 | 1.5 |
| Range | 0-19 | .5-44 | .5-6 |
| TOTAL NONTRIAL TIME | | | |
| Mean | 4.0 | 12.5 | 4.8 |
| Median | 3.9 | 7.0 | 4.0 |
| Range | 0-40 | 1.5-102 | 1.2-13.5 |
| Average trial length | 1.4 days | 2.0 days | 1.3 days |

**Note:** The "mean" is the result of dividing the sum of all instances by the number of instances. In this setting, it is the sum of all time spent on all cases divided by the number of cases. The sum of the mean time reviewing the record and preparing findings does not equal the mean total trial time because different numbers of cases were used in the calculation of these figures.

The "median" value is the value in the exact middle of the range, when all the cases are ranked in ascending order by that variable. In this setting, it is the amount of time for which half the cases require more and half require less time.

resources the trial referees provide, but at the end of this evaluation it is clear that the court has made substantial progress toward solving its backlog problems in both the civil court-trial and jury-trial lists.

The contribution of the trial referee program is apparent, but as in the Phoenix court of appeals *pro tempore* judge program, all of the improvement cannot be attributed to the adjunct program alone. Connecticut's judicial leadership emphasized the need to reduce delay in processing civil cases; the trial referee program was one part of the effort. Its impact was significant, but not the sole basis for the fairly dramatic results achieved.

# Qualitative Assessment

Two related tasks were undertaken at each of the three study sites to assess the attitudes of the participants in the program (court administrative personnel, judges, attorneys serving as trial referees, attorneys litigating cases before trial referees, and their clients.) The first task was to interview a sample of members of the first four groups. The second was to sample the opinions of judges, referees, litigating attorneys, and their clients through questionnaires.

### Questionnaire Response Rate
The response rate for the questionnaires was best for judges and trial referees; between 70 and 80 percent of the questionnaires sent to these groups were returned. The response rate for litigating attorneys was approximately 45 percent and for parties, approximately 10 percent. Results of the interviews and questionnaire responses are combined here to give an overall assessment of the reactions of each of these groups to the program.

### Overall Assessment
Although the vast majority of the respondents of each group support the program, there was a small but vocal minority of judges and litigating attorneys who strongly oppose it. Support from the trial referees themselves is the most positive. In their questionnaire responses, they rate the program as being very worthwhile (4.8 on a scale of 1 to 5 with 5 being "very worthwhile" and 1 "definitely not worthwhile"). On this same scale, litigating attorneys give the program a rating of 4.25 and judges a 3.7 (close to the neutral position of 3).

Figure 9 contains the judges', referees', and litigating attorneys' reactions to some specific statements about the program.

### Comments of Litigating Attorneys
All participants agreed that the one element that is most critical to the continuing success of the program is that the quality of the attorneys serving as trial referees remain at its current high level. There was some concern that if the program were to be made permanent, the continuing time demands on the referees would force some to withdraw from the program.

Although the litigating attorneys are predominantly supportive, their support is not without some reservations. Many of the litigating attorneys offered suggestions for improving the program.

They prefer that their trials be scheduled for a day certain and do not like the practice in all three sites of overscheduling court trials in the belief that not all the cases will proceed to trial.[8] Some would prefer a more formal atmosphere for the refereed trials but the majority think that the facilities used for them are comparable to those used for judge-conducted trials. They believe that the trials themselves are appropriate in tone and demeanor. Some mentioned that the powers of the referees should be clarified. Some litigators would like referees to be able to accept stipula-

## FIGURE 9
### Opinions of program participants toward referee program

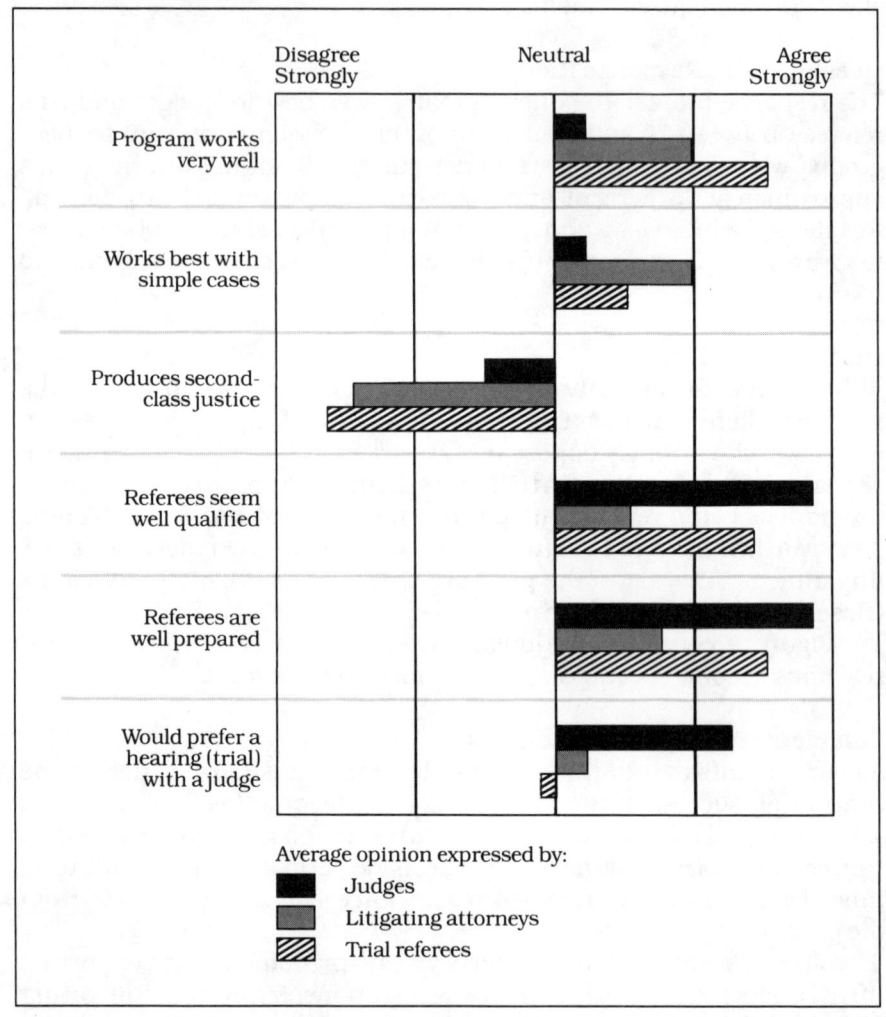

[Bar chart showing opinions on a scale from "Disagree Strongly" to "Neutral" to "Agree Strongly" for the following statements, with responses from Judges, Litigating attorneys, and Trial referees:
- Program works very well
- Works best with simple cases
- Produces second-class justice
- Referees seem well qualified
- Referees are well prepared
- Would prefer a hearing (trial) with a judge

Average opinion expressed by:
- Judges
- Litigating attorneys
- Trial referees]

tions of judgment, which they cannot do at the present time because of the state constitutional restrictions on the exercise of judicial powers, and to impose sanctions on litigating attorneys who do not abide by the time frames for submitting documents established for the program.

One attorney noted that even though the program is reducing the backlog, he believes it is not doing anything to correct the underlying problems that had caused the backlog to develop originally. He hoped the energy and resources used to run the program would not take away from the effort needed to solve the continuing, underlying calendar problems.

## Comments of Referees

Attorneys who serve as referees are even more supportive of the program than are litigating attorneys. Most are willing to serve the court, some for lengthy periods of time, for little or no compensation so long as they feel that their service is benefiting the court. Although few expressed any interest in becoming a judge, they enjoy the experience of serving in a judicial capacity.

Some noted that they had learned some things while sitting on the bench that would improve their practice of law. (This was a common observation in the Tucson and Portland judge *pro tem* programs, too.) Most said that they would continue to serve if the program were continued. The only referees expressing some reluctance are either solo practitioners or those who have already been called on extensively. Some indicate that serving has cost them or their partners lost business and income, but so long as the time commitment is kept within reasonable limits, they are willing to continue.

# Costs and Administrative Issues

The major cost of the program has been paying the fees requested by some of the trial referees. Referees are permitted to be paid $20 per hour up to a maximum of $100 per day of trial. Payment is made only on request.

In all three sites some trial referees have requested to be paid. A total of $32,778 was requested by trial referees serving in fiscal years 1984 and 1985 for the entire state. During FY 1985, the average fee for each case disposed by trial at each of the three study sites, including dispositions by referees who did not request payment, was: Bridgeport, $209.01; New Haven, $90.26; and Waterbury, $196.74. As stated previously, referees serving in New Haven spent almost twice as much time on each case as referees in the other two sites, but they requested less than half the fees per case.

There were other costs incurred at each of the sites as a result of the program. Some costs actually represented the reallocation of already existing resources, such as the portion of the salaries of the administrative staff at each court location who were responsible for administering the program.[9] Other costs represented shifting costs of court support staff such as court reporters, who would have been needed eventually. None of these costs involved spending any "new money." "New money" costs included the cost of making duplicate copies of the file of each case for the referee, the cost of preparing necessary notices for the refereed trial, and postage for sending them. Neither the reallocation nor the "new money" costs has been estimated by court officials, but they are all believed to be insignificant when compared to the referees' fees.

A not-insubstantial indirect administrative cost involved the time of the civil caseflow manager of the state Judicial Department. He estimates spending an average of about 10 hours per week on this program assisting trial courts throughout the state with administrative and calendar questions, supervising data collection, and coordinating with the National Center. His time represents an annual indirect cost, including fringe benefits and associated overhead, of about $16,125.

At the outset of the program it was thought that there might be a need to construct facilities and convert courtrooms. The presiding judge at one of the study sites said that he would like to acquire a portable bench for his court that could be carried to one or another of the hearing rooms to add a measure of formal atmosphere to refereed trials, but there were other items his courthouse needed more. Through mid-1985, no money had been spent by any of the three evaluation courts on capital improvements for the trial referee program.

## Overall Assessment

In the past three years, the court-trial list has been reduced in size at all three study sites and across the state as a whole. Time from being placed on the court-trial list to disposition has decreased, dramatically in some court locations. It is not possible, however, to state how much of this reduction is the result of the implementation of the trial referee program, how much is an extension of a trend started in the early 1980s and how much was caused by the factfinding program implemented in two of the study sites approximately one year before the trial referee program began. The trial referee and the factfinder programs are targeted at different portions of the civil caseload; the combination of the two appears to have been very effective.

The improvement noted in the three sites seems to be greater than can be attributed to the trial referee program alone or in combination with the factfinder program. Nonetheless, one Connecticut observer pointed out that the results of the trial referee program were the most dramatic and were needed statewide to convince some judges that calendar management might be effective in reducing delay. We understand that the trial referee program was managed more tightly in some courts than the general calendar. Their combined success demonstrated that the court *could* assume general calendar control. Once it became apparent that delay was not inevitable, improvement accelerated and gained a momemtum of its own. As in other sites the judicial adjunct program was only part of the reason for the magnitude of improvement, but it seems to have been a critical catalyst.

A majority of the legal community, both attorneys and judges, support the program. Some of the problems that were anticipated at the start of the program, such as excessive challenges to the referees' reports and conflicts of interest that would not be identified and would result in tainted proceedings, have not developed.

The program has brought about significant reductions in the size of the pending court-trial caseload in courts, like Bridgeport, that have made extensive use of it. There have been associated reductions, albeit not yet as large, in the jury-trial-list pending caseload, as well. Nonetheless, there are some modifications in the program that might improve it.

1. An orientation program was offered to the trial referees at the start of the program, but many said that additional training would have been helpful. For example, one referee found it necessary to review the rules of evidence before making some rulings. This and other topics could be covered briefly in an expanded training program. Orientation of litigating attorneys also could be expanded. Descriptions of the program and how it was designed to operate were printed in local bar publications. The procedures that were to be followed in refereed cases had been specified as early as 1969 in an opinion of the Supreme Court.[10] But this was not sufficient. Court staff reported that there still is some confusion concerning what options are available for objecting to a trial referee's report. This confusion might be eliminated by further efforts to educate litigating attorneys about the program.
2. The powers of the trial referees need to be specified with regard to accepting stipulated judgments and imposing sanctions on litigating attorneys who do not file their required papers on time. If these powers were clarified, trial referees probably would have less trouble completing cases and dispositions would be more timely.
3. The court needs to clarify the priority of refereed trials in relation to other court business. Both trial referees and litigating attorneys stated that judges from other judicial districts have refused to acknowledge that the litigating attorneys were in trial when the trial in question was being conducted by a referee. This is a particular problem in larger jurisdictions.
4. Some attempt should be made to simplify the procedures for accepting the referee's memorandum of decision. The current potentially three-stage procedure is unnecessarily cumbersome and could be modified to eliminate some of the redundancy, especially since experience shows it is not being used frequently.

Trial referees will continue to be a significant part of Connecticut's effort to bring the civil caseload under control. When the National Center's involvement in the evaluation of the program at the three court locations ended, there were indications that the size of the pending jury-trial list had leveled off (Waterbury) or begun to decrease (Bridgeport and New Haven).

## Notes to Chapter Ten

1. In 1986 the Governor recommended an additional six judgeships for 1987.

2. Within twelve months of case filing the litigating attorneys notify the court that the case is ready for trial by requesting that it be placed on either the court-trial list or the jury-trial list. The court monitors whether and when attorneys place matters on a trial list; it concentrates its attention on monitoring the size and age of these two trial lists.

3. Even more cases were disposed by being threatened with being referred to a trial referee. These cases do not appear in the caseload data as referee dispositions but they could be attributed to it were data-gathering capacity more sophisticated.

4. By January 1985, the court-trial list in Bridgeport had been reduced so much (see Figure 4), that the proportion of older cases in the pending caseload increased. From this list the court tended to dispose of newer cases, so the median age of the cases remaining on the court-trial list began to increase. By the end of 1985 the median age of the pending caseload was back to the same low level it had been in January 1985, indicating that during 1985 the older pending cases were disposed.

5. The rate of decrease was even greater in New Haven (as shown by the greater negative slope of the New Haven line in Figure 6) yet New Haven did not use the referee program as much as Bridgeport. This suggests that the statewide effort to reduce delay through general improvements in calendar management as well as special programs such as the trial referee program contributed to the improvements seen in the three evaluation sites and in the state.

6. *Cf.*, B. Mahoney, L. Sipes, & J. Ito, *Implementing Delay Reduction and Delay Prevention Programs in Urban Trial Courts: Preliminary Findings from Current Research* (National Center for State Courts, Williamsburg, Va., 1985), pp. 1-2, 33.

7. *Seal Audio, Inc. v. Bozak, Inc.*, 199 Conn. 496, 508 A.2d 415 (1986); and *Midland Ins. Co. v. Universal Technology, Inc.*, 199 Conn. 518, 508 A.2d 427 (1986).

8. This preference is common among trial attorneys across the country. They generally prefer a "firm" date with only their case or their case and one other scheduled to start so that the court bears the risk of last-minute settlements. Urban courts, on the other hand, generally prefer to shift the risk of last-minute settlements back to the bar by scheduling more cases for trial than the court's resources can handle, because so often some of the scheduled cases settle.

9. Connecticut staff estimate that time needed ranged from less than one hour in a typical week in New Haven to half of one full-time employee in a typical week in Bridgeport.

10. *Harbor Construction Corp. v. D.V.Frione & Co.*, 158 Conn. 14, 255 A.2d 823 (1969).

CHAPTER ELEVEN

# The Minneapolis Mandatory, Court-Annexed Arbitration Program

The Fourth Judicial District Court in Hennepin County (Minneapolis) is the largest general jurisdiction court in Minnesota. It has original civil and criminal jurisdiction and also appellate jurisdiction from the limited jurisdiction county courts. In Hennepin and Ramsey (St. Paul) counties the district court also has jurisdiction in probate and juvenile cases. In these two counties only, the limited jurisdiction courts are municipal courts with jurisdiction in civil actions under $15,000, forcible entry and unlawful detainer, misdemeanors, and ordinance violations.

There are 25 district court judges in Hennepin County. Six judges are assigned to criminal cases, two to juvenile, one to probate, one to family court, and one to mental commitments. The remaining 14 judges are assigned civil cases on an individual calendar basis when the case is filed with the court.[1] All but six of the judges rotate between the civil and criminal divisions, spending six weeks on criminal cases and twelve weeks on civil cases. At present, a municipal court judge serves as chief judge of the judicial district, including the district court.

## Developing the Program

In 1983 a special task force was created to review the civil court-trial calendar in Hennepin County. The 12-member task force was composed of a retired chief judge of the Hennepin County district court, a retired Minnesota Supreme Court justice, seven attorneys, and three nonlawyer public members. Its final report was made January 31, 1984. Following are some of the major conclusions reached by the task force:

1. The elapsed time from filing of the note of issue[2] to the time of final disposition of a civil court case in Hennepin County increased substantially from 1980 to 1983. According to statistics of the state court administrator, this time increased from 310 days to 475 days.
2. The number of pending civil cases in Hennepin County also increased substantially from 1980 to 1983. Table 22 shows the number of pending cases in Hennepin County as of September in the years 1980 through 1983.
3. Neither the number of civil complaints filed nor the number of notes of issue filed increased significantly during the period 1980 through 1982 (see Table 23).
4. An increase in judicial time needed for the criminal, juvenile, family, and mental health divisions of the court together with the growing complexity of civil litigation in the district also contributed to delay in civil case processing.

**TABLE 22**
**Trend in pending civil cases,**
**September 1980 through September 1983**

| Year | Civil cases pending | Percent increase over previous year |
|---|---|---|
| **1980** | 2,136 | — |
| **1981** | 2,600 | 22 |
| **1982** | 3,619 | 39 |
| **1983** | 3,566 | −1 |

**TABLE 23**
**Civil filings, 1980 through 1982**

| Year | Civil complaints filed | Notes of issue filed |
|---|---|---|
| **1980** | 13,828 | 3,404 |
| **1981** | 14,033 | 3,852 |
| **1982** | 14,000 | 3,370 |

The major task force recommendation was to switch from master to individual calendaring for the civil judges. It was also suggested that the court consider adopting an alternative dispute resolution mechanism such as mandatory, nonbinding, court-annexed arbitration.

District court judges began immediately to plan for implementation of the major task force recommendations. By mid-1984, the Minnesota state legislature had passed Minnesota Statutes, section 484.73, authorizing the establishment, on a local-option basis, of nonbinding, mandatory arbitration programs in the state's district courts, allowing the Hennepin County district court to proceed with development of its arbitration program.

Under the auspices of the Hennepin County Bar Association, rules were drafted for the arbitration program. National Center for State Courts project staff reviewed the rules and offered suggested forms for use in operating the program. The rules were submitted to the supreme court for approval in January 1985.

The district court set July 1, 1985, as the date it would switch to individual calendaring and the official beginning of the arbitration program. It was announced to the local bar members that applications to serve as arbitrators were open to all attorneys who had been admitted to practice in Minnesota for a minimum of five years. About five hundred attorneys applied to be arbitrators; 396 were placed in the available pool.

# Description of the Program

The arbitration program was designed to accept the referral of civil cases within 30 days of the filing of the note of issue or after the expiration of the 90-day nonreadiness period, allowed if a party files a certificate of nonreadiness for trial when the opposing party has filed a note of issue. All civil cases are eligible for the program with some exceptions:

- Those within the money-damage jurisdiction limit of the Hennepin County Conciliation Court ($2,000)
- Those asking more than $50,000 in money damages[3]
- Those that include a claim for equitable relief that is neither insubstantial nor frivolous
- Those removed from the conciliation court for a trial *de novo*
- Class actions
- Those involving family law matters[4]
- Unlawful detainer actions
- Those involving title to real estate

The arbitration hearing is to be conducted within 60 days of a case's referral to arbitration (or upon expiration of the discovery period when a certificate of nonreadiness has been filed). Hearings are conducted by a single arbitrator in courtrooms provided by the court, with the rules of evidence construed liberally in favor of admission. (The rules of the arbitration program are reproduced in Appendix D.)

The arbitrators have the following powers:

- To administer oaths or affirmations to witnesses
- To take adjournments upon the request of a party or upon his or her own initiative when deemed necessary

- To permit testimony to be offered by deposition
- To permit evidence to be offered and introduced as provided in the rules
- To rule upon the admissibility and relevancy of evidence offered
- To invite the parties, on reasonable notice, to submit prehearing or posthearing briefs or prehearing statements of evidence
- To decide the law and facts of the case and make an award accordingly
- To award costs, not to exceed the statutory costs of the action
- To view any site or object relevant to the case
- Any other powers agreed upon by the parties

The last item is used liberally to grant arbitrators powers that parties believe would assist their arbitration. The arbitrators have 10 days after a hearing within which to file their awards with the court administrator unless an extension is granted. In practice, many arbitrators file their awards immediately after the hearing. If no party files a request for trial within 20 days of the award, the court administrator enters the award as a judgment in the case.

Either party may without penalty appeal the decision of the arbitrator for a jury or nonjury trial. The trial is conducted as originally scheduled, that is, cases sent to arbitration do not "lose their place in the line" of cases waiting for trial. A record of the arbitration hearing is to be made only upon request of the arbitrator. Such record is deemed the arbitrator's personal notes and is not subject to discovery. Information stemming from the arbitration hearing is not put in the case file until after final disposition of the case.

Arbitration hearings were first conducted on Tuesdays and Thursdays with four or five arbitrators hearing a total of eight to ten cases per day (two cases per arbitrator). Referrals to the arbitration program were greater than initially expected, and hearings are now conducted Monday through Friday, with each arbitrator initially assigned three cases.

The court has limited computer support for civil case management. The arbitration program is therefore monitored through a manual system integrated with the existing manual civil case processing system. Information collected on a face sheet by the court includes:

Case number
Date of filing
Type of case
Dollar amount requested
Type of trial requested
Estimate of trial time
Date of filing note of issue/certificate of readiness

Date of filing certificate of nonreadiness
Date case sent to arbitrator
Date of arbitration hearing
Date arbitration award filed
Amount of arbitration award and for whom
Date of subsequent request for trial
The party making the trial request
Type of disposition
Date of disposition

When the case is sent to arbitration, a copy of the face sheet is sent to the arbitration office. This office enters relevant information and when the arbitration process is complete, sends a copy of the face sheet, including the results of the arbitration, back to the court administrator. If the case has been disposed of, the arbitration information will be transferred to the original face sheet contained in the case file. For cases that go to trial, the arbitration information will be added to the court file only after the case has been disposed of. The purpose of this delay is to limit the possibility that the judge to whom the case is assigned will learn the outcome of the arbitration hearing.

## Program Goals

As noted, the court implemented the arbitration program at the same time that it changed from a master to an individual calendar (locally referred to as "the Block") system for its civil cases. Both changes were being made in order to reduce case processing times, reduce the backlog of civil cases, and introduce more court control over the civil caseload. The extent of improvement in processing times and the amount of backlog reduction were not quantified by the court.

## Quantitative Evaluation

Figure 10 is a graph of the caseload of the arbitration program from its inception in September 1985 through June 1986, when data collection for this evaluation ended. "Cases added" includes all cases referred to the program by the block judges. "Cases removed" includes cases disposed by settlement before or during the arbitration hearing or as a result of the arbitrator's award and cases returned to the court either before the arbitration hearing or after completing arbitration with a request for a trial. The "pending" line indicates the number of cases awaiting arbitration or the arbitrator's decision at the end of each month.

This graph shows that the program was eventually effective. Although the average number of cases added per month is higher than the average number removed, by January 1986 the program had achieved enough momentum to show that more cases were removed than added for four of the first five months of 1986, and the number of pending cases was reduced.

**FIGURE 10**
**Arbitration caseload history, September 1985 through June 1986, Hennepin County District Court**

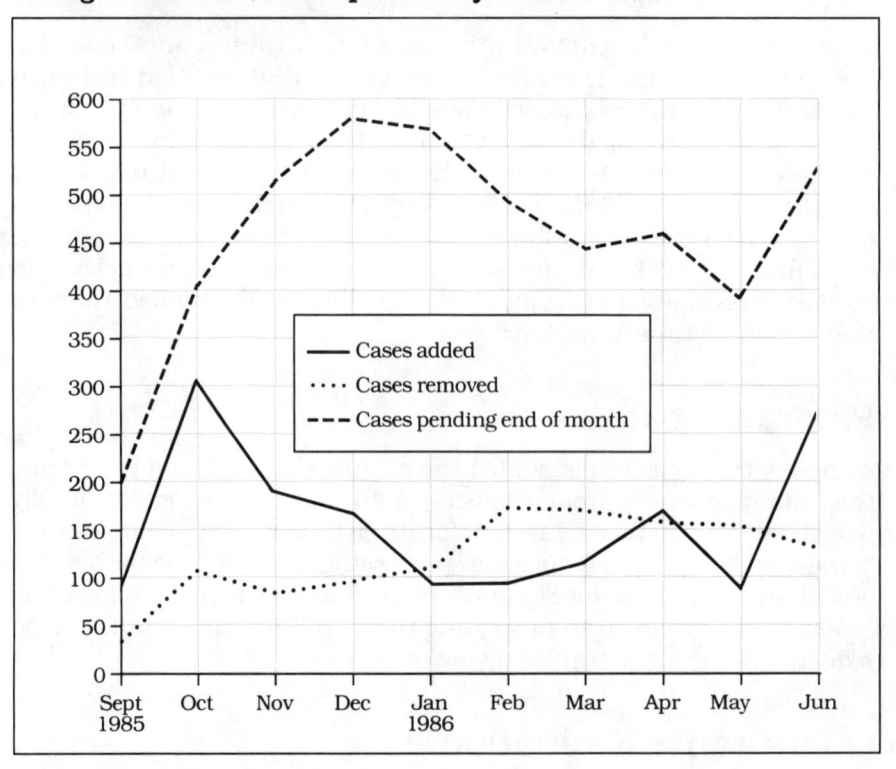

This evaluation will concentrate primarily on the cases removed from the arbitration caseload by any of the means of disposition listed above between September 1985 and end of June 1986.

### What Kinds of Cases Have Been Assigned to Arbitration?
Half of the cases referred for arbitration from September 1985 through June 1986 had originally requested a jury trial; the other half originally

requested a court trial. More than half the jury-trial cases involve a personal injury; one-quarter involve a contract dispute. Almost three-quarters of the nonjury cases are contract disputes. Table 24 gives a list of the types of cases that were referred to arbitration during the period.

In 75 percent of these cases the requested amount was $50,000 or less, and in 90 percent it was less than $60,000. The median original dollar demand was less than $20,000.

## How Are Cases Disposed Of?

The majority of cases removed through arbitration during the study period (56 percent) reached a final disposition either by settlement before or during the arbitration hearing (38 percent) or by accepting the arbitrator's award at the end of the hearing (18 percent) (see Table 25). A small number of cases were returned to the court before arbitration because of bankruptcy, or an appeal being filed in a related matter, or for

### TABLE 24
### Types of cases referred to arbitration, September 1985 through June 1986

|  | TOTAL CASES || Jury demand || Nonjury demand || |
|---|---|---|---|---|---|---|---|
|  | Number | Percent | Number | Percent | Number | Percent | Unknown |
| Contract | 582 | 49 | 149 | 26 | 425 | 75 | 8 |
| Personal injury | 349 | 30 | 329 | 56 | 19 | 3 | 1 |
| Property damage | 103 | 9 | 46 | 8 | 55 | 10 | 2 |
| Other/unknown | 148 | 13 | 60 | 10 | 69 | 12 | 19 |
| TOTAL | 1,182 | 100 | 584 | 100 | 568 | 100 | 30 |

### TABLE 25
### Results of arbitration, September 1985 through June 1986

|  | Percentage |
|---|---|
| Settled before or during arbitration | 38 |
| Accepted arbitrator's award | 18 |
| Requested trial after arbitrator's award | 36 |
| Other (bankruptcy, returned to court, etc.) | 6 |

some other reason the case being no longer thought suitable for arbitration. Slightly more than one-third of the cases removed from arbitration (36 percent) appealed for a trial *de novo*.

### What Factors Are Related to Arbitration Results?

*The amount of money in controversy.* As the original dollar amount demanded increased, case outcomes shifted from accepting the arbitrator's award for the "smallest" cases, to settlement for "medium-sized" cases, to requesting a trial for the "largest" cases (see Table 26). For all but the "more than $50,000" group of cases, more than half were disposed by arbitration or settlement.

As Table 27 shows, the type of disposition shifts from arbitration to settlement to trial requests as the average dollar amount of the demands increases. Defendants demand a trial at a lower threshold of claimed damages than plaintiffs.

Differences this large between the four outcome groups in Table 27 can be expected to be caused by chance only 5 percent of the time (usually expressed as a "probability value" of .05) when there are no differences between the underlying populations these groups represent.

**TABLE 26**
**Arbitration program results compared with original dollar demand, September 1985 through June 1986**

| Original demand | Accepted arbitrator's award Percent | Settlement Percent | Trial request Percent | Other Percent |
|---|---|---|---|---|
| Less than $1,000 | 44 | 36 | 16 | 4 |
| $1,000 to $10,000 | 25 | 45 | 25 | 5 |
| $10,000 to $50,000 | 16 | 35 | 44 | 5 |
| More than $50,000 | 9 | 35 | 47 | 9 |

**TABLE 27**
**Average original dollar demand for various outcomes**

| | |
|---|---|
| Cases disposed by arbitration | $21,294 |
| Cases disposed by settlement | 24,190 |
| Trial request filed by defendant | 33,561 |
| Trial request filed by plaintiff | 47,042 |

*The type of case.* The percentage of cases removed from the court's list of active cases varies with the type of case and whether or not a jury trial is demanded. See Table 28.

Property damage cases, both jury and nonjury demand, had the highest percentage of final dispositions; personal injury cases had the lowest. Generally, a larger percentage of nonjury cases were finally disposed by arbitration than jury-demand cases.

**TABLE 28**
**Percent of cases with final disposition in arbitration process**
*Case outcomes for casetype/trial-type pairs*

| Case type | Jury demand or nonjury | Arbitration award accepted | Settlement | Total |
|---|---|---|---|---|
| Property damage | nonjury | 40 | 38 | 78 |
| Property damage | jury | 20 | 54 | 74 |
| Contract | nonjury | 24 | 41 | 65 |
| Other/unknown | nonjury | 19 | 41 | 60 |
| Contract | jury | 14 | 38 | 52 |
| Personal injury | jury | 10 | 37 | 47 |
| Other/unknown | jury | 12 | 30 | 42 |
| Personal injury | nonjury | 20 | 16 | 36 |

**TABLE 29**
**Settlement figure as a percent of original demand for 10 percent of cases**

| Percent of original demand | Percent of cases settled |
|---|---|
| <0 (costs to defendant) | 4 |
| 0-20 to plaintiff | 31 |
| >20-40 to plaintiff | 19 (median)* |
| >40-60 | 13 |
| >60-80 | 15 |
| >80-<100 | 4 |
| 100 | 6 |
| >100 | 8 |

*Half the cases received a higher percent and half were awarded less.

*Case age.* The time between filing and assignment to arbitration affects the type of result from the arbitration process. Cases that accepted the arbitration award were referred to arbitration an average of 8.2 months after filing. Cases that were settled before or during arbitration had been referred an average of 9 months after filing. Cases that requested a trial after arbitration were an average of 11.6 months old when they were referred to arbitration. This third group was significantly older than the other two groups.[5]

*Comparison of the arbitration award to the original demand.* The dollar amount agreed to at settlement was known for approximately 10 percent of all the cases that were settled. Comparing this figure to the original dollar demand produces the numbers in Table 29.

A settlement figure or arbitrator's award of more than 100 percent of the original dollar amount demanded indicates that either the original demand was expressed as "in excess of $50,000," as personal injury cases are in this court, or that there were additional figures such as interest and attorneys' fees added to the award.

The pattern of arbitrators' awards to the original dollar demand is similar to but slightly higher than the pattern of settlements. Arbitration award figures were available for all cases that went through arbitration (see Table 30).

As larger percentages of the original demand were awarded by the arbitrators, the percentage of plaintiffs who requested a trial *de novo* decreased and the percentage of defendants who requested a trial increased. An anomaly in the data is that 7 percent of the plaintiffs awarded 100 percent or more of the amount they originally demanded

**TABLE 30**
**Arbitrator's award as a percent of the original demand**

| Percent of original demand | Percent of all cases arbitrated |
|---|---|
| <0 (costs to defendant) | 3 |
| 0-20 to plaintiff | 32 |
| >20-40 to plaintiff | 12 (median) |
| >40-60 | 10 |
| >60-80 | 7 |
| >80-<100 | 10 |
| 100 | 7 |
| >100 | 19 |

nevertheless filed a trial request. We can only speculate as to why. They may have expressed their original demand as "in excess of $50,000" and when they were awarded $50,000—or less than they thought the case was "worth"—filed a trial request in the expectation that they could get more either in a later settlement or as the result of a jury's verdict or judge's decision. Similarly, some defendants who were awarded costs, with no recovery by plaintiff, requested a trial. The rationale in these cases is unknown to us, unless the defendants had counterclaims on which they did not prevail and so appealed to pursue these counterclaims (see Table 31).

When one examines the four possible ways arbitration cases can be resolved, relates each of these to the average amounts awarded, and compares the results in percentages of the original demand, there are statistically significant differences, as shown in Table 32.

## TABLE 31
### Actions of parties in response to arbitrator's awards

| Percentage of original demand awarded | Both parties accept award; case disposed Percent | Plaintiff requests trial Percent | Defendant requests trial Percent | TOTAL Percent |
|---|---|---|---|---|
| <0 (costs to defendant) | 41 | 55 | 5 | 100 |
| 0-20 to plaintiff | 31 | 52 | 17 | 100 |
| >20-40 | 23 | 24 | 53 | 100 |
| >40-60 | 29 | 11 | 60 | 100 |
| >60-80 | 43 | 2 | 54 | 100 |
| >80-<100 | 38 | 9 | 53 | 100 |
| 100 | 51 | 2 | 47 | 100 |
| >100 | 36 | 5 | 59 | 100 |

## TABLE 32
### Average percent awarded of original demand

| | Percentage of recovery (mean contained in range) |
|---|---|
| Plaintiff requests trial | >10-20 |
| Cases disposed by settlement | >30-40 |
| Cases disposed by arbitration | >50-60 |
| Defendant requests trial | >60-70 |

The average percent of recovery for cases in which the plaintiff filed a trial request was significantly lower than the average percent for all other groups; the average percent for cases with a trial request filed by the defendant was significantly higher than the average percent for all other groups. (The probability value was once again .05, or less than 1 chance in 20 that these differences are only statistical aberrations.)

*Estimated trial length.* The estimated trial length is an indication of the complexity of a case, as perceived by the litigating attorneys. The estimated length of trial is related with strong significance statistically to the disposition achieved, except for the differences between cases with a trial request and miscellaneous cases with other types of disposition (see Table 33).

*Conclusions.* The above analyses allow construction of profiles of cases more likely to be disposed by arbitration or settlement, and those more likely to file a trial request (see Table 34).

## TABLE 33
### Disposition compared with estimated trial length

| Disposition | Estimated trial length |
|---|---|
| Cases disposed by arbitration | 1.3 days |
| Cases disposed by settlement | 1.6 days |
| Trial requested after arbitration | 2.0 days |
| Other manner of disposition | 2.2 days |

## TABLE 34
### Likelihood of arbitration or trial request

|  | More likely to be disposed by arbitration or settlement | More likely to request a trial |
|---|---|---|
| Casetypes | Contract, property damage | Personal injury |
| Type of trial requested | Nonjury | Jury |
| Level of dollar demand | Lower | Higher |
| Estimate of trial length | Shorter | Longer |
| Age of case at assignment to arbitration | Younger | Older |

## Outcome of cases with a trial request filed

*Outcome of cases.* In the first five months of arbitration hearings, September 1985 through January 1986, requests for a trial were filed in 145 of the 374 cases processed.[6] By the end of June 1986, 80 percent of these 145 cases had been disposed.[7] Their dispositions were distributed as indicated in Table 35.

The trial rate for this first group of cases processed is at least 5.9 percent (22 trials in 374 cases processed). This trial rate will probably rise somewhat after the 29 cases that were still pending at the end of June have been disposed. Even if all the pending cases were disposed by trial, the highest the trial rate could be is 13.6 percent ((22 + 29) into 374). The trial rate for the total civil caseload before the start of the arbitration program was 5 percent. Although the trial rate for cases passing through arbitration appears to be somewhat higher than before the program, the post-arbitration trial rate also may reflect the possibility that the post-arbitration caseload now contains more cases that are "hard" from the standpoint of needing a trial to be disposed.

The median tort disposition times for the court in 1983, 1984, and 1985 were 23.2, 26.0, and 18.5 months, respectively.[8] The cases that went through arbitration and then filed trial requests were disposed of considerably sooner than this. Half the cases that were settled after filing a trial request were disposed within 10.7 months of being filed; the 75th percentile for this group was 17.4 months. The significance of the comparisons between cases disposed between 1983 and 1985 and those in 1986 is limited, however, because the court was operating under two different case management systems during the two time periods. In 1983, 1984, and part of 1985, the court used a master calendar system; it changed to the individual calendar "block" system during the summer of

**TABLE 35**
**Outcomes of requests for trial between September 1985 and July 1986**

|  | Number of cases | Percent of cases |
|---|---|---|
| Settled or dismissed | 91 | 62.8 |
| Trial | 22 | 15.0 |
| Accepted arbitration award | 2 | 1.4 |
| Summary judgment granted | 1 | 0.7 |
| TOTAL DISPOSED | 116 | 80.0 |
| Still pending on 6/30/86 | 29 | 20.0 |
| TOTAL REQUESTS FOR TRIAL | 145 | 100.0 |
| TOTAL CASES PROCESSED | 374 |  |

1985. The effect of this change cannot be separated from the effect the implementation of the arbitration program had on cases referred to arbitration or on the rest of the caseload.

The time to disposition for cases disposed by trial after arbitration cannot be estimated accurately because there were only 7 cases for which filing-to-disposition figures are available, but all but one of these cases were disposed in less time than the trial list figures available from the National Center's separate, independent delay studies. In 1983 the median time to disposition from the civil trial list was 26.8 months; it had been reduced to 19.8 months by 1985. The time-to-disposition-by-trial figures for the 7 trial cases that went through arbitration are 5.5, 6.6, 6.9, and 8.0 months for court trials, and 7.9, 10.6, and 30.3 months for jury trials.

Half of the cases with a trial request filed through January 1986 and still pending at the end of June 1986 were already at least a year old. This mirrors the trend found among the cases disposed after arbitration. Most cases tend to be settled or otherwise disposed early, while a small, select group of older cases tends to put off disposition.

*Relationship between original dollar demand and case outcome.* One reason hypothesized for putting off disposition is that parties with more at stake (i.e., with a higher amount of money in dispute) may want to prolong the case until they are convinced that they have achieved the most favorable or least unfavorable result possible. If cases with larger amounts of money in controversy are prolonged, they may not be appropriate for arbitration. We know that parties in cases with a demand of $50,000 or more are more likely to request a trial after arbitration. Are these requested trials pursued? In large measure they are not, whether the original dollar amount sought is more or less than $50,000 (see Table 36). The trial rate for cases with an original demand of $50,000 or more was slightly lower by the end of June 1986 than it was for cases with a demand less than $50,000. The $50,000 or more group had a higher settlement rate and also had a slightly larger percentage of cases still pending by June 1986, but none of these differences is statistically significant.

Trials occurred both for cases involving as little as $2,017 and for those in excess of $50,000. One case with an original demand of more than $600,000 was settled. These results suggest that money is a relative commodity. Parties to these cases use factors other than or in addition to the absolute number of dollars at stake when deciding how to proceed with their individual cases. For this reason it appears that if the court has the resources to arbitrate cases demanding more than $50,000, it can continue to include these cases in the program without increasing the final trial rate. Those cases demanding more than $50,000 that request a trial do not behave differently from cases with smaller dollar demands that request a trial.

**TABLE 36**
**Outcomes of cases requesting trial according to original dollar demand, by percent**

|  | Demand less than $50,000 | Demand of $50,000 or more |
|---|---|---|
| **Case outcome** | | |
| Settled or dismissed | 59 | 65 |
| Trial | 17 | 12 |
| Other | 3 | 0 |
| TOTAL DISPOSED | 79 | 77 |
| Still pending | 21 | 23 |
| TOTAL CASES | 100 | 100 |

### Outlook for the Future

Although data collection officially ended on June 30, 1986, the members of the project visited the court for the last time in July 1986 and were given some information on the way the court anticipated using the arbitration program during the following year.

When the arbitration program was introduced in Hennepin County, there were a number of other reforms under way as well. The court had recently converted to an individual calendar system and was in the process of deciding whether to unify the jurisdiction of its general and limited jurisdiction courts. Additionally, it was requiring that all active civil cases either file a certificate of readiness by July 1, 1986, show reason why such a certificate could not yet be filed, or be dismissed. The court expected that this third reform would result in the filing of a substantial number of readiness documents as the July 1 cutoff date approached, and their expectations were met. During the month of June more certificates of readiness were filed than had been filed during a whole year in the past. The cases were immediately assigned to their block judge, who then referred many of them to arbitration. The number of cases referred to arbitration in June (263) was more than twice the number of cases that had been assigned in each of five of the last six months. The number of cases removed through the arbitration process maintained its recent level, so the number of cases pending at the end of the month shot up. During July another 1,119 cases were referred and the pending total reached a level almost three times as high as it had been in recent months.

The arbitration staff reacted quickly to the increased demand, planning to increase the number of arbitration hearings each day and thus increase their capacity. The court assigned them temporary staff from the clerk's office to help keep up with the paperwork. But as a result of the increased demand for service, the dynamics of the program may have changed.

We were able to observe this program during its organization and start-up phases. Before a final evaluation of its work can be made we recommend that another study be done at the end of its second year of operation to see whether it was able to continue to give satisfactory service to litigants as it matured and, in particular, under the new pressures brought about by the substantial increase in its caseload.

## Qualitative Evaluation

Project staff visited Minneapolis three times to interview people involved with the arbitration program. The first visit, in September 1985, was made one month after arbitration hearings began; the second was four months later, in January 1986, followed by a final visit in July 1986. The interviews in September 1985 provided an initial impression of the arbitration program. Three arbitrators, two litigating attorneys, two judges, the court administrator, and the arbitration administrator were interviewed during this visit. In addition, project staff attended a day and a half of arbitration hearings. In January, six judges, sixteen arbitrators, nine of whom had litigated cases before other arbitrators, and seven litigating attorneys were interviewed. These interviews included return visits to those people interviewed during the September site visit. During the final site visit five judges, thirteen arbitrators (seven of whom had had hearings before other arbitrators), and ten attorneys who had not served as arbitrators were interviewed.

In general, those interviewed were very supportive of the arbitration program. During the first two site visits, they recognized that it was too early to analyze statistically what the long-term effect of the arbitration program on the caseload would be, so support of the program was, in some cases, slightly guarded.

In July, those interviewed were still uncertain of the quantitative value of the arbitration program. Some statistics had circulated through the local grapevine about the percentage of awards accepted, cases settled, and cases appealed; but statistically, at least, there remained a question whether the program was successful. There was now a significant shift in attitude, however. Most considered arbitration to be a permanent, valuable program within the court. The early reviews of the program during the first two site visits were favorable but tentative. By July, this tentativeness had disappeared.

### Quality of the Pool of Arbitrators

Most arbitrators favored a pool of arbitrators representing a competent cross-section of the local bar. It was thought the current pool fulfilled these criteria. There was a minority opinion that the present pool was not experienced enough and that although a "blue-ribbon" pool was not necessary, a cross-section of attorneys with significant litigating experience was needed.

Strict qualifications for arbitrators were seen by some to be undesirable, that the draw of an arbitrator for one's case should be more like the draw of a jury—high expertise should not be sought and is not desirable. A slightly larger number of interviewees expressed exactly the opposite position, the belief that arbitrators should be experts in specific areas of the law and should be matched to case types. One arbitrator thought that even though the pool of arbitrators is four hundred strong it is a "blue ribbon" pool because it represents attorneys who care enough about the system to offer their services and who meet the selection criteria.

**Why Lawyers Agree to Serve as Arbitrators**
As noted, almost four hundred attorneys were placed on the original list of available arbitrators. With a group of judicial adjuncts so large, it is not quite the honor to serve as it might be in a program where a select number of attorneys are personally asked to serve as judicial adjuncts. It becomes increasingly interesting to assess why attorneys volunteer to place their names on the list of available arbitrators when there is such a large group and the prestige of serving may thus be lessened.

Those serving were virtually unanimous in saying that they offered to serve as a public service. Most recognized that the district court calendar was backlogged and needed help. The court was taking the initiative in developing programs and systems to reduce the backlog and speed case processing. Rather than being resistant to change within the system, these attorneys saw their participation as an offer to help make the system work more efficiently. Some were not optimistic that the arbitration program would improve case processing, but felt a duty nonetheless to do their part.

Although a few arbitrators have aspirations to become judges, none acknowledged a belief that his or her service as an arbitrator would be a stepping stone to appointment.

Many arbitrators also recognized that helping the court reduce its backlog would speed their own cases. There is a general feeling of frustration with the delay in Minneapolis, as many attorneys find it more and more difficult explaining delay to their clients.

The opportunity to learn from the experience as an arbitrator was not widely recognized as a significant motivating factor in service; yet most arbitrators, after serving, were surprised at the value of the experience in learning about the presentation of a case from the judge's perspective.

**Positive and Negative Aspects of Serving as an Arbitrator**
The vast majority of arbitrators interviewed thought that the knowledge they had gained from serving as arbitrators was the most positive aspect of service.

Certain aspects were mentioned particularly:

- More sensitivity to the client's needs
- Being able to analyze more clearly how facts are presented
- Quick recognition of "the spine of the case"
- The amount of "effluvia" presented
- Greater understanding of a judge's decision-making process
- Seeing younger lawyers litigate

The arbitrators who did not include learning as the most positive aspect of the program to them concentrated on the resolution of disputes. There was considerable pleasure in knowing that "their" awards were accepted or that "their" cases had settled. A significant number of arbitrators took pride in their ability to facilitate settlements. Involvement in the settlement process was also considered an important experience to some arbitrators.

Negative aspects of the program were not so clearly defined as positive ones. Certain cases presented problems of time, either because they could not be adequately argued in the three hours allotted or they took too much time to prepare for and decide. Some cases are too complex and thus unsuited for the arbitration program as it is structured. Most other problems noted during the first two site visits were associated with the newness of the program. It is believed that some attorneys were testing the program, others did not know what to expect, and some were not preparing for their hearings. There was also some concern expressed by arbitrators about the ease with which continuances were granted by judges (but not by the arbitration administrator, to whom the initial decision on continuances was later delegated). In July, attorneys continued to test the program to see how it might be manipulated to their benefit, but problems related to their being unfamiliar with the program no longer existed.

## Case Assignment and Selection

There was a broad range of opinion regarding which cases are most appropriate for arbitration and which are clearly inappropriate. The arbitrators have heard a great variety of cases: personal injury, contract, medical malpractice, property damage, landlord/tenant, tax, employment, and slander. They feel that arbitrators can hear most civil cases, particularly if the cases are matched to each arbitrator's legal specialty, as the court is trying to do. Most arbitrators think child custody issues should not be arbitrated, but there was a split regarding dissolution cases—some think dissolution is particularly appropriate, others are opposed to including any family law matters. Similarly, there are a few persons who would exclude personal injury cases in the belief that these cases should go before a jury. Others think they can arbitrate personal injury cases as well as other civil cases, especially given the relaxed rules of evidence.

A few interviewees mentioned some types of cases that they thought were not appropriate for arbitration, either because the cases tend to be too complex and require more time than is available, or because the issues raised are sensitive and should be handled by judges. In the first category are complex multiparty suits, construction, condemnation, and cases with a dollar demand in excess of $50,000. (This last was a minority view. When asked specifically in another context, many arbitrators said that the $50,000-dollar limit was artificial and should be eliminated. They would rather have the judges screen *all* the cases for complexity and assign those to arbitration that they think are appropriate. Cases in this jurisdiction are directed to be pled as "in excess of $50,000" in order to eliminate some of the notoriety that large dollar-demands bring to some cases. Some over-$50,000 cases are actually simple; some under-$50,000 cases are very complex.) Cases that should not be assigned to arbitration because of their sensitive nature include slander, defamation of character, and paternity cases.

**Compensating Arbitrators**
There was only one person interviewed who thought arbitrators should not be paid. Half of the arbitrators commented that the $150 a day that is paid makes the service essentially *pro bono* and that the pay does not affect the court's ability to attract qualified attorneys to serve. The overwhelming majority, thus, believed that pay was appropriate, even if the amount of pay was like a recognition for service rather than adequate compensation for services rendered. It was thought that pay legitimizes the service, makes it a professional obligation, and makes lawyers more "honest" about their commitment to the program. Three attorneys said the pay made no difference whatsoever to their willingness to volunteer their time.

Without pay for services there is a fear that arbitrators from small firms and sole practitioners would be less likely to serve. The pool of arbitrators would then be made up of attorneys from larger firms.

**Training and Orientation**
After the pool of arbitrators was selected, the court conducted an orientation and training session. The arbitration program administrator and staff also developed an arbitration manual, commonly known as the "blue book." Interviews with arbitrators confirmed that the initial training session was very well run and was useful. Even more positive marks were given to the blue book, a number of arbitrators noting that they have read it more than once and refer to it to familiarize themselves with rules and regulations of the arbitration program. The single

criticism of the blue book is that it could be more precise and should be updated to incorporate changes in the arbitration program.

Since the orientation session took place before arbitration hearings were actually held, some of the changes in operations and procedures were not included. It was suggested by at least three arbitrators that the court should hold another, updated orientation session. One arbitrator thought that the orientation program should be extended from about three hours to a full day's session. A few arbitrators thought training was not necessary for themselves, based on their experience with the court and other arbitration programs. Even these arbitrators did not discount the possible value of training for others, however.

## Conduct of the Hearings

There was unanimous approval of the level of judicial decorum associated with arbitration hearings. As noted, the arbitrators wear judges' robes, the hearings are held in courtrooms, and arbitrators are most commonly referred to as "your Honor" during the proceedings. A number of arbitrators initially did not like the formality of the arbitration hearing, felt uneasy wearing judges' robes, and would rather have conducted the hearing in an informal manner. In every instance they came to recognize that it is important to have a significant degree of formality in order to have an appropriate atmosphere for arbitration. The arbitrators felt that courtroom-style decorum increased respect and credibility for the program. Litigating attorneys agreed. Finally, the emphasis on formality was said to allow parties to perceive that they were receiving a "day in court" through the arbitration process.

Before the start of the hearing the arbitrators ask the litigating attorneys to meet with them in chambers. Some ask the litigants if it would be helpful for the arbitrator to participate in settlement negotiations. If the answer is yes, the litigants sign a form stating that they have requested the arbitrator to help with settlement. Some arbitrators also ask the parties if they would like to stipulate that the arbitration be binding. If the parties agree, they sign another form to that effect (few have done so to this point).

The degree to which arbitrators participate in settlement discussion varies considerably. Some are reluctant to participate and do little more than tell the attorneys that they have an opportunity to talk settlement before the hearing if they so desire. The majority of arbitrators have recognized that settlement is more likely if the arbitrator takes an active role in bringing the parties together. These arbitrators view the settlement discussion process as an increasingly important part of the arbitration procedure. Some feel that they are only successful when they are able to settle the case before the hearing.

Before the hearing some arbitrators ask for a review of the evidence that will be presented. For the most part, testimony during the hearing is limited to facts, skipping foundation. Many of the cases in arbitration are estimated to need three days for trial, but they can be arbitrated in the two-hour period available if the testimony is limited to the central witnesses and foundation is eliminated.

Normally there are no closing statements. If the arbitrator has some questions remaining after completion of the hearing he or she may request the litigants to submit letter briefs focusing on particular points of their case. Some arbitrators are able to decide cases immediately; others must wait for the submission of additional materials or do additional legal research themselves before they make their award.

Most arbitrators give their decision only in the form of an award. This may include a list of the components of the award, such as so many dollars for medical expenses and lost wages, and interest to be paid at a certain percent from a certain date until the award is satisfied. A few arbitrators said they also write brief memos explaining the rationale behind their awards, even though the court does not favor this practice. In one case involving multiple issues, the arbitrator felt he had to write such a memo so that the parties would know how he had decided each issue and how he had arrived at the award.

**Time Required of Arbitrators**
Time demands on arbitrators vary considerably, depending upon the complexity of their cases and the amount of time they are willing to commit. Some arbitrators took as little as one-half hour to review two cases before the hearings and others as much as twelve hours to review one case.

Most arbitrators report spending between four and four and a half hours on each case: between one-half and one and one-half hours prehearing, approximately two hours in hearing, and one hour posthearing. One reported requiring as little as two-and one-half hours to complete the total case; the longest time reported was between twenty and twenty-five hours on each case. (This was one of the semi-retired attorneys.) Arbitrators are normally assigned three cases; in most instances at least two will settle before arbitration and the arbitrator will be left with one case to hear.

**Conflicts of Interest**
None of the arbitrators has had any problems with conflicts of interest; none is aware of being challenged. One arbitrator said she would recuse herself if she were assigned to arbitrate a case in which her husband, also an attorney, represented one of the parties, but if a member of her

husband's law firm was involved, she would disclose this relationship but not recuse herself unless she had a close professional or social relationship with that attorney. This was typical of the way the arbitrators said they handle situations with the potential for an appearance of a conflict of interest. They review the names and associations of all attorneys and parties to all cases upon assignment to them and disclose any relationships that they find. When appropriate they withdraw completely from the case. It was noted that there is a very active board of professional responsibility that has educated the bar well. Actual conflicts of interest and the potential for conflict are not seen as a major problem area, therefore.

## Costs and Administrative Issues

### Costs

The court administrator of the Hennepin County district court, in a report prepared in September 1986 on the arbitration program, reviewed the costs of the program as follows:

> The cost of the arbitration program for a first 12 months was $75,750, which translates into $110.58 per disposition. From a productivity standpoint, it appears that the arbitration program is equivalent to two judges at the cost of $75,000 versus $400,000.

The bases for this conclusion are as follows.

The arbitration program recorded 685 dispositions during its first year of operation. The cost per case was figured by dividing the $75,750 cost of arbitrators by the 685 dispositions.

The statement that 685 dispositions is roughly equivalent to two judges is based on a district court judge's responsibilty for an average of 342.5 civil dispositions annually. An average cost of a judge of the district court of $200,000 includes salaries and benefits for the judge, a court reporter, and a law clerk.

The following comments add further perspective to the court administrator's analysis.

Disposition data during ten months in 1985 and 1986 show that the district court disposed of 2,867 civil cases through means other than the arbitration program. Projecting this number to a full year, the district court would dispose of 3,440 civil cases. Dividing this number by the 14 judges assigned to hear civil cases results in a figure of 246 civil case dispositions per judge per year. The 685 arbitration program dispositions in this analysis thus equal the work of 2.78 district court judges.

If a district court judge costs $200,000 a year, then the cost savings to the court would be $557,000 (the dollar equivalent of 2.78 judgeships annually), less the cost of the arbitration program. Using the administrator's figure of $75,750 (the total dollar amount paid to arbitrators during the first year of operation of the arbitration program), the first-year cost savings equal $481,250, even more than the administrator indicated.

The court in its September 1986 report did not include the cost of staff of the arbitration program, as the figure used for a judge's annual cost of $200,000 did not include any clerical support or administrative costs.

There are two reasons these support costs were not included. First, although technically possible, the calculations that would be required to factor the dollar amount of clerical and administrative support provided by the clerk's office and the court administrator's office in support of each individual judge would be overly time-consuming to justify their inclusion in this cost analysis. Second, it is asserted that the staff assigned to the arbitration program were existing court employees who would be assigned elsewhere if they were not running the arbitration program; thus they do not represent additional expense to the court for purposes of running the arbitration program. It is also noted that in jurisdictions with smaller caseloads, particularly rural jurisdictions in Minnesota where judges ride circuit and courts have sitting judges only on a part-time basis, the administration of an arbitration program could be assumed by existing clerical employees, typically those clerks who perform calendaring duties for the court.

The project team recognizes the limitations that led to the court's first-cut cost comparison in September 1986. We have the luxury of time not available to court staff. Furthermore, the project team's perspective in all project sites has been to determine costs from an accountant's rather than a budget analyst's perspective. Therefore, we ascribe costs to the program beyond those included in the court's preliminary analysis.

Some arbitration staff members are full-time court employees assigned exclusively to the arbitration program. The arbitration program has a director and deputy whose combined annual salaries, including fringe benefits at a rate of 35 percent, equal approximately $76,000. The arbitration program also has four contract and part-time employees whose annual costs would be $33,000, if their employment remains as it is now. For the first year of the arbitration program the cost for these four employees was approximately $15,000, as two of them did not work with the program from its inception.

The arbitration staff notifies litigants of their assignment to the arbitration program. Annual costs for production of forms, notification of litigants, and other correspondence are not insignificant. Paperwork that uniquely involves the arbitration program as a separate part of the processing of civil cases through the court should be attributed as a direct cost of the program.

The Hennepin County district court has housed its arbitration program in unused courtrooms of the Minneapolis City Hall. The cost of these facilities has not been included in our cost analysis of the arbitration program. Jurisdictions that do not have space to house an arbitration program might have to factor in costs for such facilities.

The National Center project staff would include the following direct costs for the arbitration program:

| | |
|---|---|
| $75,750 | fees paid to arbitrators |
| 76,000 | salaries and benefits for full-time staff |
| 15,000 | part-time staff |
| 5,000 | project team estimate of approximation of mailing, notification costs |
| $171,750 | Total annual arbitration program direct costs |

Even with these additional costs ascribed to the program, it is cost effective. The $171,750 costs compare to projected judicial costs of $500,000, even without clerical and administrative costs factored into the cost of a judge. The net fiscal savings exceeds $300,000 a year for the first year.

**Program Administration**

The administration of the arbitration program is highly commended. Most arbitrators report that there are absolutely no administrative problems in conducting their hearings. The two administrative problems identified are not attributed to those administering the program. First, arbitrators note that files they receive for their cases are sometimes incomplete. This appears to be a relatively common phenomenon in the court, at least partially due to the lack of clarity in the rules for filing documents with the court and also to the local practice of filing a certificate of readiness without having completed all discovery and motions. Arbitrators also note some concern with the procedures for allowing continuances of arbitration hearings. In addition, there was some early confusion as to what they should do with exhibits that had been entered during the arbitration hearing.

## Overall Assessment

The arbitration program has proven itself statistically to be disposing of a significant number of cases either through settlement or acceptance of the arbitration award at a demonstrably lower cost to the court. The program has achieved widespread acceptance by the bench and bar. Most notably, the court has enthusiastically supported the program, and remains flexible enough to institute minor modifications to improve its operations.

The vast majority of judges, arbitrators, and litigating attorneys interviewed in Minneapolis think that arbitration should be made a permanent fixture in the court. Should the court ever have more judges than it actually "needs," they still think that arbitration can play an important role. One arbitrator thinks that the arbitration program will be more important to the court in the coming year than it was during its first year of operation because of the large number of cases that have been filed in response to the new certificate of readiness rule.

All but one of the arbitrators is happy with the concept of arbitration and is satisfied with the way it has been implemented. They see it as providing a great benefit to the court in a cost-effective manner. They have no negative comments to make about it from the perspective of arbitrators. Some, who represent mostly plaintiffs in their own practices, complained that the defense bar does not take the program seriously and does not present a defense at hearings, since their strategy is to appeal; the defense attorneys complain that some plaintiffs' attorneys use the program as a dress rehearsal for trial and plan to appeal any decision that is not entirely favorable. (Note that the quantitative data do not support either view.)

One arbitrator said he has changed his mind since forming his original, favorable opinion. He now thinks that the program is a waste of time and money and only adds another, unnecessary step to his cases, since all the awards he has won as a litigator have been appealed and are still pending before judges. He wishes the court would put more emphasis on binding arbitration. He would be much happier knowing that cases he arbitrated were going to be disposed of at the end of the arbitration process. But his was a singular view. All the other arbitrators and litigating attorneys are moderately to ecstatically satisfied with the current program.

In March 1986 (after nine months of operation) the court adopted amended rules that addressed problem areas. (See Appendix D.) There was a problem with attorneys who did not appear for their hearings and simply appealed the award. The new rules impose reasonable costs on a nonappearing party. There was a problem with judges granting too many continuances; the new rules allow continuances to be granted only by the court administrator. There was a problem with the timing of exchange of evidentiary documents between the parties; the new rules shorten the time allowed.

It could be counterproductive if a court changed its rules every time a small problem developed. There could be considerable confusion and resistance to change. The changes made by the Hennepin County district court were all made at one time, were well publicized, and reflect the continued support of the program by the court. There is every reason to believe that if the court continues to support the program as it has to this point, the arbitration program will continue to serve it well.

# Notes to Chapter Eleven

1. In Minnesota, a civil complaint is commenced when a summons and complaint are served or are delivered to the proper officer for service upon the defendant. The court does not know that a civil case has been commenced until some document is filed with the court. Ordinarily, this first document is a pretrial motion or the note of issue requesting a trial date.

2. When a note of issue/certificate of readiness is filed with the court, certifying that the case is ready for trial, this places the case on the active trial calendar.

3. Cases seeking more than $50,000 in damages may be referred to the program at the discretion of a trial judge or by stipulation of the parties. Between the start of the program and the end of June 1986, 23 percent of the cases assigned were seeking damages in excess of $50,000. In early January 1986, because the program was being used beyond its capacity, the judges agreed to temporarily reduce the number of referrals of cases seeking over $50,000 in damages.

4. A few exceptions have been referred to the program for all case categories except for family law matters.

5. The probability value that this difference is no more than a chance difference is .005 (5 chances in 1,000). In other words, the older the case the more likely it is to request a trial *de novo*.

6. Cases processed include those settled before or during the arbitration hearing or that completed the arbitration process. They do not include cases removed from arbitration before their hearing and returned to the block judge.

7. Cases with trial requests filed after January 1986 are not included in the following discussion because too small a percentage of them had been disposed by the time data collection ended.

8. All comparable time-to-disposition data referenced here were collected and analyzed by the Implementation of Delay Reduction Programs in Urban Trial Courts project funded by the National Institute of Justice and conducted by the Institute for Court Management of the National Center for State Courts. A report on this project will be published in 1987.

CHAPTER TWELVE

# The Seattle Early Disposition Program

The Superior Court of King County, Washington, serves the largest city in the state, Seattle. It is a general jurisdiction trial court, with jurisdiction over all types of civil cases,[1] felonies, and appeals of civil and criminal cases from lower courts. Thirty-nine judges serve the court.

The court has used mandatory settlement conferences in domestic relations cases and mandatory and voluntary settlement conferences in civil cases. When it instituted its Early Disposition Program (EDP), settlement conferences for general civil cases were voluntary and available anytime before trial upon request. In 1983, the court became concerned about the growing number of civil cases ready for trial that did not yet have a trial date assigned, so it implemented the Early Disposition Program in an effort to make up for some of this shortfall.

## Description of the Program

Programs similar to EDP have been implemented in several courts, each with its own distinctive characteristics. Seattle's program is based on the program that has been operating successfully for several years in the Superior Court of Alameda County (Oakland), California.

Alameda County's EDP is held several times a year. The original design in Seattle was for a one-time effort in the fall of 1983 to reduce the number of cases ready for trial to a more manageable size. Civil cases on the jury-trial calendar were identified as candidates for the early disposition program. Cases were selected that within the following two months were due to be assigned a date for jury trial. Half of these cases were randomly identified for inclusion in the EDP experimental group. The remainder were used as a comparison group; their processing continued to follow the procedures normally used by the court. In addition to the assigned cases, the court also allowed attorneys to volunteer their cases for participation. Approximately 25 percent of the total cases included in the 1983 hearings were "volunteered" into the program. These also were distributed approximately half to the EDP and the balance to the comparison group. The EDP hearings were held during the short Thanksgiving week. The majority were scheduled for Monday and Tuesday, leaving Wednesday free to finish hearings that were left over or continued from the previous two days.

Conferences were conducted by three-member panels made up of a judge and two attorneys. Panels were established for four major case types: personal injury (torts), medical malpractice, contracts and commercial, and domestic relations. When the bar normally is divided into plaintiff's and defense bar (torts, medical malpractice, and to a lesser degree commercial), there was one plaintiff's attorney and one defense attorney on the panel with the judge. In domestic relations cases attorneys normally represent both husbands and wives in separate cases, so the court tried only to place two well-regarded and experienced attorneys on the domestic relations panels. The attorneys from among whom the panels were established were named by an advisory group of senior bar members; they were highly experienced and respected members of the bar whose opinions regarding the value of a case for settlement would be respected by their peers.

Six to twelve cases were scheduled in 1983 for each of 14 panels sitting on two days.[2] (Although it was expected that these panels could hear only 192 cases, 250 cases were scheduled for settlement conferences either by specific time or on a "stand-by" list to accommodate for preconference settlements and other expected fall-out.) Hearings were held on 226 cases in 1983.

Each litigating attorney was required to submit a memorandum one week prior to the settlement conference containing the following:

- Designation of the trial attorney
- A statement of facts, including agreed facts, agreed issues, and an itemized statement of medical bills, loss of income, and other special damages claimed
- All police, medical, and other reports on which any attorney wished to depend
- The date when the last face-to-face settlement discussion was held
- The nature and extent of injury in personal injury cases
- Any special barriers to settlement

The court's local rules for settlement conferences applied to the EDP program. The parties or, in the case of an insured party, an authorized representative of the insurance company, were required to appear at the panel hearings.

The panel reviewed the memoranda prior to the settlement conference. In the hearings observed, each case was informally presented to the three-member panel. The hearings normally took place in the courtroom of the judge presiding. Most panels allowed each side about ten minutes to present its case. The panel then questioned the attorneys on key issues. All panel members participated actively. The panel retired and discussed the case, normally in the judge's chambers. It returned with its shared view of the probable outcome of the case and of an appropriate settlement figure. If the panel disagreed, normally the views of each panel member were presented along with their reasoning, or, in the case of disagreement on amount of damages only, an average figure might be given. The litigating attorneys were then encouraged to settle the case in light of the panel's opinions. Some panels asked the parties to meet immediately to discuss settlement based on the panel's comments. Other panels allowed the parties to disperse, but asked them to advise the court if settlement were achieved.

Attorneys volunteered their time to sit on the panels. Some administrative and suppport personnel costs were incurred.

In the spring of 1984, after the court had obtained opinions about the program directly from attorneys and after reviewing memoranda from the National Center for State Courts on opinions about the program gained through interviews and questionnaires, the court decided to have a second EDP in Thanksgiving week of 1984. The 1984 EDP was set up to mirror the 1983 program in structure and the types of cases eligible for the program. In 1984, 149 cases were assigned to EDP, 43 of which (29 percent) were volunteered for the program.

In June 1985, the court reviewed its two years of experience with EDP. It had available to it a statistical analysis completed by the Washington office of the administrator for the courts on both the experimental and control cases from 1983 and 1984, the results from the National Center for State Courts' questionnaires and interviews, and the National Center's supplementary thoughts regarding the statistical analysis. Upon reflection and for reasons discussed more fully below, the court decided to terminate the program.

## Goals

When the program was implemented, the court enumerated five goals:

1. Provide an expeditious, cost-effective manner of providing disposition to noncriminal cases.
2. Reduce the pending caseload of the Superior Court, providing quicker, more accurate trial dates.

3. Settle cases as soon in the process as possible, reducing costs to the taxpayers.
4. Reduce the number of civil jury cases going to trial.
5. Reduce the time to disposition for cases with EDP hearings.

The principal qualitative goal specified at the beginning of the program was to create a positive exchange between attorneys and judges, providing attorneys with a first-hand, behind-the-scenes look at the problems faced by the judiciary in dealing with thousands of attorneys and *pro se* litigants on a variety of different issues and cases. More generally, the court also hoped for improved relations between the bench and bar and an enhanced recognition within the bar and in the community at large of its efforts to improve its efficiency.

## Quantitative Evaluation

The participation of the National Center for State Courts in evaluating EDP began only after the design of the program and its companion caseload data evaluation had been planned. The Washington office of the administrator for the courts agreed to use its computerized, statewide data processing system, SCOMIS (Superior Court Management Information System), which collects statistical caseload data from each superior court location in the state, and additional data provided by the court in King County to evaluate the impact that EDP had on the court's caseload.

The National Center agreed to offer its perspective on the quantitative evaluation but to focus its resources on the qualitative and fiscal aspects of an evaluation.

The Washington office of the administrator for the courts prepared its evaluation for the June 1985 meeting of the court. At the request of the National Center, it extended the collection of data and its analysis through July 1986. It also expanded its evaluation report in response to requests by National Center project staff. The expanded analysis and evaluation of data is Appendix E. The discussion that follows reflects the National Center project staff's analysis of data provided by the office of the administrator.

A "controlled" evaluation was planned. As indicated, cases were selected as eligible for the program and then randomly assigned to either the EDP hearings or to the control group. Volunteer cases were also randomly assigned, half to EDP and half to the control group. The number of cases in each group for the 1983 and 1984 hearings is given in Table 37. Following the EDP hearings, cases in both the EDP and the control groups were followed by the evaluation staff at the state office of the administrator, and the date and type of disposition for each case were noted. The results must be examined against the court's two key

## TABLE 37
### Distribution of cases in EDP evaluation, 1983 and 1984

|  | Number of cases |  |  |  |
|---|---|---|---|---|
|  | 1983 Program |  | 1984 Program |  |
|  | EDP | Control | EDP | Control |
| **Civil case type** |  |  |  |  |
| Assigned | 142 | 166 | 104 | 199 |
| Volunteer | 56 | 46 | 37 | 48 |
| *Subtotal* | *198* | *212* | *141* | *147* |
| **Domestic relations case type** |  |  |  |  |
| Volunteer | 28 | — | 6 | — |
| TOTAL | 226 | 212 | 147 | 147 |

quantitative goals: to reduce the number of trials and to improve the time to disposition for cases assigned to the EDP.

### Number and Rate of Trials

The court was most interested in learning whether the EDP would reduce the trial rate substantially. After two programs, no clear conclusions emerge.

Thirty-two months after the 1983 EDP hearings, the trial rate for control cases was 12.3 percent and for EDP (exclusive of domestic relations cases) 9.6 percent, a total reduction of more than 20 percent. Less than 10 percent of the cases remaining in each group had not yet been disposed. Most of the reduction in the trial rate was attributable to the volunteered cases—EDP volunteer cases had a trial rate that was 77 percent lower than control-volunteer cases (see Table 38).[3] The trial rate for cases assigned to EDP was higher than for control-assigned cases.

Twenty months after the 1984 EDP hearings, the overall trial rate was 3 percent *lower* for EDP cases than for control cases. In contrast to 1983, the trial rate was lower for cases assigned to EDP than for control-assigned cases (8.7 percent versus 11.8 percent), but it was substantially higher (almost 50 percent) for volunteered cases put through the EDP (24.3 percent for EDP-volunteer cases versus 16.7 percent for control-volunteers). A large number of the trials for the 1984 EDP cases were held within six months of the EDP hearing; this pattern is very different from 1983. During the following 14 months, more trials were held for control group cases. The relationship between trial rates for 1984 EDP and control group cases may change further as the remaining cases are disposed. (Between 13 and 20 percent of each group was still active when

## TABLE 38
### Trials in EDP and control cases

| 1983 PROGRAM | TOTAL CASES | Trials held | Percent tried | Percent of cases remaining active |
|---|---|---|---|---|
| **EDP cases** | | | | |
| Volunteer | 56 | 3 | 5.4 | 1.8 |
| Assigned | 142 | 16 | 11.3 | 4.2 |
| TOTAL FOR EDP | 198 | 19 | 9.6 | 3.5 |
| Domestic relations | 28 | 3 | 10.7 | 0.0 |
| **Control cases** | | | | |
| Volunteer | 46 | 11 | 23.9 | 2.2 |
| Assigned | 166 | 15 | 9.0 | 6.6 |
| TOTAL FOR CONTROL | 212 | 26 | 12.3 | 5.7 |
| **1984 PROGRAM** | | | | |
| **EDP cases** | | | | |
| Volunteer | 37 | 9 | 24.3 | 13.5 |
| Assigned | 104 | 9 | 8.7 | 13.5 |
| TOTAL FOR EDP | 141 | 18 | 12.8 | 13.5 |
| Domestic relations | 6 | 0 | 0.0 | 16.7 |
| **Control cases** | | | | |
| Volunteer | 48 | 8 | 16.7 | 18.7 |
| Assigned | 119 | 14 | 11.8 | 19.3 |
| TOTAL FOR CONTROL | 167 | 22 | 13.2 | 19.2 |

the trial rates were calculated for the 1984 cases.) All of these rates are likely to rise. Questions remain, however, why there were so many trials so soon after the 1984 EDP hearings.

In considering this question, the age distributions of the cases in each of the four 1984 groups were compared. Cases in the EDP and control groups in 1983 were "younger" than cases in the 1984 hearings (see Table 39). Trials in this court usually occur about 540 days after filing; in 1984 there were more cases in three of the four groups at or beyond this critical age than there had been in 1983. When cases were scheduled for EDP, they did not lose their place on the trial calendar. As a result, older cases might have had more time (and money) invested in the case when the EDP hearing occurred and thus be more willing to test the value of the case at trial.[4] When data collection for this evaluation closed (July 1986) it was too early to estimate what the final difference between the trial rates for the 1984 EDP and control cases will be.

**TABLE 39**
**Age at EDP hearing date for EDP and control cases, 1983 and 1984**

|  | 1983 |  | 1984 |  |
| --- | --- | --- | --- | --- |
|  | No. | Percent | No. | Percent |
| **EDP volunteer** |  |  |  |  |
| 540 days or less | 37 | 66 | 20 | 54 |
| More than 540 days | 19 | 34 | 17 | 46 |
| **EDP assigned** |  |  |  |  |
| 540 days or less | 87 | 61 | 67 | 63 |
| More than 540 days | 55 | 39 | 39 | 37 |
| **Control volunteer** |  |  |  |  |
| 540 days or less | 31 | 67 | 27 | 56 |
| More than 540 days | 15 | 33 | 21 | 44 |
| **Control assigned** |  |  |  |  |
| 540 days or less | 111 | 67 | 56 | 47 |
| More than 540 days | 55 | 33 | 63 | 53 |

The court hoped that the reduction in total trial time would be sufficient to offset the time the judges devoted to the EDP. Judges spent 23 judge days in EDP hearings in 1983 and 27 judge days in hearings held in 1984. According to the jury clerk, most civil jury trials last three days. The number of trial days saved by the 1983 EDP can be estimated. Almost 5.5 trials probably were avoided as result of the EDP hearings. If each had required the average three days, the EDP saved about 16.5 days of trial. By similar calculations, there was a savings of almost two days from the 1984 program. It is not known whether the trials held for EDP cases were any shorter than other civil jury trials. If they were, this would add to the savings, helping to further offset the time judges spent preparing for and participating in the EDP hearings.

In 1983 the trial rate appears to have been lower for EDP cases but not sufficiently to offset fully the days spent by judges in EDP hearings. The 1984 data must be considered preliminary, but they show only a small trial-rate saving through the end of the data collection period. At the time that data collection ended, it does not appear possible that the reduction in the trial rate for EDP cases in either 1983 or 1984 will be sufficient to offset the time judges spent in preparation for the program.

**Time to Disposition**

The time to disposition for the EDP and control cases was measured from the date the case was assigned to either the EDP or control group to the date of filing the document that finally closed the case in the court's records. The rate of disposition is determined by dividing the number of cases disposed at a given point by the total number of cases in the group (EDP or control, assigned or volunteer).

Figure 11 gives the cumulative disposition rates for the four groups of cases for the 1983 program; Figure 12 gives these rates for the 1984 program. For both 1983 and 1984, cases that went through the EDP were

**FIGURE 11**

**EDP and control cases disposed 1983, 30-day periods, all cases**

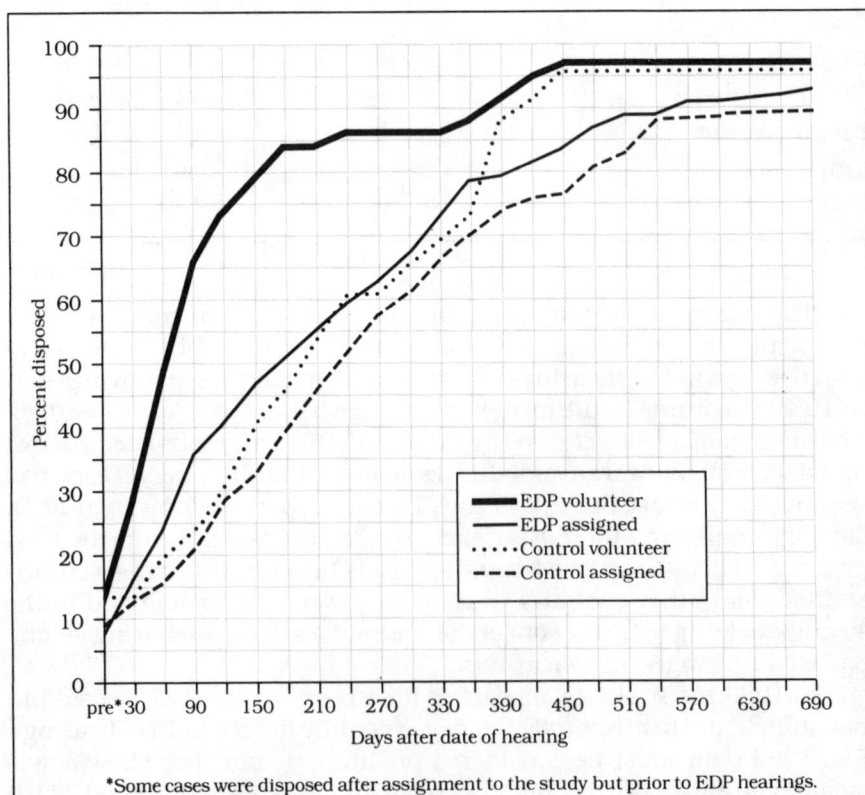

*Some cases were disposed after assignment to the study but prior to EDP hearings.

disposed of in less time than cases in the control group. The time savings are indicated in Table 40.

Comparisons of cumulative disposition rates between the EDP- and control-assigned groups and between the EDP- and control-volunteer groups are both statistically significant for 1983 data.[5] Cases that had EDP hearings were disposed at a faster rate than those that did not have hearings. The effect of the EDP program was most pronounced shortly after the EDP hearing. The effect decreased over time, but it lasted until 390 days (almost 13 months) after the hearing for cases volunteered into the program, and for more than 540 days (17 months) for cases assigned, although by that time the residual effect was small. The same positive advantage for cases going through the EDP is apparent from examining how long it took 50 percent, 75 percent, and 90 percent of each group to be disposed. In each instance, the 1983 EDP groups reached the 50th, 75th, and 90th percent levels for disposition markedly sooner than their related

**FIGURE 12**

**EDP and control cases disposed 1984, 30-day periods, all cases**

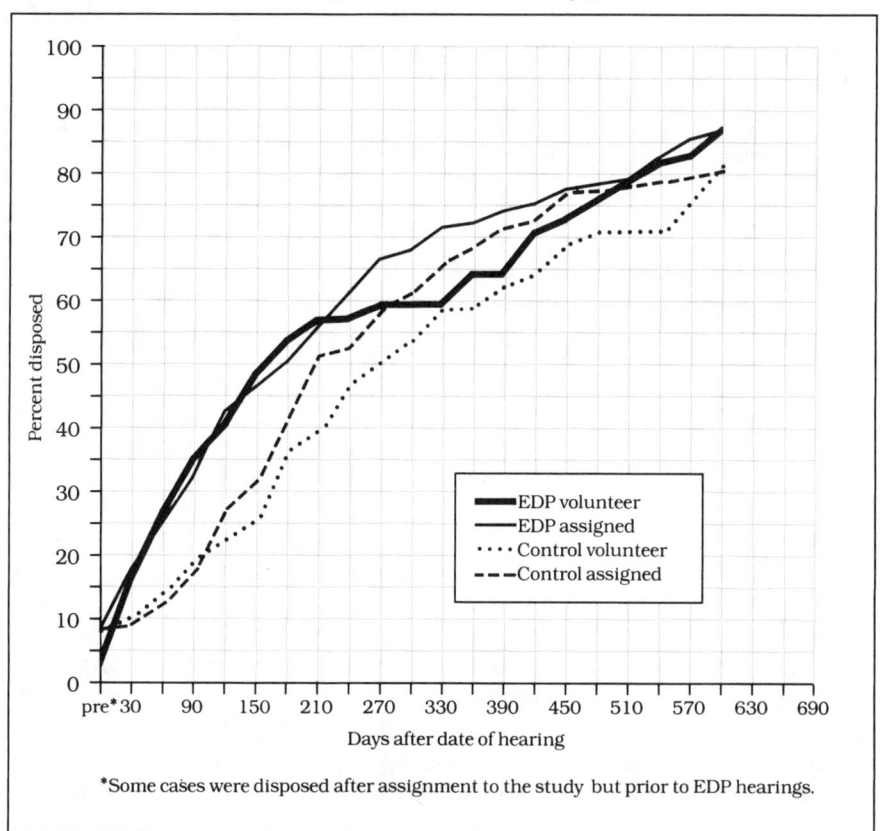

*Some cases were disposed after assignment to the study but prior to EDP hearings.

## TABLE 40
## Comparison of days to reach disposition, by percentiles

### Assigned cases

| 1983 cases | EDP | Control | Difference |
|---|---|---|---|
| 50th percentile | 175* days | 240 days | 65 days |
| 75th percentile | 340 days | 410 days | 70 days |
| 90th percentile | 555 days | 800 days | 245 days |

| 1984 cases | | | |
|---|---|---|---|
| 50th percentile | 180 days | 215 days | 35 days |
| 75th percentile | 420 days | 440 days | 20 days |
| 90th percentile | (not yet reached) | | |

### Volunteer cases

| 1983 cases | EDP | Control | Difference |
|---|---|---|---|
| 50th percentile | 60 days | 190 days | 130 days |
| 75th percentile | 130 days | 360 days | 230 days |
| 90th percentile | 390 days | 410 days | 20 days |

| 1984 cases | | | |
|---|---|---|---|
| 50th percentile | 150 days | 270 days | 120 days |
| 75th percentile | 470 days | 570 days | 100 days |
| 90th percentile | (not yet reached) | | |

*Days were estimated from the lines plotted on Figures 11 and 12.

control group. Similar results were achieved for the cases included in the program in 1984. These results are summarized in Table 40.

For the cases included in the 1983 program, the lines on Figure 11 for the volunteer cases are very different from those for the assigned cases. On Figure 12 (for the 1984 data), the roles of volunteer and assigned cases appear to have been reversed. Initially, the disposition rates for the 1984 cases most closely resemble those for the EDP and control-assigned cases from 1983. After 180 days, disposition rates for assigned cases are higher than for volunteer cases.

It is possible that the attorneys who volunteered cases for the program in 1983 were all anxious to dispose of their cases and wanted the court's assistance to accomplish this. The EDP hearing provided sufficient assistance for most of these EDP volunteer cases; most of the volunteered cases put in the control group were resolved by the opposing attorneys on their own, but not as fast as the volunteer-EDP cases were resolved.[6] Other courts may also find that there is a substantial difference in disposition rates between volunteer and assigned cases the first one or two times EDP hearings are held, as was the case the first year in Seattle. This effect dissipated in Seattle, replaced by a much clearer distinction between disposition rates for EDP- and control-group cases, whether or not volunteered.

The increased disposition rates for cases that had EDP hearings were found for all types of cases. The biggest disposition-rate differential within 90 days of the EDP hearing was found for vehicle torts (dispositions for EDP cases were 37 percentage points higher than for control cases in 1983; EDP dispositions were 27 percentage points higher in 1984), but smaller differences were also found in both 1983 and 1984 for personal injury, medical malpractice, commercial, and "other" cases (see Table 41). There was no comparison possible for domestic cases—all were assigned to the EDP program—but their rates of disposition during the first 90 days after the hearing were substantial, at 36 percent in 1983 and 67 percent in 1984.

The increased disposition rate for EDP cases was also found for cases grouped by age (see Table 42). Cases between 18 and 21 months old[7] (541 to 630 days) had the largest difference in disposition rates between EDP and control cases—a 36 percent difference in 1983 and 25 percent in 1984—but the disposition rate for EDP cases was higher for all other age groups, as well. Differences were larger for the groups in 1983.

**TABLE 41**

**Percentage of all cases disposed within 90 days of EDP hearing dates, by case type, 1983 and 1984, compared with dispositions in control group**

| | 1983 Program | | | 1984 Program | | |
|---|---|---|---|---|---|---|
| Case type | EDP | Control | Percentage points difference (EDP-Control) | EDP | Control | Percentage points difference (EDP-Control) |
| Motor vehicle tort | 51 | 14 | 37 | 35 | 8 | 27 |
| Personal injury | 28 | 11 | 17 | 28 | 11 | 17 |
| Medical malpractice | 19 | 8 | 11 | 18 | 10 | 8 |
| Commercial | 34 | 21 | 13 | 26 | 12 | 14 |
| Other civil | — | 0 | — | — | 50 | — |
| Domestic relations | 36 | — | — | 67 | — | — |
| ALL CASES | 35 | 13 | 22 | 28 | 10 | 18 |

—=No cases of this type included in this group.

**TABLE 42**

**Percentage of all cases disposed within 90 days of EDP hearing dates, by age of case, 1983 and 1984, compared with dispositions in control group**

| Days from filing to EDP hearing | 1983 Program EDP | 1983 Program Control | 1983 Percentage points difference (EDP-Control) | 1984 Program EDP | 1984 Program Control | 1984 Percentage points difference (EDP-Control) |
|---|---|---|---|---|---|---|
| 360 days or less | 27 | 7 | 20 | 30 | 0 | 30 |
| 361 to 450 days | 34 | 10 | 24 | 16 | 4 | 12 |
| 451 to 540 days | 39 | 16 | 23 | 26 | 14 | 12 |
| 541 to 630 days | 50 | 14 | 36 | 28 | 3 | 25 |
| 631 days or more | 28 | 15 | 13 | 38 | 15 | 23 |
| ALL CASES | 35 | 13 | 22 | 28 | 10 | 18 |

## Qualitative Evaluation

We conducted an assessment of the attitudes of the program participants toward the program. Questionnaires were sent out to all judges, attorney-panelists, and litigating attorneys and their clients from the 1983 hearings and a sample of these same groups from the 1984 hearings. In addition, we observed a selection of EDP hearings in 1983 and in 1984, and interviewed members of each group of participants—judges, attorney-panelists, litigating attorneys, parties who attended the conferences, and court administrative staff—in the course of our site visits. The questionnaire responses will be reviewed first.

### Questionnaire Responses

*Response rates.* Response rates for both mailings of questionnaires were similar. The highest response rates were achieved for judges and attorney-panelists, 79 percent and 78 percent, respectively (once voided questionnaires had been removed).[8] The response rates for litigating attorneys and their clients were much lower—47 percent and 16 percent, respectively. Many of the returned clients' questionnaires were attached to those of their attorneys, so there is some question about the independence of the clients' and litigating attorneys' responses.

Participants in the 1983 implementation were given the option of signing their questionnaires. Sixty-three percent of the clients, 66 percent of the litigating attorneys, and 80 percent of the judges and attorney-panelists signed them. As a result of this high voluntary return it was decided to reduce the number of questionnaires for the evaluation of the 1984 program, identify those who had returned them, and increase follow-up of the judge and attorney returns in an effort to improve the response rate. Despite a reminder letter to nonrespondents to the 1984 questionnaires, the overall response rates for the two years were approximately the same.

Analysis of the questionnaires is based only on those questionnaires returned. Items left blank have not been included in the percentages reported unless specified (i.e., "of all questionnaires returned,..."). Therefore, all percentages should be considered as, "of those answering this item, ___ percent agreed," unless specified otherwise.

*Expressions of support.* In both years all groups were largely supportive of the program. Judges and attorney-panelists rated the program 1.6 on a 5-point "worthwhileness" scale (1-very worthwhile, 3-neutral, 5-definitely not worthwhile). Litigating attorneys and their clients were less enthusiastic, but still rated the program as worthwhile (2.1 and 2.2 scores respectively, both on the worthwhile side of neutral). Attorneys and clients who volunteered to participate in the program and attorneys and clients whose cases were settled as a result of the program thought the program was more worthwhile. Client representatives of insurance companies thought the program was more worthwhile than did private clients, perhaps because the insurance company representatives had more experience with traditional court procedures and likely case outcomes.

All respondents thought that for the most part the program had lived up to their expectations. Over half (54 percent) of the litigating attorneys reported that their cases had settled before, during, or after the hearings as a direct result of the program. Many of those whose cases were not disposed reported that the program had helped to narrow issues and, as a result, would probably save some trial time, estimated at approximately 1½ days per case. The general attitudes of the three groups toward fourteen statements about the program are given in Figure 13. All three groups of respondents shared the same opinions about the program—their answers are all on the same side of the neutral position for each statement—but they hold these opinions with varying degrees of conviction. The judges and attorneys who served as panelists usually represented the most supportive position, requiring the fewest restrictions on the program. For example, they agreed most strongly of the three groups that the program worked best with cases ready for trial, but were closest to neutral on whether discovery should be complete prior to the conference.

Perhaps not surprisingly, since their experience is most limited, parties held the least strong opinions. Their answers went in the same direction as those of the panelists and litigating attorneys, but not as far.

170 FRIENDS OF THE COURT

**FIGURE 13**
**Opinion chart**
**King County Settlement Program**

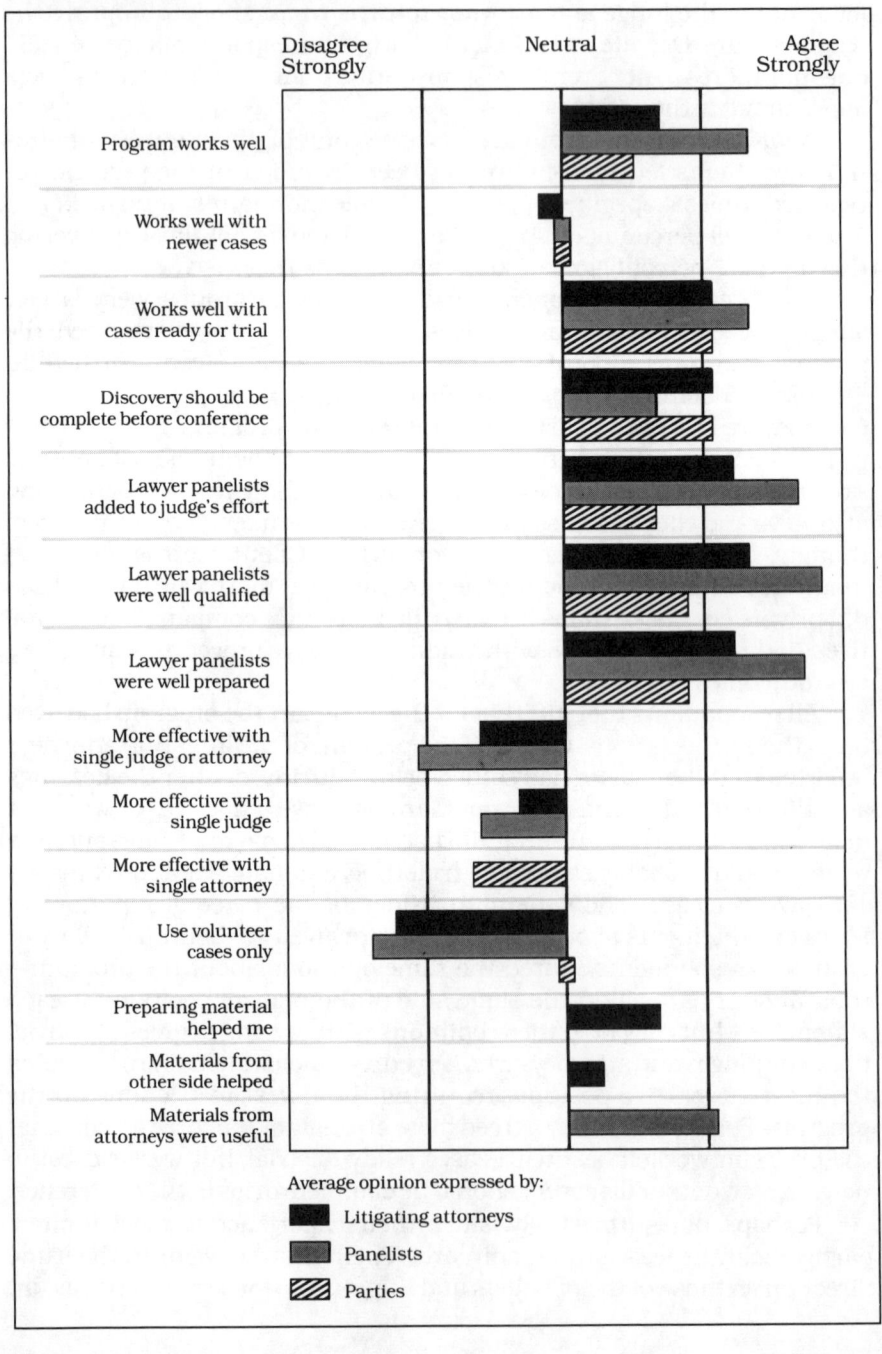

| Statement | Disagree Strongly — Neutral — Agree Strongly |
|---|---|
| Program works well | |
| Works well with newer cases | |
| Works well with cases ready for trial | |
| Discovery should be complete before conference | |
| Lawyer panelists added to judge's effort | |
| Lawyer panelists were well qualified | |
| Lawyer panelists were well prepared | |
| More effective with single judge or attorney | |
| More effective with single judge | |
| More effective with single attorney | |
| Use volunteer cases only | |
| Preparing material helped me | |
| Materials from other side helped | |
| Materials from attorneys were useful | |

Average opinion expressed by:
■ Litigating attorneys
▓ Panelists
▨ Parties

On most items, the pattern of responses showed the panelists farthest away from neutral, then the litigating attorneys, with clients closest to a neutral position.

### Interview Responses

*Composition of the panel.* The interviews with the panelists and litigating attorneys reflected much the same information that was collected on the questionnaires. The program participants all continued to make supportive statements. They liked the design of the program, in particular the composition of the panels: one judge, one plaintiff's attorney, and one defense attorney. This arrangement was thought to strike a good balance, increasing the credibility of the recommendation of the panel to both sides of a case. One of the panelists said that he thought an opinion about weaknesses or problems with a case carried more weight when it came from an attorney on the same side. The composition of the panels was cited as the reason for many of the settlements that occurred.

*Quality of attorney-panelists.* All participants were satisfied on the whole with the quality of the attorneys who served on the panels. They were described as being well qualified and, by some, as a "blue ribbon" group.[9]

*Presence of a judge on the panel.* Litigating attorneys stated that it was important to them to include a judge on the EDP panels to help "sell" the opinion of the panel to their clients. The judge served as a balance and in many instances was a key to settlement. Judge-panelists echoed this view. The presence of the judge on the panel, they said, requires that the participants take the recommendation of the panel seriously.

*Preparation time and materials submitted.* The panelist-attorneys spent varying amounts of time preparing for the EDP hearings. One attorney estimated that he spent up to two hours preparing each case for the conference. Most found the materials submitted by the opposing sides to be helpful, although in some cases they also were thought to be too voluminous. A few of the panelists indicated that they were dismayed at the quality of the briefs submitted and the oral presentations of some of the attorneys at the EDP hearings. This is a concern that was echoed at most of the study sites in this project. This increased awareness by experienced attorneys of the work product normally provided to the court is one of the incidental positive aspects of improved relations between bench and bar from this type of program.

Litigating attorneys reported that preparing materials and briefs for the hearings had helped them focus their thinking about their own cases. The materials prepared by the opposing side had been helpful to them and they assumed that what they had prepared was useful to their opponents, as well.

*Conflicts of interest.* Resolving conflict of interest situations did not constitute the major problem that program participants had anticipated it might be. There were many instances of potential conflicts of interest, but when major relationships between panel attorneys and litigators or parties surfaced, they were resolved by transferring the case in question to another EDP panel. There were a few instances in medical malpractice panels, because the medical malpractice bar is fairly small, where a junior member of a law firm sat on a panel that heard a case presented by one of the firm's senior members, but neither the panelists nor the other litigating attorneys reported any undue discomfort with the situation.[10]

*Reflections of parties.* Clients who attended the EDP hearings and were interviewed appeared to have benefited from the experience. Their observation of the process and their hearing the presentation of the panel were instrumental in convincing many clients to accept a settlement offer. Many cases settled at or near the figure recommended by the panel.

*Perceived effect of program.* Litigating attorneys whose cases were settled after the EDP hearings were unable to say whether they thought that without the program their case would have gone to trial. Even before the EDP program this court had a reasonably low trial rate, so most of these cases would have been expected to be disposed without trial anyway.

*Secondary effect of EDP.* One proposition tested in both the questionnaires and interviews was that settlement conferences may have a beneficial effect on cases that are not settled by narrowing the issues to the dispute and, as a consequence, saving trial time. Although the questionnaire responses indicated that some trials might have been shortened, few of the litigating attorneys interviewed whose cases were not yet disposed at the time of their interview thought that this had taken place. The EDP hearings may have been scheduled too far in advance of the scheduled trial date (four to six months) for this type of effect to be apparent.

*Differences between 1983 and 1984 programs.* Panelists and litigating attorneys who had participated in both the 1983 and 1984 EDP hearings noted that the cases heard in 1984 seemed to be less "mature" and to some extent not as significant in terms of dollars at issue as those heard in 1983.[11] The interviewers also sensed that participants in the 1984 program felt it had not been as successful as the one in 1983. There seemed to have been fewer cases reported as settled immediately after the hearings and many of the cases presented did not seem to be as prepared to discuss settlement as in 1983.

*Concerns of judges.* Although the judges of the court were very supportive of the program in their questionnaire responses, they identified some of their concerns about and objections to it during interviews.

These objections surfaced particularly in interviews conducted at the conclusion of the hearings held in 1984. The judges thought that fewer cases had been disposed immediately after this set of hearings than they had observed the previous year and they were beginning to question whether the amount of time they were taking away from their regular duties was producing any real benefit. They recognized that disposing of cases earlier might save the litigants money and might be appreciated by the litigants, but thought that the number of litigants and the amount of money saved was insignificant in relation to the size of the civil caseload of the court and the amount of time they had devoted to the program. One judge pointed out that any litigant who wants a judge to conduct a settlement conference can get one without the EDP.

The judges thought that some of the unique features of this program—the three-member panel, the requirement that the litigants report back to the court if they arrived at a settlement, and the assignment of cases to the program—were valuable, but not sufficient to merit its continuation. At the end of the second set of EDP hearings, most of the judges interviewed were opposed to it in varying degrees. The questions included in the questionnaire did not elicit these negative responses, probably because they did not focus on the relationship between the benefits and costs of the program.

## Costs and Administrative Issues

In designing a program like this, many decisions must be made on how the program is to be implemented. Although they are administrative in nature, they have a direct effect on the outcome of the program. Participants in the program were asked for their opinions on how the program had been designed.

### Costs

Project staff asked the participants involved in the planning, implementation, and monitoring of the 1984 EDP to estimate the amount of time they spent to support the program.

Attorney-panelists served without compensation, so this potential cost was not incurred by the court.

Probably the major cost to the court, in terms of time spent, was the time the judges devoted to reviewing documents submitted and participating on the panels. In 1983, judges of the court spent approximately 23 days on the program; they spent 27 days in 1984. Some of this time was offset by the trial days that are assumed to have been saved as a result of the reduced trial rate in 1983 and length of trials brought about by the program.

The chief judge estimated he spent between 20 and 30 hours in program administration each year, including participation in the initial discussions of establishing the program and formulating its design, reviewing the necessary forms and notices, and responding to individual requests from litigants to be excused from participation. The trial court administrator estimated that he spent between 20 and 30 hours performing tasks related to EDP administration in 1983 and 10 to 15 hours in 1984.

The arbitration supervisor coordinated the attorney-panelist list and supervised the distribution of all necessary notices and forms to judge- and attorney-panelists and litigating attorneys. After the hearings, she coordinated the distribution of the questionnaires and follow-up reminders to a sample of each group of program participants. She also served as a liaison for the court with the staff at the state office of the administrator for the courts who prepared the caseload analysis. These tasks took 618.5 hours, including 36.5 overtime hours. She was supported in these tasks by two temporary clerical employees who spent a total of 625.3 hours. The combined costs of the salaries for these three was $11,062. Staff of the administrative office spent between 50 and 60 days each year helping to set up the program and conduct the caseload portion of the evaluation. (These are not out-of-pocket expenses, as the salaries would have been paid anyway, but they represent the cost of deferring other tasks.) The court also spent $212 for postage and $177 for printing and copying.

There was no estimate of the amount of time the arbitration coordinator, the arbitration secretary, and court bailiffs contributed to program support.

### Administrative Issues

*Timing of the hearings in relation to the trial date.* Cases selected for EDP could be expected to have a jury trial scheduled for a date within the next 12 months. Several of the attorneys interviewed said that they had not yet begun to prepare for trial before the EDP hearing. Discovery was complete for a larger proportion of cases assigned to EDP in 1983 than in 1984. Some attorneys in both 1983 and 1984 said that their case was not appropriate for the program because of the absence of substantial discovery and, therefore, the absence of a basis for making a reasoned settlement decision. Some for whom discovery was only partially complete had found the conference to be worthwhile nonetheless.

*Mandatory vs. voluntary participation.* Timing of the conferences is related to whether participation should be voluntary or mandatory. Most attorneys interviewed thought that EDP should continue to be a mandatory program. Some thought that attorneys whose cases have been assigned to the program should be permitted to remove their cases if they think that the conference is not appropriate at that time because discovery is not sufficiently complete. This outlet, if strictly monitored, could add to the "appearance of justice" aspect of EDP. Few attorneys thought that the program would be effective if it became entirely voluntary. The majority of judges agreed.

*Time of year conference held.* Most attorneys and judges thought that holding the hearings once a year was sufficient. There were a few suggestions to move the program to the summer, when attorneys usually are less busy, but most preferred to keep to the fall schedule. One attorney said he thought that Thanksgiving week was a good time for the conferences because people are in a more "generous" and "giving" mood at that time of the year.

*Types of cases assigned.* There were some perceived differences, mentioned above, between the types of cases assigned to the program in 1983 and 1984. Beyond those observations, there were two contrasting views on what types of cases should be emphasized. One group wanted to concentrate EDP hearings on complex cases that are expected to require lengthy trials. In contrast, several attorneys suggested that simpler cases be assigned to the program since they make up the bulk of the court's caseload. This question can be answered only by new research, in which each case is identified by its degree of complexity.

*Notifying the bar.* A few of the lawyers did not think that there had been adequate information given to the bar about the program. Many, even some attorney-panelists, were unaware that cases could be volunteered.

## Overall Assessment

The program met one of its caseload-related goals, reducing the average time from at-issue to disposition, but it did not result in enough of a reduction in the number of trials held to offset sufficiently the time required of the judges to conduct the EDP hearings. In the course of their discussions about whether to continue the program in 1985 and beyond, it became clear that significantly reducing the number of trials was the judges' main goal for the program. Because that goal was not achieved, the program was discontinued.

The program provided some positive effects on case processing, however. The time to disposition for cases participating in the program, especially in 1983, was shortened materially. Attorneys report that they and their clients view this improvement as a positive achievement. A number of attorneys also believe clients saved some money as a result. Relations between the bench and bar, as represented by the attorney-panelists, were fostered. The bar was almost universally supportive of the program and was happy to see it continued after the first year. Even those who were not happy initially to have their cases assigned to the program felt that they had received some benefit from participation—an increased understanding of their case, anticipated reduced trial time for some, and, in some instances, disposed cases.

The experience of this court demonstrates that, in addition to setting goals for a program before it is implemented, it is equally important to establish priorities among those goals. All the goals for EDP in 1983 and 1984 were met, but after the program had been in use it became clear that one goal, reducing the number of trials, had not been met sufficiently. The goals of reducing time to disposition, improving bar relations, and improving efficiency were important to the program participants, but reducing trials was most important to the judges and this was not fully understood—perhaps even by some of the judges—until after the second EDP. When the program was extended into 1984, this heightened expectations among the bench and bar. The court may have experienced a slight complacency or diminution in bar support during the program's second year specifically because the question of priorities among goals was not fully addressed at the outset.

If improved time to disposition has a higher priority in other courts, the use of adjuncts in an early settlement program may be more attractive. Other courts might benefit, however, by keeping the following in mind:

1. EDP may not reduce trial rates significantly. The trial rate for 1983 cases had been reduced at the time this report was written (fall 1986) from 12.3 to 9.6 percent and for 1984 cases from 13.2 to 12.8 in this court. Most cases settled as a result of an EDP hearing probably would not have gone to trial anyway. Other courts (notably, the Superior Court of Alameda County, California) have noticed a substantial drop in the number of trials for cases exposed to EDP.
2. EDP has the greatest impact on "mature" cases and cases that ask to be included in the program.
3. The program can foster improved relations between the bench and bar and enhanced regard for the court both among litigating attorneys and attorneys who serve as panelists.

# Notes to Chapter Twelve

1. Civil jurisdiction is concurrent with the limited jurisdiction courts up to $7,500 and exclusive above.

2. There were 9 panels for personal injury, 2 for medical malpractice, 2 for commercial, and 1 for domestic relations cases.

3. EDP in other courts has resulted in reduced trial rates as well. The trial rate for EDP cases in the Superior Court of Alameda County (Oakland), California, was half that of the trial rate for control cases, 5 percent and 10 percent, respectively. ("Early Disposition Program," a memorandum prepared by Stanley Collis, Executive Officer, Alameda County Superior Court, page 5.)

4. See, e.g., D. Dodge & S. Hathaway, "Waiting, Waiting for the Court," *Judges Journal*, vol. 24, no. 3 (Summer 1985), at p. 22.

5. The Kolmogorov-Smirnov test statistic produced a probability level of between .1 and .05 for the assigned cases and less than .001 for the volunteer cases. This test is not distribution-specific and is used to measure differences between cumulative distribution functions like those graphed here.

6. We note, too, that the rate of disposition prior to the hearing was higher for both groups of volunteer cases than it was for either the EDP- or control-assigned cases, cases that the attorneys presumably were not as anxious to dispose.

7. Most civil jury trials occur in this court when the case is between 18 and 21 months old.

8. Questionnaires were voided for two major reasons—lost in the mail prior to delivery to the potential responder and case dropped from the program or disposed before the settlement conference.

9. One attorney objected to the use of the term "blue ribbon" because he felt that this suggested that all or most of the participants were from larger law firms. Most respondents understood the term to mean "highly qualified and more respected" attorneys.

10. This occurred in 1983. It was reported after the 1984 program by an attorney *not* in the firm involved that there was "talk" that this situation caused problems within the firm after the 1983 EDP hearings.

11. In fact, the age distribution of cases in the two years indicates that 1984 cases generally were older than 1983 cases.

APPENDIX A

# The Use of Judges Pro Tempore as Mental Health Judges in the Pima County (Tucson, Arizona) Superior Court

A paper prepared by Roberta L. Tepper

## Introduction and Background

The use of judges *pro tempore* to conduct mental health hearings in the Pima County (Tucson, Arizona) Superior Court lasted six months, from January through June 1984. Previously, a judge *pro tem* would be used occasionally to conduct mental health hearings, but strictly on an emergency basis. The use was relatively uncommon, despite the fact that the superior court made frequent use of (and continues to use) judges *pro tempore* for other matters.

Shortly before January 1984 the superior court was faced with both a temporary shortage of court commissioners and a period of budgetary constraint that made appointment of any new court commissioners impossible. The fiscal outlook made it obvious that the judicial ranks would not be replenished until at least July 1984.

With this in mind, Judge Alice Truman, a probate judge (who, pursuant to local rule, was responsible for mental health adjudications), and Judge William Sherrill proposed the use of judges *pro tempore* to conduct mental health hearings on a more regular basis. Though the use was planned, it was never intended for the judges *pro tem* to become an integral part of the judiciary of the superior court; the use of the judges *pro tempore* was minimal and only temporary, ending with the appointment of a new court commissioner.

Judge Sherrill was a court commissioner prior to his appointment to the superior court bench, had served as a mental health judge on many occasions, and was familiar with the needs and requirements of those hearings. After his elevation to the bench, Judge Sherrill continued to conduct a large number of the mental health hearings because of his familiarity with the area and the lack of a replacement. This burdened the superior court bench, which was already relying on the services of judges *pro tem* to take up the slack in the other areas. Even after the implementation of the judge *pro tem* program for mental health hearings, Judge Sherrill continued to hear a substantial number of the mental health matters.

The then presiding judge, William Druke, gave his consent to the proposed use. Judges Truman and Sherrill then selected a number of attorneys who had already been approved and appointed as judges *pro tempore* for other matters and requested their assistance. Some other attorneys, also already serving as judges *pro tem*, volunteered for this use and were accepted.

This use of judges *pro tem*, though necessary at the time, was viewed with some reservations by Judge Truman on account of the complexity of the law in the area. This hesitancy may explain why the use of judges *pro tempore* was always viewed as merely a temporary solution and not the creation of a new and continuing judicial resource, as well as why the judges *pro tem* were never used as frequently as possible. Despite her reservations, the use was begun and continued until July 1984, when Margaret Houghton (one of the judges *pro tem*) was appointed as the newest court commissioner.

## Actual Use

In January through June 1984, a total of 41 mental health commitment hearings were actually conducted. A varying number of cases each month were set for hearing; some scheduled hearings were canceled (also in varying numbers), usually after the voluntary commitment of the patient.

**TABLE A-1**
**Mental health hearings, January-June 1984**

| Month | Total number of hearings | Hearings by judges/commissioners | Hearings by judges *pro tem* |
|---|---|---|---|
| January | 12 | 7 | 5 |
| February | 10 | 4 | 6 |
| March | 2 | 1 | 1 |
| April | 2 | 1 | 1 |
| May | 8 | 5 | 3 |
| June | 7 | 6 | 1 |
| TOTAL | 41 | 24 (59%) | 17 (41%) |

Superior court judges or commissioners conducted a total of 24 hearings (59 percent of the 41 total) and judges *pro tempore* conducted the remaining 17 (41 percent). Of the 24 hearings conducted by judges or commissioners, Judge Sherrill conducted 9.

Time spent in preparation for each case varied with the complexity of the case and the size of the client's file. Some judges *pro tem* reviewed the statutes before each hearing, others did not. Preparation time for those *pro tems* conducting their first mental health hearings ranged from 30 minutes to a few hours. Those *pro tems* who had experience were able to review a case and prepare in an average of 15 minutes per case.

## Selection

Selection of *pro tem* judges was made informally from among those attorneys already appointed and serving as judges *pro tem* for the court. Judge Truman and Judge Sherrill recruited those *pro tem* judges they felt had some familiarity with either the probate field or mental health law, and/or could quickly gain the required knowledge—in other words, attorneys they had confidence in. Two of the judges *pro tem* volunteered once they learned of the proposed use for mental health matters.

Although experience in probate or with mental health law was a factor in the judges' decision, it was not determinative. In fact, a number of *pro tem* judges interviewed had neither exposure to nor experience in mental health law prior to conducting these hearings, although some had done a bit of probate work. All of the attorneys selected had practiced law locally for a number of years in private or government practice.

Only two of the *pro tem* judges had substantial experience in the field of mental health law. One had been the Pima County public fiduciary before returning to private practice. The other had been a magistrate in the Tucson City Court and had been exposed to competency determinations. In that context, however, her determinations had been based on reports and recommendations submitted by the court clinic or local mental health services.

## Training

Minimal training was provided to some of the judges *pro tem* at a lunchtime meeting with Judges Truman and Sherrill. It covered mostly administrative matters: how to complete the required forms, minute entries, the use of the tape recorders used to record the proceedings, and a brief review of the applicable statutes. Other *pro tem* judges serving in this capacity received no training. All found their own "style" with experience.

All judges *pro tem* reviewed the applicable statutes and law prior to conducting their first hearings and felt competent in the area. Of course, since they were already serving as judges *pro tem* for other matters in the superior court, they were not inexperienced in filling the judicial role. The time each *pro tem* judge spent in preparing varied with each case.

As all the judges *pro tem* had previous experience in serving a judicial function, they all had experience in decision-making under pressure and in relatively short periods of time. None expressed concern over his or her ability to make fair and equitable decisions regarding the client's status or continued commitment.

Though the minimal training was considered sufficient overall by the judges *pro tem*, some expressed their initial discomfort in serving the first time. One *pro tem* judge suggested that a walk-through of a simulated hearing would have been helpful. It is a matter of speculation, however, whether additional training would have alleviated the feelings of initial discomfort.

## Why They Volunteered or Agreed to Serve

Most of the *pro tem* judges were flattered to have been asked to serve for mental health hearings; that sense of flattery played a large role in their acceptance. Similarly, most were already interested in the field. A number of the judges *pro tem* have or had ambitions to the judiciary in the future and this was seen as a way of "auditioning" and gaining some valuable experience. Some were in need of time away from the grind of practice and this was an interesting break. A number cited their belief that attorneys should provide some kind of service to the community.

## Benefits in the Use of Judges *Pro Tempore*

### To the Court and System

Obviously, the most immediate benefit of using *pro tem* judges was the extension of the limited judicial resources of the court. This extension could have been greater, however, had the decision been made to integrate the judges *pro tem* into the regular assignment for mental health hearings rather than use them solely as an emergency resource. A number of the *pro tem* judges expressed some frustration at having been underutilized during this period. They felt that had a more organized scheduling mechanism been established, with each judge *pro tem* assigned to a different day or a certain time slot, their utilization might have increased. Of course, this betrays the *pro tems*' erroneous assumption that they were to be an integral part of the judiciary, much the way judges *pro tem* are used for other matters in the court. As it was, only when a judge or commissioner could not be scheduled to conduct a hearing would the judges *pro tem* be called upon. As most of the *pro tem* judges were willing to volunteer larger amounts of their time, this would seem to be a waste of a potential (and permanent) resource.

Another benefit to the system in general was cited by one of the *pro tem* judges, who felt that not having been routinely exposed to the mental health adjudication process, and therefore not "hardened" to it, the judges *pro tem* were more likely to view their role as problem-solving rather than adjudicative. This "fresh perspective" was viewed as a benefit, not only by a number of the judges *pro tempore* but also by the other attorneys involved in the process.

It was the general consensus that the judges *pro tem* tended to be less of a "rubber stamp" for the state and truly addressed the merits of the petition and the client's presentation, rather than giving the client's claims perfunctory attention before granting the action requested in the petition. Related to this was the perception that *pro tem* judges tended to be more concerned and conscientious regarding the client's civil liberties and due process rights. This perception was that the judges *pro tem* were more likely to "put the state to its proof" than the judges or commissioners. One wonders whether this was not a kind of "honeymoon," as none of the judges *pro tem* served more than a couple of times.

An interesting observation by one attorney interviewed was that commissioners were generally viewed as taking the "better-safe-than-sorry" route and tended to commit patients more easily. One of the *pro tem* judges cited an example that brought great satisfaction and illustrates a problem-solving approach. At the *pro tem's* request, the hospital staff drew up an alternative treatment plan to avoid committing the patient. The plan of supervised therapy was so successful that the patient was released to an outpatient treatment facility.

The number of mental hearings conducted during the period *pro tems* were used is too small to provide a basis for a reliable statistical analysis of the dispositions of the cases. Nevertheless, the dispositions do not indicate, on their face, an inclination on the part of the *pro tems* to be any less likely to commit the clients than the judges and commissioners. The dispositions of the 41 hearings held for January through June 1984 show similar patterns between *pro tems* and judges/commissioners.

In almost all cases, the clients were not told of the status of the judge *pro tem*. Most of the attorneys felt that even if the client had been informed, it would not have made a difference, for a number of reasons. Among the reasons were clients' generally tenuous mental state and their lack of knowledge about the court system. The only problem was encountered when clients did not believe that the women *pro tem* judges were judges because they were women. This is a problem not limited to judges *pro tem*, however, nor to mental health hearings.

## TABLE A-2
### Mental health hearing dispositions

| Dispositions | Guardian appointed, no commitment | Petition dismissed | Commitment ordered | TOTAL |
|---|---|---|---|---|
| Pro tems | 1 | 2 | 14 | 17 |
| Judges/ Commissioners | 4 | 1 | 19 | 24 |

**Length of commitment ordered**

| | 60 days or less | 90 days or less | 180 days or less | 1 year or less | Undetermined |
|---|---|---|---|---|---|
| Pro tems | 3 | 4 | 5 | 2 | 0 |
| Judges/ Commissioners | 1 | 7 | 6 | 4 | 1 |

### To the Judges *Pro Tem*

This utilization of judges *pro tem* enabled the individuals involved to get either their first or increased exposure to this area of the law, an area most private practitioners do not get the opportunity to be involved in; it was also seen as an opportunity to be involved in the area. It was seen, too, as a way to get training toward ambitions of eventually entering the judiciary. One *pro tem* judge found it useful in gaining perspective into a judge's role. Another cited being a *pro tem* judge as an acceptable way to get away from the daily grind of private practice yet remain legally active. Most continued to hear other matters as judges *pro tem* during this time.

# Problems in the Use of Judges *Pro Tempore*

### The Court's View

There were no major problems in the use of the judges *pro tem* in conducting mental health hearings. The minor problems encountered were difficulty in contacting the judge *pro tem* when necessary regarding follow-up approval of treatment plans, and in completing additional paperwork. This meant that Judge Truman usually had to complete that extra work, rather than delay processing of the case. Thus, additional work was created for Judge Truman, though in general the system benefited. Occasionally a *pro tem* judge would take a case under advisement, causing a delay in either releasing or committing the individual. This was rare, however, and not much of a problem.

## The Attorneys' View

The judges *pro tem* were criticized by the attorneys involved on a limited number of grounds. Perhaps feedback by the attorneys or the court could have solved these relatively minor problems. One attorney felt that the judges *pro tem* had control problems, both in controlling the flow of the hearing and in controlling their own reactions when faced with the aberrant behavior of the clients. The same attorney felt that the *pro tem* judges were not sufficiently removed from their role as advocates and found that they would criticize the participating attorneys or tend to "take sides." This was seen not necessarily as a deliberate decision but rather as an unconscious inability to relinquish the role of advocate. One attorney felt that in that way the judges *pro tem* tended to interfere with one party's presentation and handling of the case. Had there been more supervision or feedback to the judges *pro tem*, these nondeliberate mannerisms possibly could have been eliminated.

## The *Pro Tem* Judges' View

There was no feedback from the court on the performance of *pro tem* judges, either positive or negative, making improving their performance or changing their "style" difficult. For some, with little prior experience in the mental health area, that would have been helpful. Usually the judge *pro tem* had no later information about the progress of a case he or she had presided over, and this lack was mildly frustrating for some of them. The problems of scheduling were more troubling to some of the *pro tems*. A request to be scheduled on a specific day was usually ignored or forgotten. As most of the *pro tems* understood the last-minute nature of some of the hearings, however, this was a minor irritant.

None of the judges *pro tem* felt that cases were "dumped" on them. Had they been used more often, perhaps that perception might have arisen. With their minimal use, though, no one felt that the only reason they were being used was to get rid of unpopular cases.

## Administrative Problems

A number of the recurring problems have already been discussed in previous sections. Since most of the judges *pro tem* had relatively flexible schedules, the lack of advance notice of need for their service normally was not a problem. Because of the small number of judges *pro tem* being used, only 5 out of a possible 8 to 10, the scheduling clerk was able to call the attorneys to confirm availability before scheduling them to conduct a hearing.

Neither the county attorney, public defender, nor the public fiduciary ever objected to the scheduling of a *pro tem* judge, other than some nonserious, idle complaining. Filing for a change of judge never occurred, according to the scheduling clerk. As cases were rarely, if ever, continued, notice problems did not occur. The staff of the court administrator's office had no problems with the paperwork completed by the *pro tem* judges or with contracting them for any necessary revisions.

## Are Lawyers Especially Good or Bad for This Purpose?

As discussed previously, most attorneys involved had relatively few complaints about the performance of the judges *pro tem*. In fact, for most, a *pro tem* judge would be as good as, if not preferable to, a judge or commissioner, for the reasons discussed above, complaints notwithstanding. The general perception was that *pro tem* judges tended to take the proceedings very seriously and gave them their total concentration, perhaps because they were inexperienced in the field. The "fresh perspective" of the *pro tems*, their willingness to hear the clients out, and their enthusiasm were considered advantages. Despite the misgivings of Judge Truman, it seems that *pro tem* judges helped the court and the process and were positive factors in these matters.

APPENDIX B

# Administrative Orders of Division One of the Arizona Court of Appeals

IN THE COURT OF APPEALS
STATE OF ARIZONA
DIVISION ONE

IN RE THE USE OF JUDGES PRO
TEMPORE IN DIVISION ONE,
ARIZONA COURT OF APPEALS  **ADMINISTRATIVE ORDER**

**1. Preamble.** The Court of Appeals, Division One, is currently facing a substantial delay in the disposition of civil appeals where oral argument has been requested. In order to relieve this backlog and to expedite the disposition of such appeals, the Court has determined to enlist the assistance of state bar members to serve as judges *pro tempore*. This procedure is authorized by A.R.S. § 12-146. By administrative order dated April 13, 1984, the Arizona Supreme Court has authorized a temporary department of Division One for this purpose. This department has been designated Department E.

**2. Composition.** Department E shall be composed of one judge currently serving on Division One and two judges *pro tempore*. Assignments of judges and judges *pro tempore* to Department E shall be made by the Chief Judge. The Division One judge shall be the presiding judge.

**3. Cases.** Department E shall consider only civil appeals in which oral argument has been requested. A normal weekly calendar for Department E shall consist of three such civil appeals.

**4. Meetings.** Department E shall hear cases once a week for the period September, 1984, through December, 1985. Department E may meet more or less frequently as the Chief Judge deems necessary.

**5. Memorandum Decisions.** All cases assigned to Department E shall be disposed of by memorandum decisions as provided for in Rule 28, Arizona Rules of Civil Appellate Procedure.

**6. Selection of Judges *Pro Tempore*.** The Chief Judge shall be responsible for maintaining a list of qualified individuals to serve as judges *pro tempore*. Requests for appointment as a judge *pro tempore* shall be made by the Chief Judge to the Chief Justice of the Arizona Supreme Court who shall, in his discretion, make the appointment. Judges *pro tempore* shall have the qualifications required by A.R.S. §12-146.A. and shall have the appropriate demeanor, reputation and knowledge of the law which, in the opinion of the Chief Judge and Chief Justice, qualify them to serve.

**7. Disqualification.** Judges *pro tempore* shall disqualify themselves from cases in accordance with Canon 3(c) of the Code of Judicial Conduct. In addition, judges *pro tempore* shall otherwise comply with the Code of Judicial Conduct where applicable. Prior to permanent assignment of a judge *pro tempore* to an individual case, a proposed list of *pro tempore* judges shall be submitted to all the parties to that appeal. Within ten days after mailing of the list to the parties, any party to the appeal may disqualify a specified number of the judges *pro tempore* submitted by so advising the Court in writing.

DATED this 7th day of May, 1984.

EINO M. JACOBSON, Chief Judge

# ARIZONA COURT OF APPEALS, DIVISION ONE TEMPORARY DEPARTMENT E INTERNAL OPERATING GUIDELINES

**Introduction.** In accordance with administrative orders of this Court and the Arizona Supreme Court, effective with the Court's September 1984 calendar there shall be established a temporary Department E. The administration of this Department shall be governed by these guidelines and this Court's administrative order of May 7, 1984.

**Timetable.** In order for Department E to be operational by September 1984 the following timetable is established.

| Activity | Completion Date |
| --- | --- |
| Each Division One judge recommends 20 names to Chief Judge | April 1 |
| Invitations sent by Chief Judge | May 1 |
| Invitation to serve as judges *pro tempore* accepted | May 15 |
| Chief Justice appoints judges *pro tempore* | July 1 |
| Cases for Department E identified (September-December) | July 1 |
| List of cases and counsel sent to judges *pro tempore* to identify conflicts | July 1 |
| List of *pro tempore* judges sent to parties for disqualifications | July 1 |
| Panels set and cases for Department E calendared internally | July 15 |
| The process repeats itself for the period January 1985 through June 1985 | |

**Selection of Judges *Pro Tempore*.** The primary means which will be used to select *pro tempore* judges will be through recommendation by present Division One judges. By April 1, 1984, each Division One judge should suggest twenty attorneys to the Chief Judge. In making these recommendations, judges should consider the statutory qualifications of A.R.S. §12-146.A. as well as the attorney's demeanor, reputation and knowledge of the law. These names, and others which may be received by the Chief Judge, will be screened by him and invitations sent to such attorneys by May 1, 1984. Invitations shall be accepted by May 15, 1984. Appointment will be made by the Chief Justice effective July 1, 1984, for a six-month period in accordance with A.R.S. § 12-147.B.

**Selection of Cases.** Cases to be assigned to Department E shall be evaluated by the following criteria. First, cases should be those which would likely be disposed of as memorandum decisions. Second, cases should be of moderate difficulty, according to our internal weighting guidelines. In this way, the more difficult cases will be heard by panels of three judges as well as the relatively simple matters which should be handled pursuant to our "decision by the court." Third, cases should be chosen from the "oldest" on our at-issue list. The staff should identify these cases by July 1, 1984.

**Disqualification.** In order to assure maximum acceptance of this project, liberal procedures for disqualification will be followed. This will be true both from the standpoint of *pro tempore* disqualifications and disqualifications requested by the litigants.

By July 1, 1984, the judges *pro tempore* will have been identified and a list of such individuals will be mailed to counsel for cases calendared for Department E. Each party separately represented shall be entitled to peremptorily challenge any *pro tempore* judge appearing on the list. When the list is returned to the Court, the panel for each case shall be made up of individuals who have not been challenged by any party.

Similarly, judges *pro tempore* shall be sent a list of all cases to be calendared during September through December. The list will include names of parties and counsel appearing. Each *pro tempore* judge shall indicate each case in which he or she should be disqualified. Judges *pro tempore* shall disqualify themselves in accordance with the same standards applicable to judges.

**Presiding Judge Duties.** The presiding judge for each Department E panel will be a Division One judge. Each judge will serve on Department E once every twelve weeks. By June 15, the clerk shall advise each presiding judge of the proposed date for his or her panel and the tentatively assigned *pro tempore* judges. The presiding judge shall confirm with each *pro tempore* judge his or her availability to sit on the date in question. Once confirmed, that information will be forwarded to the clerk who will then prepare the calendar by July 15. The presiding judge will be responsible for sending one set of the briefs to the *pro tempore* judge prior to argument. The presiding judge will be responsible for scheduling conferences, monitoring the post-argument procedures and distributing all post-decision motions. *Pro tempore* judges who desire to review the record prior to oral argument should do so in the clerk's office. Judges *pro tempore* may take the record with them after oral argument.

**Clerk's Responsibilities.** The clerk will carry out all functions in support of Department E as is currently done with respect to existing departments. In addition, the clerk will be responsible for distributing invitations to attorneys, receiving responses and preparing supreme court appointments, doing all mailings necessary to identify disqualifications and calendaring panels so as to avoid conflicts.

# IN THE SUPREME COURT OF THE STATE OF ARIZONA

IN RE THE USE OF JUDGES PRO TEMPORE
IN DIVISION ONE, ARIZONA COURT
OF APPEALS

**ADMINISTRATIVE ORDER 84-3**

Pursuant to Article 6, §3 of the Arizona Constitution and A.R.S. §12-147.A. (Supp. 1983), it is

ORDERED, there is established a temporary department of the Arizona Court of Appeals, Division One. This temporary department shall be designated as Department E and shall be convened as of September 1, 1984, and shall remain convened until December 31, 1985.

Upon request of the Chief Judge of the Court of Appeals, Division One, the Chief Justice may appoint judges *pro tempore* to Department E in accordance with A.R.S. § 12-146.

DATED this 13th day of April, 1984.

WILLIAM A. HOLOHAN, Chief Justice

# Letter to
# Prospective *Pro Tem* Judges

Dear _____

Division One of the Arizona Court of Appeals, in an attempt to reduce the backlog of civil cases in which oral argument has been requested, has decided to enlist the aid of the State Bar through the use of judges *pro tempore*.

This effort has been approved by the Arizona Supreme Court and has been implemented by the attached administrative order. In order for this program to succeed, we need the assistance of members of the State Bar to serve as judges *pro tempore* in the Court of Appeals.

Because I believe that you meet the qualifications described in the enclosed administrative order, I cordially invite you to serve as such a judge *pro tempore* and participate in this national demonstration project.

Before accepting this invitation, please consider the following:

1. That you will be asked to sit on one court calendar, consisting of three civil cases.

2. You will be expected to read all the briefs for your calendar and be prepared to rule on the issues presented.

3. You will be required to attend a pre-oral argument conference, oral argument and a post-oral argument conference. These conferences will all be scheduled on Wednesday of each week.

4. You will be required to write a proposed disposition in one of the civil cases heard, and distribute that proposed draft within 30 days of the argument.

5. You will be performing this service *pro bono* and the court will be unable to reimburse you for any expenses incurred, including travel expense.

6. While serving as a judge *pro tempore*, you will be bound by the applicable provisions of the Code of Judicial Conduct.

If you are still with me after reading the above and if you desire to accept this invitation, the court is enthusiastic about the prospect of using judges *pro tempore* and looks forward to sitting with you. All participants will receive a certificate reflecting the court's appreciation; a reception will be held at the conclusion of the program to further acknowledge the assistance of all attorneys participating.

Will you please notify me by returning the attached acceptance letter by May 21, 1984. If you accept this invitation, your expected participation would be during the period September through December, 1984.

                                              Cordially yours,

                                              EINO M. JACOBSON
                                              Chief Judge, Division One

APPENDIX C

# Rules and Guidelines for the Connecticut Trial Referee Program

## Connecticut Practice Book, Superior Court—Civil

**Sec. 431.** Appointment of Committee or Referee

It is the function of the court or judge to determine and appoint the person or persons who shall constitute a committee, or the referee to whom a case shall be referred. Recommendations by counsel shall be made only at the request of the court or judge. If more than one person shall constitute the committee, the first person named by the court shall be the chairman of the committee.

**Sec. 432. Effect of Reference**

When any case shall be referred to a committee, no trial will be had by the court unless the reference be revoked upon stipulation of the parties or order of court. Any reference shall continue in force until the duties of the committee thereunder have been performed or the order revoked.

In making a reference in any domain proceeding, the court shall fix a date not more than sixty days thereafter, unless for good cause shown a longer period is required, on which the parties shall exchange copies of their appraisal reports. Such reports shall set forth the valuation placed upon the property in issue and the details of the items of, or the basis for, such valuation. The court may, in its discretion and under such conditions as it deems proper, and after notice and hearing, grant a further extension of time, beyond that originally fixed, to any party confronted with unusual and special circumstances requiring additional time for the exchange of appraisal reports.

### Sec. 433. Pleadings

No case shall be referred until the issues are closed and a trial list claim filed. Thereafter no pleadings may be filed except by agreement of all parties or order of court. Such pleadings shall be filed with the clerk and by him transmitted to the committee.

### Sec. 434. Report

The report of a committee shall state, in separate and consecutively numbered paragraphs, the facts found and the conclusions drawn therefrom. It should not contain statements of evidence or excerpts from the evidence. The report should ordinarily state only the ultimate facts found; but if the committee has reason to believe that his conclusions as to such facts from subordinate facts will be questioned, he may also state the subordinate facts found proven; and if he has reason to believe that his rulings will be questioned, he may state them with a brief summary of such facts as are necessary to explain them; and he should state such claims as were made by the parties and which either party requests him to state.

The committee may accompany his report with a memorandum of decision including such matters as he may deem helpful in the decision of the case, and, in any case in which appraisal fees may be awarded by the court, he shall make a finding and recommendation as to such appraisal fees as he deems reasonable.

### Sec. 435. Request for Finding

Either party may request a committee to make a finding of subordinate facts or of his rulings, and of the claims made, and shall include in or annex to such request a statement of facts, or rulings, or claims, he desires the committee to incorporate in the report.

### Sec. 436. Alternative Report

If alternative claims are made before the committee, or he deems it advisable, he may report all the facts bearing upon such claims and make his conclusions in the alternative, so that the judgment rendered will depend upon which of the alternative conclusions the facts are found legally to support.

### Sec. 437. Amending Report

A committee may, at any time before a report is accepted, file an amendment to it or an amended report.

### Sec. 438. Motion to Correct

If either party desires to have the report or the finding corrected by striking out any of the facts found, or by adding further facts, or by stating the claims of the parties made before the committee, or by setting forth rulings upon evidence or other rulings of the committee, he shall within two weeks after the filing of the report or finding file with the court a motion to correct setting forth the changes and additions desired by him. He shall accompany the motion with a brief statement of the grounds of each correction asked, with suitable references to the testimony. The file shall then be returned to the committee for consideration of the motion to correct. As soon as practicable the committee shall file with the court the motion to correct, together with his decision thereon.

### Sec. 439. Exceptions to Report or Finding

If a committee fails to correct a report or finding in compliance with a motion to correct, the moving party may, within ten days after the decision on the motion to correct, file exceptions seeking corrections by the court in the report or finding. The court will not consider an exception unless its subject matter has been submitted to the committee in a motion to correct, provided that this requirement shall not apply to exceptions taken to corrections in the report or finding made after it was filed; nor will the court correct a finding of fact unless a material fact has been found without evidence or the committee has failed to find an admitted or undisputed fact, or has found a fact in such doubtful language that its real meaning does not appear. A party excepting on these grounds must file with his exceptions a transcript of the evidence taken before the committee, except such portions as the parties may stipulate to omit.

### Sec. 440. Objections to Acceptance of Report

A party may file objections to the acceptance of a report on the ground that conclusions of fact stated in it were not properly reached on the basis of the subordinate facts found, or that the committee erred in rulings on evidence or other rulings or that there are other reasons why the report should not be accepted.

If an objection raises an issue of fact the determination of which may require the consideration of matters not appearing in the report or stenographic notes of proceedings before the committee, the adverse party shall, within two weeks after the filing of the objection, plead to it by a motion to strike, answer or other proper pleading.

### Sec. 441. Time to File Objections

Objections to the acceptance of a report shall be filed within two weeks after the filing of the report or finding, or if a motion to correct the report or finding has been made, within two weeks from the filing of the decision on the motion.

### Sec. 442. Judgment on the Report

After the expiration of two weeks from the filing of the report, if no motion to correct and no objections to the report have been filed and no extension of time for filing either has been granted, either party may, without written motion, claim the case for the short calendar for judgment on the report of the committee, provided, if the parties file a stipulation that no motion to correct or objections will be filed, the case may be so claimed at any time thereafter. If exceptions or objections have been seasonably filed, the case should be claimed for the short calendar for hearing thereon; and the court may, upon its decision as to them, forthwith direct judgment to be rendered.

### Sec. 443. Function of the Court

The court shall render such judgment as the law requires upon the facts in the report as it may be corrected. If the court finds that the committee has materially erred in his rulings or that by reason of material corrections in his findings the basis of the report is subverted or that there are other sufficient reasons why the report should not be accepted, the court shall reject the report and refer the matter to the same or another committee for a new trial or revoke the reference and leave the case to be disposed of in court.

The court may correct a report at any time before judgment upon the written stipulation of the parties or it may upon its own motion add a fact which is admitted or undisputed or strike out a fact improperly found.

### Sec. 444. Extensions of Time

The committee for good cause shown may extend the time for filing motions to correct with him, and any judge of the court in which the report is filed may for good cause shown allow extensions of time for filing such motions to correct and for taking any of the other steps herein provided.

January 31, 1984
# Guidelines for Attorney State Trial Referees

You have been appointed a state trial referee by the Chief Justice under General Statutes Section 52-434. Initial appointments to this office will be effective until July 1, 1984, and thereafter will be made on a yearly basis. You will be involved in either the *semi-retired attorneys* program or the *practicing attorneys* program outlined below.

### Goals of Programs

The goals of the programs are to accelerate the disposition of cases on the court trial list and to free judges assigned to the Civil Division Part C (court matters) so that they can adjudicate a greater number of civil jury cases than is now possible.

### Oath of Office

Because of the importance of this position you will be required to take the following oath of office:

"You do solemnly swear (or affirm, as the case may be) that you will support the Constitution of the United States, and the Constitution of the State of Connecticut, so long as you continue a citizen thereof; that you will faithfully discharge, according to law, the duties of the office of state trial referee to the best of your ability; and that you will, in addition to complying with the provisions of the Code of Professional Responsibility, comply with the provisions of Canons 1, 2, and 3 of the Code of Judicial Conduct concerning the matters in which you serve as a state trial referee. So help you God." (See attached)

### Semi-Retired Attorneys Program

Semi-retired attorneys, who should be able to serve for a continuous period of not less than one month, will be assigned by the Chief Court Administrator to Judicial District court locations. During the period of their assignment, they will be available to the Presiding Judge of the Civil Division for trials in much the same manner as an additional judge would be available.

When cases are reached on the assignment list for trial, the Presiding Judge, subject to the procedure set forth below, will refer as many cases as feasible to the assigned attorney referee for immediate trial. Contract cases, which fall within the purview of the fact-finding program, as defined in General Statutes Section 52-549n, however, generally will not be referred to attorney referees.

The consent of the parties is not required for a case to be referred to an attorney referee. If the parties agree to the appointment of a particular attorney referee, the Presiding Judge may order the case referred to said referee. If there is no such order, the presiding civil judge will give the parties the names of three attorney referees who may hear the case. Each party, starting with the plaintiff, will reject one of the three. In cases involving multiple parties each side will strike one.

### Practicing Attorneys Program

The attorney referees serving under this program have agreed to set aside periods of time within their schedules to hear cases which have been referred to them. Because such attorneys are full-time practitioners, they may have difficulty in devoting full and continuous days to the trial of these cases. Thus, unlike the semi-retired attorneys, they will not be assigned full-time to a particular Judicial District for a specific period of time. Rather, working within their schedules, they will set aside time, which should be as continuous as possible, to hear and decide cases as soon as possible after they have been referred. After receiving notice of a reference, the attorney referee should consult promptly with the parties to set an early date certain for the commencement of the trial and to establish a trial schedule. Once a date certain has been fixed, it should not be changed unless there are compelling reasons to do so. The referee should also arrange with the administrative judge to have a courtroom made available.

Generally, the types of cases to be referred under this program are those civil nonjury trial list cases which are not within the purview of the fact-finding program and which fall into the following categories:

| **MAJOR DESCRIPTION** | **MINOR DESCRIPTION** |
| --- | --- |
| **Contracts** | Construction—*State or Local* |
|  | Construction—*All Other* |
|  | Insurance Policy |
|  | Specific Performance |
|  | Collections |
| **Torts** (Other than Vehicular) | Defective Premises—*Private—Snow or Ice* |
|  | Defective Premises—*Private—Other* |
|  | Defective Premises—*Public—Snow or Ice* |
|  | Defective Premises—*Public—Other* |
|  | Products Liability Other Than Vehicular |
|  | Malpractice—*Medical* |

Malpractice—*Legal*
Malpractice—*All Other*
Assault and Battery
Defamation
Animals—*Dogs*
Animals—*Other*
False Arrest
Fire Damage

**Vehicular Torts**   Motor Vehicles*—*Driver and/or Passenger(s) vs. Driver(s)*
Motor Vehicles*—*Pedestrian vs. Driver*
Motor Vehicles*—*Property Damage Only*
Motor Vehicles*—*Products Liability Including Warranty*
Motor Vehicles*—*All Other Motor Vehicles*
Boats
Airplanes
Railroads
Snowmobiles

**Wills, Estates and Trusts**   Construction of Wills and Trusts

---

*(Motor Vehicles include cars, trucks, motorcycles, and motorscooters).*

---

Cases which require a flexible trial schedule to accommodate out-of-state and expert witnesses or have complex, specialized issues are particularly suitable for reference to attorney referees under the practicing attorney program, but any trial list case may be referred to such a referee.

There are three sources from which cases can be referred under this program. Although cases on the assignment list should normally be referred under the semi-retired attorneys program, special circumstances may exist when a case cannot go forward immediately and it is prudent to make the reference under this program. Most references under this program will be made, however, from specially prepared lists of particular types of cases as described above. A list of such cases would be prepared by the clerk and sent to counsel together with a notice that the court on a date certain would consider referring such cases to attorney referees under this program. The notice should encourage the attorneys to agree upon an attorney referee (not a semi-retired attorney) to whom the reference could be made and announce that a list of attorney referees would be available in the clerk's office. Motions for reference to an attorney state trial referee constitute the final source from which reference can be made under this program.

The consent of the parties is not required for a case to be referred for trial to an attorney referee. If the parties agree to the appointment of a particular attorney referee, the Presiding Judge may order the case referred to said referee subject to the referee's acceptance.

A list of attorney trial referees serving under this program will be available in each Judicial District clerk's office. Parties are encouraged to stipulate to the appointment of a particular attorney referee after having ascertained that the referee is available. If no order is entered to refer the case to a particular attorney referee pursuant to an agreement, the Presiding Judge of the Civil Division will give the parties the names of three attorney referees who may hear the case. Each party, starting with the plaintiff, will reject one of the three. In cases involving multiple parties, each side will strike one.

### Guidelines Applicable to Both Programs

The Practice Book rules concerning references to committees shall be followed (Practice Book Sections 434 through 444) except that the attorney referee shall file a memorandum of decision in each case. *Harbor Construction Corporation v D.V. Frione & Company*, 158 Conn. 14 (1969), is an informative case concerning this procedure.

As a general proposition, it is anticipated that many of the practicing attorneys who serve as referees will serve pro bono. However, payment for services to an attorney referee under both programs may not exceed $20 an hour up to a maximum of $100 a day. Invoices must be approved by the Administrative Judge or the Presiding Judge of the Civil Division.

Attorney referees shall have a court reporter or court recording monitor in the courtroom during trial proceedings.

The disqualification of an attorney referee shall be for cause only. The procedure shall be that set forth in Practice Book Sections 546E and 546O concerning the disqualification of fact-finders and arbitrators.

The Presiding Judge shall establish time standards for the revocation of a reference. References will be subject to revocation by the court when there has been excessive delay in completing a trial.

MAURICE J. SPONZO, Judge
Chief Court Administrator

# APPENDIX D

# Fourth Judicial District Court (Minneapolis, Minnesota) Rules Regarding Mandatory, Nonbinding Arbitration

## Effective July 1, 1985

## RULE 5. ARBITRATION

**RULE 5.01. Authority**

Pursuant to Minn. Stat. § 484.73, the Fourth Judicial District has authorized the establishment of a system of arbitration for civil cases.

**RULE 5.02. Actions Subject to Arbitration**

(a) All Civil actions are subject to arbitration except:
1. Actions for money damages in excess of $50,000.00;
2. Actions for money damages within the jurisdictional limit of the Hennepin County Conciliation Court;
3. Actions that include a claim for equitable relief that is neither insubstantial nor frivolous;
4. Actions removed from the Hennepin County Conciliation Court for trial de novo;
5. Class actions;
6. Actions involving family law matters;
7. Unlawful detainer actions; or
8. Actions involving the title to real estate.

(b) The Chief Judge or the judge that the case is assigned to shall have authority to order that particular actions otherwise excluded shall be submitted to arbitration.

(c) Any action otherwise excluded above may be submitted to arbitration by agreement of all parties.

**RULE 5.03.   Qualifications of Arbitrator**

Unless otherwise ordered by the Chief Judge or his/her designee or agreed to by all parties, an arbitrator must be admitted to practice in the State of Minnesota for a minimum of five years and must sign and file an Oath of Office with the Chief Judge of the District Court.

**RULE 5.04.   Selection of Arbitrators**

(a) Arbitrators shall be selected from members of the Bar who reside or practice in Hennepin County and who are qualified in accordance with Rule 5.03.

(b) The Court Administrator shall randomly assign arbitrators from a list of qualified arbitrators maintained by the Court.

(c) Any party or his attorney may file with the Court Administrator within five days of the notice of appointment and serve on the opposing party a notice to remove. Upon receipt of a notice to remove, the Court Administrator shall immediately assign another arbitrator. After a party has once disqualified an arbitrator as a matter of right, a substitute arbitrator may be disqualified by that party only by making an affirmative showing of prejudice to the Chief Judge or his/her designee.

**RULE 5.05.   Arbitrator's Fees**

(a) The arbitrator's award or a notice of settlement signed by the parties or their counsel, must be timely filed with the Court Administrator before a fee may be paid to the arbitrator.

(b) On the arbitrator's verified ex parte application, the court may for good cause authorize payment of a fee when the award was not timely filed.

(c) The arbitrator's fee statement shall be submitted to the Court Administrator promptly upon the completion of the arbitrator's duties, and shall set forth the title and number of the cause arbitrated, the date of the arbitration hearing, and the date the award or settlement was filed.

(d) The arbitrator's fee will be set by the court with a maximum of $150.00 per day.

**RULE 5.06.   Communication with the Arbitrator**

No disclosure of any offers of settlement by any party, other than contained in the court file, shall be made to the arbitrator prior to the filing of the award. There shall be no ex parte communication by counsel or the parties with the arbitrator or a potential arbitrator except for the purpose of scheduling the arbitration hearing or requesting a continuance.

**RULE 5.07. Arbitration Hearing**

(a) Thirty (30) days after filing of a Note of Issue/ Certificate of Readiness, or 120 days after the filing of a Certificate of Non-Readiness, the Court Administrator shall schedule an arbitration hearing, which hearing shall be set for not more than 60 days thereafter at a specified time and place. No further extensions for discovery shall be allowed unless granted by the Chief Judge or his/her designee on motion.

(b) By agreement of all parties, an action may be submitted to arbitration before the filing of the Note of Issue/Certificate of Readiness.

(c) Failure to appear at the arbitration hearing may subject the nonappearing party or counsel, or both, to imposition by the assigned judge of reasonable costs to the party who did appear at the arbitration hearing.

**RULE 5.08. Continuances**

A continuance of the arbitration hearing may be granted only by the Court Administrator.

**RULE 5.09. Rules of Evidence at Hearing**

(a) All evidence shall be taken in the presence of the arbitrator and all parties, except where any of the parties has waived the right to be present or is absent after due notice of the hearing.

(b) The Rules of Evidence, construed liberally in favor of admission, apply to the conduct of the arbitration hearing, except:

    1. Any party may offer, and the arbitrator shall receive in evidence written medical and hospital reports, records and bills (including physiotherapy, nursing and prescription bills), documentary evidence of loss of income, property damage, repair bills or estimates, and police reports concerning an accident which gave rise to the case, if copies have been delivered to all opposing parties at least 10 days prior to the hearing. Any other party may subpoena the author of a report, bill or estimate as a witness and examine that person as if under cross-examination. Any repair estimate offered as an exhibit, and the copies delivered to opposing parties, shall be accompanied by a statement indicating whether or not the property was repaired and if it was, whether the estimated repairs were made in full or in part, and by a copy of the receipted bill showing the items of repair made and the amount paid. The arbitrator shall not consider any opinion expressed in a police report as to ultimate fault.

    2. The written statement of any other witness, including written reports of expert witnesses not enumerated above, and including statements of opinion which the witness would be

qualified to express if testifying in person, may be offered and shall be received in evidence if: (i) they are made by affidavit or by declaration under penalty of perjury; (ii) copies have been delivered to all opposing parties at least 10 days prior to the hearing; and (iii) no opposing party has, at least 5 days before the hearing, delivered to the proponent of the evidence a written demand that the witness be produced in person to testify at the hearing. The arbitrator shall disregard any portion of a statement received pursuant to this rule that would be inadmissible if the witness were testifying in person, but the inclusion of inadmissible matter does not render the entire statement inadmissible.

3. The deposition of any witness may be offered by any party and shall be received in evidence, subject to objections, notwithstanding that the deponent is not "unavailable as a witness" and no exceptional circumstances exist, if: (i) the deposition was taken in the manner provided for by law or by stipulation of the parties and within the time provided for in these rules: and (ii) not less than 10 days prior to the hearing the proponent of the deposition serves on all opposing parties notice of his intention to offer the deposition in evidence. The opposing party, upon receiving the notice, may subpoena the deponent and if he does so, at the discretion of the arbitrator, either the deposition may be excluded from evidence or the deposition may be admitted and the deponent may be further cross-examined by the party who subpoenaed him. These limitations are not applicable to a deposition admissible under the terms of Minn.R.Civ.P.32.01.

(c) Subpoenas shall issue for the attendance of witnesses at arbitration hearings as provided in Minn.R.Civ.P.45. It shall be the duty of the party requesting the subpoena to modify the form of subpoena to show that the appearance is before an arbitrator, and to give the time and place set for the arbitration hearing. At the discretion of the arbitrator, nonappearance of a properly subpoenaed witness may be a ground for an adjournmment or continuance of the hearing. If any witness properly served with a subpoena fails to appear at the arbitration hearing or, having appeared, refuses to be sworn or to answer, proceedings to compel compliance with the subpoena on penalty of contempt may be had before the court.

(d) Notwithstanding any other provisions in these rules, a party offering opinion testimony in the form of an affidavit or other statement, or a deposition, shall have the right to withdraw such testimony, whereupon the attendance of the witness at the hearing shall not be required.

**RULE 5.10. Conduct of the Hearing**
(a) The arbitrator shall have the following powers:
1. To administer oaths or affirmations to witnesses;
2. To take adjournments upon the request of party or upon his own initiative when deemed necessary;
3. To permit testimony to be offered by deposition;
4. To permit evidence to be offered and introduced as provided in these rules;
5. To rule upon the admissibility and relevancy of evidence offered;
6. To invite the parties, on reasonable notice, to submit pre-hearing or post-hearing briefs or pre-hearing statements of evidence;
7. To decide the law and facts of the case and make an award accordingly;
8. To award costs, not to exceed the statutory costs of the action;
9. To view any site or object relevant to the case; and
10. Any other powers agreed upon by the parties.

(b) The arbitrator may, but is not required to, make a record of the proceedings. Any records of the proceedings made by or at the direction of the arbitrator shall be deemed the arbitrator's personal notes and are not subject to discovery, and the arbitrator shall not deliver them to any party to the case or to any other person, except to an employee using the records under the arbitrator's supervision or pursuant to a subpoena issued in a criminal investigation or prosecution for perjury. No other record shall be made, and the arbitrator shall not permit the presence of a stenographer or court reporter or the use of any recording device at the hearing, except as expressly permitted by this rule.

**RULE 5.11. The Award**
(a) The award shall be in writing and signed by the arbitrator. It shall determine all issues properly raised by the pleadings, including a determination of any damages and an award of costs if appropriate. The arbitrator is not required to make findings of fact or conclusions of law.

(b) Within ten (10) days after the conclusion of the arbitration hearing, the arbitrator shall file his award with the Court Administrator, with proof of service on each party to the arbitration. On the arbitrator's application in cases of unusual length or complexity, the court may allow up to 20 additional days for the filing and service of the award. Within the time for filing the award, the arbitrator may file and serve an amended award.

(c) The Court Administrator shall enter the award as a judgment forthwith upon the expiration of twenty (20) days after the award is filed if no party has, during that period, served and filed a request for trial as provided in these rules. Promptly upon entry of the award as a judgment, the Court Administrator shall mail notice of entry of judgment to all parties who have appeared in the case and shall execute a certificate of mailing and place it in the court's file in the case. The judgment so entered shall have the same force and effect in all respects as, and is subject to all provisions of law relating to, a judgment in a civil action or proceeding, except that it is not subject to appeal and it may not be attacked or set aside except as provided in subdivision d. The judgment so entered may be enforced as if it had been rendered by the court in which it is entered.

(d) A party against whom a judgment is entered pursuant to an arbitration award may, within six months after its entry, move to vacate the judgment on the ground that the arbitrator was subject to a disqualification not disclosed before the hearing and of which the arbitrator was then aware, or upon one of the grounds set forth in the Uniform Arbitration Act, Chapter 572, Minnesota Statutes, and upon no other grounds. The motion shall be heard by the court upon notice to the adverse parties and to the arbitrator, and may be granted only upon clear and convincing evidence that the grounds alleged are true, and that the motion was made as soon as practicable after the moving party learned of the existence of those grounds.

**RULE 5.12. Trial after Arbitration**

(a) Within 20 days after the arbitration award is filed with the Court Administrator, any party may request a trial by filing with the Court Administrator a request for trial, with proof of service of a copy upon all other parties appearing in the case. The 20-day period within which to request trial may not be extended.

(b) The case shall be restored to the civil calendar in the same position on the list it would have had if there had been no arbitration in the case, unless the court orders otherwise for good cause.

(c) The case shall be tried as though no arbitration proceedings had occurred. No reference may be made during the trial to the arbitration award, to the fact that there had been arbitration proceedings, to the evidence adduced at the arbitration hearing, or to any other aspect of the arbitration proceedings, and none of the foregoing may be used as affirmative evidence, or by way of impeachment, or for any other purpose at the trial.

**RULE 13.01. Objection to Referee Hearing Case**

Unless otherwise provided by law, the objection to a referee conducting a particular hearing shall be filed in writing with the judge to whom the case has been assigned or the judge who presides over the division at least one court day before the time set for the hearing.

APPENDIX E

# Analysis of King County Superior Court Early Disposition Programs, 1983 and 1984

Prepared by the Office of the Administrator for the Courts, Research and Statistics

Sharon L. Estee, Ph.D. / Robert Anson / Jenni A. Christopher

Revised October 1986

## Background of Analysis

In order to examine the efficacy of the two Early Disposition Programs (EDP) undertaken by the King County Superior Court bench and the King County bar, a classic experimental design was used. Specifically, cases that were assigned or volunteered for the program were compared with a randomly selected set of comparable cases. Cases that participated in EDP are considered the "experimental group" and those that continued in the normal court processing routine, which were used as a comparison group, are termed the "control group." Using a random selection of cases to either EDP or the control group from both assigned cases and volunteers permits an evaluation of the effectiveness of EDP relative to normal case processing procedures.

The effectiveness of EDP is to be determined by two indicators: (1) earlier time of disposition after the EDP hearing and (2) the avoidance of subsequent trials. Three characteristics of cases are examined to determine their impact on the effectiveness of EDP. They are: (1) volunteer vs. assignment status, (2) cause of action, and (3) age of case.

Since the program was conducted for two consecutive years, 1983 and 1984, and since control groups were established in both years, it is possible to examine the effectiveness of EDP for a fairly substantial number of cases (see Table E-1). Although the number of panels used and the number of cases participating in EDP were reduced in 1984 relative to those in 1983, no substantial change was made in the operation of the program between the two years.

## TABLE E-1
**Distribution of cases included in study**

| | 1983 Program* | | 1984 Program** | |
|---|---|---|---|---|
| Type of case | EDP | Control | EDP | Control |
| **Civil case type** | | | | |
| Assigned | 142 | 166 | 104 | 119 |
| Volunteer | 56 | 46 | 37 | 48 |
| *Subtotal* | *198* | *212* | *141* | *167* |
| **Domestic case type** | | | | |
| Volunteer | 28 | — | 6 | — |
| TOTAL | 226 | 212 | 147 | 167 |

*Excludes four EDP and eight control cases selected for the 1983 program that were disposed prior to the mailing of assignment notices. Also excludes six cases excused from the 1983 EDP program.

**Excludes three EDP and two control cases selected for the 1984 program that were disposed prior to the mailing of assignment notices. Also excludes eleven cases excused from the 1984 EDP program.

Data were collected through July 31, 1986. This allowed 32 months of follow-up for cases in the 1983 program and 20 months of follow-up for those in the 1984 program. During this period 95.7 percent of cases involved in the 1983 study and 83.4 percent of cases involved in the 1984 study reached disposition (see Table E-2).

# Evaluation of Early Disposition Effect

### ISSUE #1: Are cases participating in EDP disposed of sooner than those exposed to normal court processing procedures?
### Discussion
Cases that participated in EDP tended to be disposed of earlier than those that did not participate. The effect of EDP on dispositions appeared to be greatest within the 90-day period immediately following the EDP hearing. In 1983, 35 percent of the civil cases in the program were disposed of within this period compared with only 13 percent of the civil cases in the control group. In 1984, the respective percentages were 28 versus 10.

The early disposition effect is demonstrated graphically by Figures E-1 and E-2, which show the cumulative percent of cases disposed after the assignment to EDP was made and the dispositions in 30-day increments following the EDP hearings.

## TABLE E-2
## Distribution of dispositions by end of study period

| 1983 PROGRAM | TOTAL CASES | Total cases disposed | Percent cases disposed |
|---|---|---|---|
| Volunteer | 56 | 55 | 98.2 |
| Assigned | 142 | 136 | 95.8 |
| *Subtotal* | *198* | *191* | *96.5* |
| Domestic Volunteer | 28 | 28 | 100.0 |
| **Control group** | | | |
| Volunteer | 46 | 45 | 97.8 |
| Assigned | 166 | 155 | 93.4 |
| *Subtotal* | *212* | *200* | *94.3* |
| TOTAL | 438 | 419 | 95.7 |
| **1984 PROGRAM** | | | |
| **EDP group** | | | |
| Volunteer | 37 | 32 | 86.5 |
| Assigned | 104 | 90 | 86.5 |
| *Subtotal* | *141* | *122* | *86.5* |
| Domestic Volunteer | 6 | 5 | 83.3 |
| **Control group** | | | |
| Volunteer | 48 | 39 | 81.3 |
| Assigned | 119 | 96 | 80.7 |
| *Subtotal* | *167* | *135* | *80.8* |
| TOTAL | 314 | 262 | 83.4 |

**Note:** Data on case activity were analyzed through July 31, 1986.

The degree to which disposition is hastened by participation in EDP can be determined by comparing the number of days by which 50 percent of the cases in each subcategory were disposed after the dates of the 1983 and 1984 hearings. This comparison results in the difference between the median disposition times of the EDP and the control groups and can

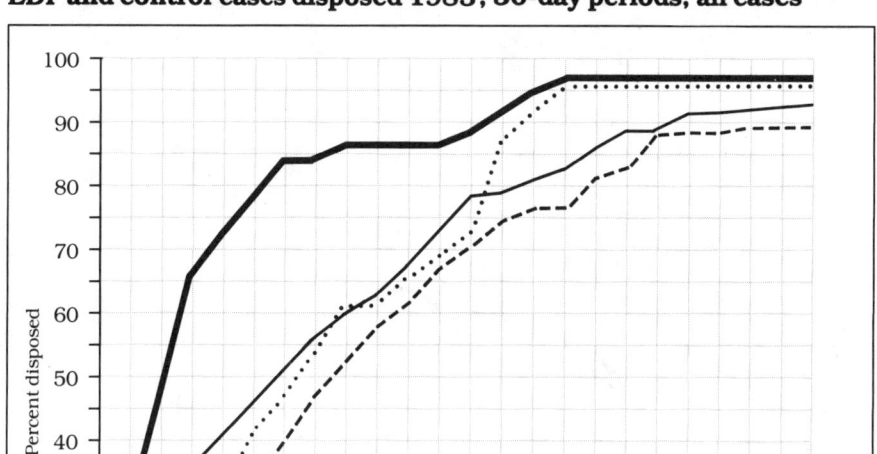

**FIGURE E-1**
**EDP and control cases disposed 1983, 30-day periods, all cases**

*Some cases were disposed after assignment to the study but prior to EDP hearings.

be calculated directly from Figures E-1 and E-2 for 1983 and 1984, respectively.

For 1983, approximately 50 percent of the volunteer cases that went to the EDP hearings were disposed within 60 days. Fifty percent of the volunteers placed in the control group were disposed within 210 days after the hearing. The difference between these figures indicates that EDP saved 150 days, or five months, for litigants who voluntarily participated in the hearings. Comparable calculations for cases assigned to the project revealed that the amount of time saved for 50 percent of the cases was 55 days, or just under two months.

A similar but somewhat weaker pattern emerges for the 1984 cases. Fifty percent of volunteer cases that went to the EDP hearings were disposed within 160 days. Since it took 270 days for 50 percent of the volunteers placed in the control group to be disposed, EDP saved 110 days

## FIGURE E-2
**EDP and control cases disposed 1984, 30-day periods, all cases**

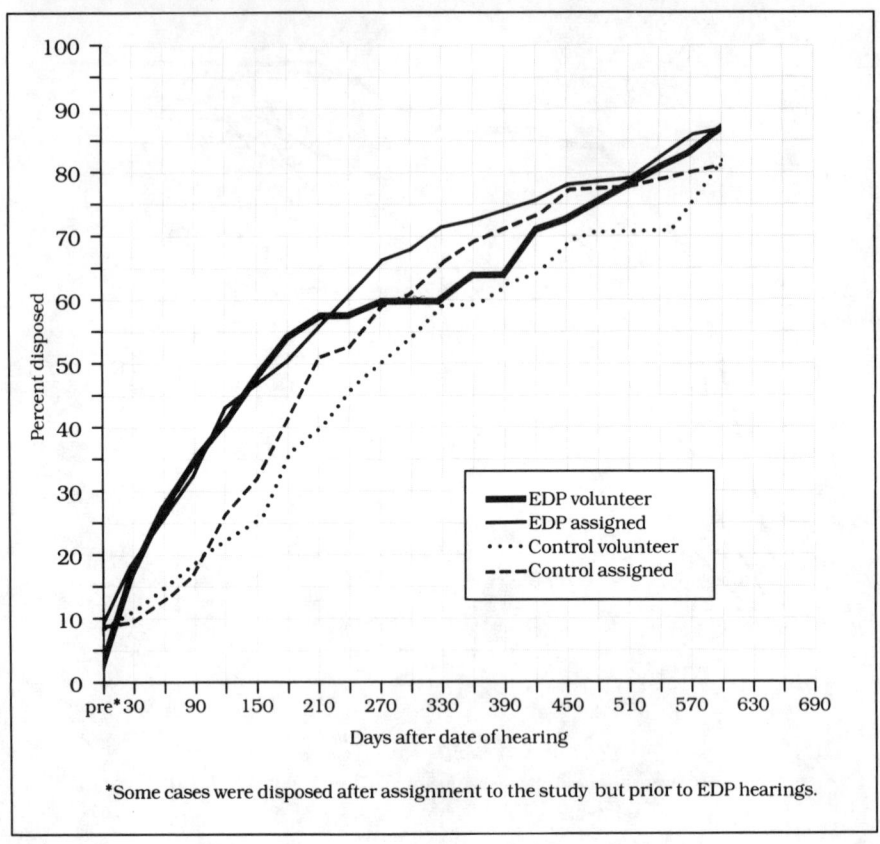

*Some cases were disposed after assignment to the study but prior to EDP hearings.

(just under four months) for litigants who voluntarily participated in the hearings. For cases assigned to the project, EDP saved 30 days (one month).

### Conclusion
EDP results in earlier disposition of civil cases than would normally occur. Volunteers in EDP were disposed between four and five months earlier than volunteers in the control group. Cases assigned to EDP were disposed one to two months sooner than they would have been under normal case processing procedures.

**ISSUE #2: Do volunteers differ from cases assigned to EDP in the time required for their dispositions?**

## Discussion

A marked difference in the time-to-disposition was found between volunteer and assigned cases in the 1983 program but not in the 1984 program. In the 1983 program, 54 percent of the volunteer civil cases were disposed of within the first 90 days following the EDP hearing, compared with only 28 percent of the assigned cases. In the same period following the 1984 EDP hearings, only 32 percent of the volunteers reached disposition relative to 26 percent of the assigned cases. (See Table E-3 for more detailed statistics.)

## TABLE E-3
### Cases disposed by time of disposition and volunteer/assignment status

|  | TOTAL CASES | Assignment to hearing No. | Assignment to hearing Percent | Post-hearing 1-90 days No. | Post-hearing 1-90 days Percent | Post-hearing 91-180 days No. | Post-hearing 91-180 days Percent | Total disposed by 180 days No. | Total disposed by 180 days Percent |
|---|---|---|---|---|---|---|---|---|---|
| **1983 PROGRAM** | | | | | | | | | |
| **EDP group** | | | | | | | | | |
| Volunteer | 56 | 7 | 13 | 30 | 54 | 10 | 18 | 47 | 84 |
| Assigned | 142 | 10 | 7 | 40 | 28 | 23 | 16 | 73 | 51 |
| *Subtotal* | *198* | *17* | *9* | *70* | *35* | *33* | *17* | *120* | *61* |
| Domestic | 28 | 6 | 21 | 10 | 36 | 9 | 32 | 25 | 89 |
| **Control group** | | | | | | | | | |
| Volunteer | 46 | 6 | 13 | 5 | 11 | 10 | 22 | 21 | 46 |
| Assigned | 166 | 14 | 8 | 22 | 13 | 30 | 18 | 66 | 40 |
| *Subtotal* | *212* | *20* | *9* | *27* | *13* | *40* | *19* | *87* | *41* |
| **1984 PROGRAM** | | | | | | | | | |
| **EDP group** | | | | | | | | | |
| Volunteer | 37 | 1 | 3 | 12 | 32 | 7 | 19 | 20 | 54 |
| Assigned | 104 | 8 | 8 | 27 | 26 | 17 | 16 | 52 | 50 |
| *Subtotal* | *141* | *9* | *6* | *39* | *28* | *24* | *17* | *72* | *51* |
| Domestic | 6 | 0 | 0 | 4 | 67 | 1 | 17 | 5 | 83 |
| **Control group** | | | | | | | | | |
| Volunteer | 48 | 4 | 8 | 5 | 10 | 8 | 17 | 17 | 35 |
| Assigned | 119 | 10 | 8 | 11 | 9 | 27 | 23 | 48 | 40 |
| *Subtotal* | *167* | *14* | *8* | *16* | *10* | *35* | *21* | *65* | *39* |

The differential effect of EDP on volunteers relative to assigned cases is shown clearly in Figure E-1. Particularly evident is the rapid rise in the cumulative percentage of dispositions for volunteers following the 1983 hearing. In contrast, the rise in dispositions for volunteer cases after the 1984 hearing shown in Figure E-2 closely parallels the disposition rates shown for the assigned cases.

## Conclusion

EDP hearings may have a greater impact on cases that volunteer than on those that are mandated to participate in settlement conferences. This conclusion, however, is supported more strongly by the data for the first enactment of the program than by the second. As a result, restructuring the project to use only volunteers could be considered but should be monitored carefully. Other factors, such as cause of action and age of case, might be useful to include in screening prospective cases for EDP.

## ISSUE #3: Does the cause of action affect the impact of EDP on the length of time to disposition?

### Discussion

Torts arising from motor vehicle accidents were more likely to reach disposition in the 90 days following the EDP hearing than cases involving other causes of action. The proportion of motor vehicle torts disposed of in this period was 51 percent after the 1983 program and 35 percent after the 1984 program. [These figures combine volunteer and assigned cases.] A summary of the percentages disposed by cause of action is shown in Table E-4, and a detailed presentation appears in Table E-5.

### TABLE E-4
### Percent of cases disposed within 90 days of EDP hearings by type of case

|  | 1983 Program | | 1984 Program | |
|---|---|---|---|---|
| Cause of action | Percent EDP | Percent control | Percent EDP | Percent control |
| Tort, motor vehicles | 51 | 14 | 35 | 8 |
| Personal injury | 28 | 11 | 28 | 11 |
| Medical malpractice | 19 | 8 | 18 | 10 |
| Commercial | 34 | 21 | 26 | 12 |
| Other | — | 0 | — | 50 |
| Domestic | 36 | — | 67 | — |

Cases involving personal injury were the next most likely to result in an early disposition following the EDP hearing when the data for both years are considered. The percentage of personal injury cases reaching disposition in the 90-day post-hearing period was 28 following both the

**TABLE E-5**
**Civil cases disposed by time of disposition and type of case**

|  | TOTAL CASES | \multicolumn{6}{c|}{Time of disposition} | | | | | |
|---|---|---|---|---|---|---|---|---|---|
| 1983 PROGRAM |  | Assignment to hearing || 1-90 days || 91-180 days || Total disposed by 180 days ||
|  |  | No. | Percent | No. | Percent | No. | Percent | No. | Percent |
| **EDP group— volunteer** | | | | | | | | | |
| Tort, motor vehicles | 42 | 6 | 14 | 22 | 52 | 7 | 17 | 35 | 83 |
| Personal injury | 6 | 1 | 17 | 4 | 67 | 0 | 0 | 5 | 83 |
| Medical malpractice | 0 | — | — | — | — | — | — | 0 | — |
| Commercial | 8 | 0 | 0 | 4 | 50 | 3 | 38 | 7 | 88 |
| **EDP group— assigned** | | | | | | | | | |
| Tort, motor vehicles | 21 | 3 | 14 | 10 | 48 | 3 | 14 | 16 | 76 |
| Personal injury | 59 | 4 | 7 | 14 | 24 | 10 | 17 | 28 | 47 |
| Medical malpractice | 32 | 2 | 6 | 7 | 22 | 6 | 19 | 15 | 47 |
| Commercial | 30 | 1 | 3 | 9 | 30 | 4 | 13 | 14 | 47 |
| **Control group— volunteer** | | | | | | | | | |
| Tort, motor vehicles | 31 | 3 | 14 | 4 | 13 | 8 | 26 | 15 | 48 |
| Personal injury | 4 | 1 | 25 | 0 | 0 | 1 | 25 | 2 | 50 |
| Medical malpractice | 5 | 1 | 20 | 1 | 20 | 0 | 0 | 2 | 40 |
| Commercial | 3 | 1 | 33 | 0 | 0 | 1 | 33 | 2 | 67 |
| Other | 3 | — | — | — | — | — | — | — | — |
| **Control group— assigned** | | | | | | | | | |
| Tort, motor vehicles | 32 | 6 | 19 | 5 | 16 | 12 | 38 | 23 | 72 |
| Personal injury | 71 | 4 | 6 | 8 | 11 | 10 | 14 | 22 | 31 |
| Medical malpractice | 31 | 1 | 3 | 2 | 7 | 6 | 19 | 9 | 29 |
| Commercial | 31 | 3 | 10 | 7 | 23 | 2 | 7 | 12 | 39 |
| Other | 1 | — | — | — | — | — | — | 0 | — |

*continued*

## TABLE E-5, *continued*
## Civil cases disposed by time of disposition and type of case

<table>
<tr><th rowspan="3">1984<br>PROGRAM</th><th rowspan="3">TOTAL<br>CASES</th><th colspan="8">Time of disposition</th></tr>
<tr><th colspan="2">Assignment<br>to hearing</th><th colspan="2">1-90<br>days</th><th colspan="2">91-180<br>days</th><th colspan="2">Total<br>disposed<br>by 180 days</th></tr>
<tr><th>No.</th><th>Percent</th><th>No.</th><th>Percent</th><th>No.</th><th>Percent</th><th>No.</th><th>Percent</th></tr>
<tr><td colspan="10">**EDP group—<br>volunteer**</td></tr>
<tr><td>Tort, motor vehicles</td><td>20</td><td>1</td><td>5</td><td>8</td><td>40</td><td>4</td><td>20</td><td>13</td><td>65</td></tr>
<tr><td>Personal injury</td><td>10</td><td>0</td><td>0</td><td>3</td><td>30</td><td>2</td><td>20</td><td>5</td><td>50</td></tr>
<tr><td>Medical malpractice</td><td>1</td><td></td><td>—</td><td></td><td>—</td><td></td><td>—</td><td>0</td><td>—</td></tr>
<tr><td>Commercial</td><td>3</td><td>0</td><td>0</td><td>1</td><td>33</td><td>0</td><td>0</td><td>1</td><td>33</td></tr>
<tr><td>Other</td><td>3</td><td>0</td><td>0</td><td>0</td><td>0</td><td>1</td><td>33</td><td>1</td><td>33</td></tr>
<tr><td colspan="10">**EDP group—<br>assigned**</td></tr>
<tr><td>Tort, motor vehicles</td><td>35</td><td>3</td><td>9</td><td>11</td><td>31</td><td>6</td><td>17</td><td>20</td><td>57</td></tr>
<tr><td>Personal injury</td><td>22</td><td>2</td><td>9</td><td>6</td><td>27</td><td>6</td><td>27</td><td>14</td><td>64</td></tr>
<tr><td>Medical malpractice</td><td>27</td><td>2</td><td>7</td><td>5</td><td>19</td><td>1</td><td>4</td><td>8</td><td>30</td></tr>
<tr><td>Commercial</td><td>20</td><td>1</td><td>5</td><td>5</td><td>25</td><td>4</td><td>20</td><td>10</td><td>50</td></tr>
<tr><td colspan="10">**Control group—<br>volunteer**</td></tr>
<tr><td>Tort, motor vehicles</td><td>16</td><td>0</td><td>0</td><td>2</td><td>13</td><td>3</td><td>19</td><td>5</td><td>31</td></tr>
<tr><td>Personal injury</td><td>9</td><td></td><td>—</td><td></td><td>—</td><td></td><td>—</td><td>0</td><td>—</td></tr>
<tr><td>Medical malpractice</td><td>5</td><td>0</td><td>0</td><td>2</td><td>40</td><td>2</td><td>40</td><td>4</td><td>80</td></tr>
<tr><td>Commercial</td><td>9</td><td>2</td><td>22</td><td>0</td><td>0</td><td>1</td><td>11</td><td>3</td><td>33</td></tr>
<tr><td>Other</td><td>9</td><td>2</td><td>22</td><td>1</td><td>11</td><td>2</td><td>22</td><td>5</td><td>56</td></tr>
<tr><td colspan="10">**Control group—<br>assigned**</td></tr>
<tr><td>Tort, motor vehicles</td><td>37</td><td>7</td><td>19</td><td>2</td><td>5</td><td>12</td><td>32</td><td>21</td><td>57</td></tr>
<tr><td>Personal injury</td><td>28</td><td>1</td><td>4</td><td>4</td><td>14</td><td>7</td><td>25</td><td>12</td><td>43</td></tr>
<tr><td>Medical malpractice</td><td>26</td><td>2</td><td>8</td><td>1</td><td>4</td><td>1</td><td>4</td><td>4</td><td>15</td></tr>
<tr><td>Commercial</td><td>28</td><td>0</td><td>0</td><td>4</td><td>14</td><td>7</td><td>25</td><td>11</td><td>39</td></tr>
</table>

1983 and 1984 programs. Although commercial cases evidenced a disposition rate of 34 percent in this period after the 1983 hearing, the rate for these cases dropped to 26 percent following the 1984 program.

All types of cases experienced a higher disposition rate in the early post-hearing period than comparable cases in the control group. Disposition rates for the control group remained roughly similar for both years.

More than one-third of the domestic relations cases that were voluntarily included in the 1983 program were disposed within 90 days after the EDP hearing. Four out of the six domestic cases in the 1984 program also settled in this period. Since comparable data for a control group are not available, it is not possible to draw a firm conclusion from these numbers. Relative to other civil cases included in EDP, the settlement rate for domestic cases appears to be substantial. Further comparison of regularly processed domestic cases would be warranted before making decisions about including domestic cases in future EDP efforts.

## Conclusion
Motor vehicle torts are likely to be more receptive to settlement following an EDP hearing than other types of cases. Settlement rates for personal injury cases also appear to be sufficiently high to merit inclusion in future programs.

Medical malpractice and commercial cases also settle at a higher rate for those participating in EDP than for those serving as controls, but at a somewhat smaller advantage. More information should be examined before deciding to include domestic relations cases.

## ISSUE #4: Is the age of a case related to the time-to- disposition following an EDP hearing?

## Discussion
The age of a case appears to have a limited effect on the likelihood of settlement in the early post-hearing period. As shown in Table E-6, there is a tendency for the proportion of cases settling in this period to increase with the age of the case. Also, disposition rates are clearly higher for cases that participated in EDP than for those in the control group at each age level.

The higher rate of disposition for 1983 EDP cases overall relative to those in 1984 reflects the higher rates of disposition for cases between 361 and 630 days old in 1983. The disposition rates for the youngest cases were equal between 1983 and 1984.

One cautionary note is necessary based on the 1983 program's data, in general, and on assigned cases in particular (see Table E-7). The oldest cases may not always settle at the highest rates. The highest settlement rate following EDP in 1983 was found for those aged 541 to 630 days [including volunteer and assigned cases] at the time of the hearing. The disposition rate was somewhat lower for those in the oldest category in that year. This pattern emerged for both years for cases assigned to EDP, while extremely old volunteer cases evidenced a rather high settlement

**TABLE E-6**
**Percent of cases disposed within 90 days of EDP hearings by age of case**

|                  | 1983 Program    |                 | 1984 Program    |                 |
| ---------------- | --------------- | --------------- | --------------- | --------------- |
| Age of case      | Percent EDP     | Percent control | Percent EDP     | Percent control |
| 360 days or less | 27              | 7               | 30              | 0               |
| 361-450 days     | 34              | 10              | 16              | 4               |
| 451-540 days     | 39              | 16              | 26              | 14              |
| 541-630 days     | 50              | 14              | 28              | 3               |
| 631 days or over | 28              | 15              | 38              | 15              |
| ALL CASES        | 35              | 13              | 28              | 10              |

**Note:** Age of case equals the number of days between the filing date and the date EDP hearings began—November 21, 1983, for the first program and November 19, 1984, for the second.

rate. Possibly, the oldest cases that did not ask to be included in the EDP hearings contain complex issues not readily resolved at a settlement conference. In contrast, older cases that did volunteer for the programs may have reached a point at which they were ready to settle. Insufficient data exist for comparing the complexity of issues or other aspects of the volunteer and the assigned cases.

**Conclusion**
As a case matures, it may become more amenable to settlement through an intensive hearing similar to those used in EDP. The oldest cases are more likely to settle after such a hearing if their participation is voluntary rather than compulsory.

## Evaluation of Trial Avoidance

**ISSUE #5: Are cases that participated in EDP less likely to require trials than those exposed to normal court processing procedures?**

**Discussion**
In the 32 months following the 1983 EDP hearings, the total number of trials recorded for civil cases in the EDP program equaled 19. Trials for the 1983 control group totaled 26. As a result, 9.6 percent of the EDP cases resulted in trial compared with 12.3 percent of the control group.

## TABLE E-7
## Civil cases disposed within 90 days of EDP hearing by age of case

| | 1983 Program | | | 1984 Program | | |
|---|---|---|---|---|---|---|
| | Disposed 1-90 days | | Total cases | Disposed 1-90 days | | Total cases |
| Age of case | No. | Percent | | No. | Percent | |
| **EDP group—volunteer** | | | | | | |
| Under 360 days | 1 | 20 | 5 | 5 | 42 | 12 |
| 361-450 days | 10 | 53 | 19 | 0 | 0 | 5 |
| 451-540 days | 8 | 62 | 13 | 1 | 33 | 3 |
| 541-630 days | 3 | 60 | 5 | 2 | 20 | 10 |
| Over 631 days | 8 | 57 | 14 | 4 | 57 | 7 |
| **EDP group—assigned** | | | | | | |
| Under 360 days | 8 | 32 | 25 | 1 | 13 | 8 |
| 361-450 days | 7 | 23 | 31 | 3 | 21 | 14 |
| 451-540 days | 9 | 29 | 31 | 11 | 26 | 43 |
| 541-630 days | 11 | 48 | 23 | 7 | 32 | 22 |
| Over 631 days | 5 | 16 | 32 | 5 | 29 | 17 |
| **Control group—volunteer** | | | | | | |
| Under 360 days | 0 | 0 | 1 | 0 | 0 | 13 |
| 361-450 days | 0 | 0 | 14 | 0 | 0 | 6 |
| 451-540 days | 1 | 6 | 16 | 1 | 13 | 8 |
| 541-630 days | 1 | 11 | 9 | 0 | 0 | 6 |
| Over 631 days | 3 | 50 | 6 | 4 | 27 | 15 |
| **Control group—assigned** | | | | | | |
| Under 360 days | 2 | 7 | 28 | 0 | 0 | 4 |
| 361-450 days | 5 | 14 | 36 | 1 | 6 | 17 |
| 451-540 days | 9 | 19 | 47 | 5 | 14 | 35 |
| 541-630 days | 3 | 15 | 20 | 1 | 4 | 23 |
| Over 631 days | 3 | 9 | 35 | 4 | 10 | 40 |

**Note:** The age of a case equals the number of days between the filing date and the date EDP hearings began. The 1983 program began hearings on November 21, 1983. The 1984 program began hearings on November 19, 1984.

The 1984 data reveal approximately equal trial rates for the EDP and the control groups. In the 20 months after the EDP hearings, 12.8 percent of the EDP cases had gone to trial compared with 13.2 percent of the control group.

## Conclusion
Participating in EDP hearings does not seem to result in a strong trial avoidance effect.

## TABLE E-8
## Cases in which trials were held, by EDP involvement

| 1983 PROGRAM | TOTAL CASES | Average age of case at EDP hearing | Total trials held | Percent cases tried |
|---|---|---|---|---|
| **EDP group** | | | | |
| Volunteer | 56 | 559.5 | 3 | 5.4 |
| Assigned | 142 | 531.9 | 16 | 11.3 |
| *Subtotal* | *198* | — | *19* | *9.6* |
| Domestic Volunteer | 28 | 344.5 | 3 | 10.7 |
| **Control group** | | | | |
| Volunteer | 46 | 506.2 | 11 | 23.9 |
| Assigned | 166 | 525.9 | 15 | 9.0 |
| *Subtotal* | *212* | — | *26* | *12.3* |
| TOTAL | 438 | — | 48 | 11.0 |
| **1984 PROGRAM** | | | | |
| **EDP group** | | | | |
| Volunteer | 37 | 478.4 | 9 | 24.3 |
| Assigned | 104 | 527.0 | 9 | 8.7 |
| *Subtotal* | *141* | — | *18* | *12.8* |
| Domestic Volunteer | 6 | 249.2 | 0 | 0 |
| **Control group** | | | | |
| Volunteer | 48 | 538.4 | 8 | 16.7 |
| Assigned | 119 | 621.8 | 14 | 11.8 |
| *Subtotal* | *167* | — | *22* | *13.2* |
| TOTAL | 314 | — | 40 | 12.7 |

**Note:** Average age of case at EDP hearings is measured as the number of days between the filing date and the date EDP hearings began. The 1983 program began hearings on November 21, 1983. The 1984 program began hearings on November 19, 1984.

## ISSUE #6: Did voluntary participation in EDP hearings affect the likelihood of avoiding trials any more than compulsory participation?

## Discussion
Volunteers to the 1983 EDP had far fewer trials in the 32 months after the hearing than their counterparts in the control group. Specifically, 5.4 percent of the volunteers to EDP resulted in trials relative to 23.9 percent of the volunteers that were placed in the control group. Trials were not avoided by cases *assigned* to EDP in 1983; 11.3 percent of those assigned to EDP subsequently required trial relative to 9.0 percent of those assigned to the control group.

In contrast, during the first 20 months following the 1984 hearings 24.3 percent of the volunteers to EDP had trials in contrast to only 16.7 percent of the volunteers in the control group. For assigned cases, the pattern reverses: 8.7 percent of those assigned to EDP had trials, in contrast to 11.8 percent of those assigned to the control category. This highest trial rate for volunteers in EDP is particularly surprising since these cases were younger at the time of the EDP hearings than cases in any of the other civil categories.

## Conclusion
Volunteers were considerably more likely to avoid trials after participating in the 1983 program. This pattern was reversed for volunteers in the 20 months following the 1984 program. The reason for the different results for the volunteers in the two programs is unclear.

## ISSUE #7: Does cause of action affect the likelihood of avoiding trials after participation in EDP?

## Discussion
Torts involving motor vehicle accidents were considerably less likely to require trials after participating in the 1983 EDP than those that did not. Only 9.5 percent of motor vehicle torts included in the EDP subsequently had trials while 20.6 percent of these tort cases in the control group had trials. Medical malpractice and commercial cases also appeared to require fewer trials after experiencing EDP hearings in 1983 (see Table E-9).

A similar effect was not found for motor vehicle torts in the first 20 months following the 1984 EDP hearing. Rather, 9 of the 18 trials held for the cases that had participated in these hearings were motor vehicle torts.

## Conclusion
Motor vehicle torts that participated in 1983 EDP hearings were less likely to require trials than similar cases that experienced normal processing by the court. In contrast, motor vehicle torts that participated in the 1984 EDP program had a higher trial rate than did their counterparts.

## TABLE E-9
## Cases in which trials were held, by type of case

| 1983 PROGRAM | Total cases | Total trials held | Percent cases tried |
|---|---|---|---|
| **EDP group** | | | |
| Tort, motor vehicles | 63 | 6 | 9.5 |
| Personal injury | 65 | 9 | 13.8 |
| Medical malpractice | 32 | 2 | 6.3 |
| Commercial | 38 | 2 | 5.3 |
| *Subtotal* | *198* | *19* | *9.6* |
| **Control group** | | | |
| Tort, motor vehicles | 63 | 13 | 20.6 |
| Personal injury | 75 | 3 | 4.0 |
| Medical malpractice | 36 | 5 | 13.9 |
| Commercial | 34 | 5 | 14.7 |
| Other | 4 | 0 | 0 |
| *Subtotal* | *212* | *26* | *12.3* |
| Domestic dissolution | 28 | 3 | 10.7 |
| TOTAL | 438 | 48 | 11.0 |
| **1984 PROGRAM** | | | |
| **EDP group** | | | |
| Tort, motor vehicles | 55 | 9 | 16.4 |
| Personal injury | 32 | 2 | 6.3 |
| Medical malpractice | 28 | 4 | 14.3 |
| Commercial | 23 | 0 | 0 |
| Other civil | 3 | 3 | 100.0 |
| *Subtotal* | *141* | *18* | *12.8* |
| **Control group** | | | |
| Tort, motor vehicles | 53 | 8 | 15.1 |
| Personal injury | 37 | 4 | 10.8 |
| Medical malpractice | 31 | 5 | 16.1 |
| Commercial | 37 | 4 | 10.8 |
| Other civil | 9 | 1 | 11.1 |
| *Subtotal* | *167* | *22* | *13.2* |
| Domestic dissolution | 6 | 0 | 0 |
| TOTAL | 314 | 40 | 12.7 |

# Comparison of 1983 and 1984 Early Disposition Programs

**ISSUE #8: Why did the results for the 1983 program differ from those for the one held in 1984?**

## DISCUSSION

The following results emerged from the analysis of the 1983 program:
1. Volunteer cases to EDP experienced both a stronger early disposition effect and trial avoidance than those assigned to EDP.
2. Motor vehicle torts experienced a much stronger early disposition effect and trial avoidance than other types of cases.
3. In general, early disposition following EDP hearings increased with the age of the cases.

None of the preceding results were found as strongly or as conclusively for the 1984 program. Some of the results, such as those for Issues 6 and 7, were actually reversed in the early analysis following the 1984 hearings.

Based on the characteristics of the cases examined in this report and shown in Tables E-1 and E-2 and in E-10, E-11, and E-12, there is relatively little difference between the types of cases included in either EDP or the control groups in the two years. The two most noticeable differences are the smaller number of cases overall and the somewhat

## TABLE E-10
### Distribution of cases among case types

| Cause of action | 1983 Program EDP | 1983 Program Control | 1984 Program EDP | 1984 Program Control |
|---|---|---|---|---|
| **Civil case type** | | | | |
| Tort, motor vehicles | 63 | 63 | 55 | 53 |
| Personal injury | 65 | 75 | 32 | 37 |
| Medical malpractice | 32 | 36 | 28 | 31 |
| Commercial | 38 | 34 | 23 | 37 |
| Other civil cases | 0 | 4 | 3 | 9 |
| Subtotal | 198 | 212 | 141 | 167 |
| **Domestic case type** | | | | |
| Dissolution | 28 | — | 6 | — |
| TOTAL | 226 | 212 | 147 | 167 |

older age of the control group in the 1984 program. The distributions of cases by cause of action and volunteer/assignment status remained similar between the two years.

## Conclusion

There is no known reason for the differences beween the results of the 1983 EDP and those of the one held in 1984. Results from 1983 would provide rather clear direction as to the types of cases most likely to benefit by participation in EDP hearings. Volunteers and motor vehicle torts would be the most likely candidates for future programs if EDP were to be continued. Results from the 1984 program do not sustain the 1983 findings.

**TABLE E-11**
**Distribution of cases between case types and volunteer/assignment status**

| Cause of action | 1983 Program | 1984 Program |
|---|---|---|
| **EDP group—volunteer** | | |
| Tort, motor vehicles | 42 | 20 |
| Personal injury | 6 | 10 |
| Medical malpractice | 0 | 1 |
| Commercial | 8 | 3 |
| Other civil cases | 0 | 3 |
| **EDP group—assigned** | | |
| Tort, motor vehicles | 21 | 35 |
| Personal injury | 59 | 22 |
| Medical malpractice | 32 | 27 |
| Commercial | 30 | 20 |
| **Control group—volunteer** | | |
| Tort, motor vehicles | 31 | 16 |
| Personal injury | 4 | 9 |
| Medical malpractice | 5 | 5 |
| Commercial | 3 | 9 |
| Other civil cases | 3 | 9 |
| **Control group—assigned** | | |
| Tort, motor vehicles | 32 | 37 |
| Personal injury | 71 | 28 |
| Medical malpractice | 31 | 26 |
| Commercial | 31 | 28 |
| Other | 1 | — |

## TABLE E-12
## Cases included in study, by age of case

| Age of case | 1983 Program EDP | 1983 Program Control | 1984 Program EDP | 1984 Program Control |
|---|---|---|---|---|
| **Civil** | | | | |
| Under 360 days | 30 | 29 | 20 | 17 |
| 361-450 days | 50 | 50 | 19 | 23 |
| 451-540 days | 44 | 63 | 46 | 43 |
| 541-630 days | 28 | 29 | 32 | 29 |
| Over 631 days | 46 | 41 | 24 | 55 |
| *Subtotal* | *198* | *212* | *141* | *167* |
| **Domestic** | | | | |
| Under 360 days | 20 | — | 5 | — |
| 361-450 days | 2 | — | 1 | — |
| 451-540 days | 2 | — | 0 | — |
| 541-630 days | 1 | — | 0 | — |
| Over 631 days | 3 | — | 0 | — |
| *Subtotal* | *28* | — | *6* | — |

**Note:** The age of a case equals the number of days between the filing date and the date EDP hearings began. The 1983 program began hearings on November 21, 1983. The 1984 program began hearings on November 19, 1984.

# The National Center for State Courts

The National Center for State Courts is a nonprofit organization dedicated to the modernization of court operations and the improvement of justice at the state and local level throughout the country. It functions as an extension of the state court systems, working for them at their direction and providing for them an effective voice in matters of national importance.

In carrying out its purpose, the National Center acts as a focal point for state judicial reform, serves as a catalyst for setting and implementing standards of fair and expeditious judicial administration, and finds and disseminates answers to the problems of state judicial systems. In sum, the National Center provides the means for reinvesting in all states the profits gained from judicial advances in any state.

**THE BOARD OF DIRECTORS**

Warren E. Burger, Chief Justice of the United States (retired)
*Honorary Chairman*

Robert C. Murphy, Chief Judge, Court of Appeals of Maryland
*Chairman*

Clement C. Torbert, Jr., Chief Justice, Supreme Court of Alabama
*Chairman-elect*

Arthur H. Snowden, II, Administrative Director of the Courts, Alaska
*Vice-chairman*

William G. Clark, Chief Justice, Supreme Court of Illinois

Stanley R. Collis, Executive Officer, Alameda Superior Court, Oakland, California

Robert L. Doss, Jr., Director, Administrative Office of the Courts, The Judicial Council of Georgia

Haliburton Fales, 2d, White & Case, New York City

Gordon R. Hall, Chief Justice, Supreme Court of Utah

Harriet P. Henry, Judge at Large, Maine District Court

Charles V. Johnson, Judge, Superior Court, King County, Seattle, Washington

Gladys Kessler, Judge, Superior Court, District of Columbia

Edward B. McConnell, President, National Center for State Courts

Margie M. Meacham, Judge, County Court of Carbon County, Rawlings, Wyoming

J. Denis Moran, Director of State Courts, Wisconsin

Robert N.C. Nix, Jr., Chief Justice, Supreme Court of Pennsylvania

John T. Racanelli, Presiding Justice, California Court of Appeal, First District

C. Kenneth Roberts, General Counsel, Exxon Company, U.S.A., Houston, Texas

Thomas J. Stovall, Presiding Judge, Second Administrative Judicial District of Texas

Gerald T. Wetherington, Chief Judge, Eleventh Judicial Circuit of Florida

## THE OFFICES AND MANAGEMENT STAFF

**Headquarters**
300 Newport Avenue
Williamsburg, VA 23187-8798
(804) 253-2000

Edward B. McConnell
*President*

Keith L. Bumsted
*Director for Administration
and Technical Services*

Linda R. Caviness
*Director for Development
and Central Services*

Geoff Gallas
*Director for Research
and Special Services*

**Northeastern Region**
Beechwood Hill
1545 Osgood Street
North Andover, MA 01845
(617) 687-0111
Samuel D. Conti, *Regional Director*

**Southeastern Region**
300 Newport Avenue
Williamsburg, VA 23187-8798
(804) 253-2000
James R. James, *Regional Director*

**Western Region**
720 Sacramento Street
San Francisco, CA 94108
(415) 557-1515
Alexander B. Aikman,
*Regional Director*

**Institute for Court Management**
1331 17th Street, Suite 402
Denver, CO 80202
(303) 293-3063
Harvey E. Solomon, *Director*

**Washington Project Office**
4001 North 9th Street, Suite 218
Arlington, VA 22203
(703) 841-0200
Thomas A. Henderson, *Director*

**Washington Liaison**
Hall of the States
444 N. Capitol Street, Suite 608
Washington, D.C. 20001
(202) 347-5924
Harry W. Swegle, *Washington Liaison*